C000059996

250 ESSENTIAL CHINESE CHARACTERS

FOR EVERYDAY USE

Vol 2

by Philip Yungkin Lee
University of New South Wales, Australia

TUTTLE PUBLISHING
Tokyo • Rutland, Vermont • Singapore

Published by Tuttle Publishing, an imprint of Periplus Editions (HK) Ltd.,
with editorial offices at 364 Innovation Drive, North Clarendon, VT 05759
and 130 Joo Seng Road #06-01, Singapore 368357

LCC Card No. 2004297990
ISBN-10: 0-8048-3360-5
ISBN-13: 978-0-8048-3360-8

Distributed by:

North America, Latin America & Europe
Tuttle Publishing
364 Innovation Drive
North Clarendon, VT 05759-9436
Tel: (802) 773 8930; Fax: (802) 773 6993
Email: info@tuttlepublishing.com
Website: www.tuttlepublishing.com

Japan
Tuttle Publishing
Yaekari Bldg., 3F, 5-4-12 Osaki, Shinagawa-ku
Tokyo 141-0032
Tel: (03) 5437 0171; Fax: (03) 5437 0755
Email: tuttle-sales@gol.com

Asia Pacific
Berkeley Books Pte. Ltd.
130 Joo Seng Road, #06-01, Singapore 368357
Tel: (65) 6280 1330; Fax: (65) 6280 6290
Email: inquiries@periplus.com.sg
Website: www.periplus.com

Indonesia
PT Java Books Indonesia
Kawasan Industri Pulogadung
Jl. Rawa Gelam IV No. 9,
Jakarta 14240, Indonesia
Tel: (62-21) 4682 1088; Fax: (62-21) 461 0207
Email: cs@javabooks.co.id

10 09 08 07 06
10 9 8 7 6 5 4 3

Printed in Singapore

TUTTLE PUBLISHING® is a registered trademark of Tuttle Publishing,
a division of Periplus Editions (HK) Ltd.

Contents

Introduction

How many characters do you need for a basic knowledge of written Chinese? This is a question people beginning to learn Chinese often ask. There is no simple answer because it depends on what you mean by "basic knowledge." You need around 250 characters for simple sentence construction and some 500 to construct more complex sentences so that you can speak in everyday contexts.

The second volume of *250 Essential Chinese Characters for Everyday Use* continues to teach the basic skills in writing basic Chinese characters. Following the same format, each unit introduces ten new characters, presented in simplified form, along with pinyin romanization and the English meaning. Just over a third of the selection have traditional forms and they are listed alongside the simplified form. There are short notes on the origin of the character, some explanations of how the traditional form was constructed and, in some cases, a guide to pronunciation. The aim is to demystify characters and make the task of learning them less arduous. Each character is combined with other characters to form compounds that are placed in sample sentences to illustrate their use. Pinyin romanization is written next to the characters so that you can identify and pronounce the words. The English translation provides a general guide to meaning.

The book is arranged in 25 units of 10 characters, each with a quiz in both characters and pinyin so that learners can progress at their own pace. At the end of each 5 units or 50 characters there is a **Character Building** section where characters are grouped together based on their meaningful parts (known as radicals). This also shows how character components are recycled to form other characters. A **Review** of characters and compounds, arranged according to parts of speech, helps learners develop their skills in building sentences. The **Word and Sentence Puzzles** section uses all the characters that have been introduced, and challenges you to identify characters in meaningful combinations. Don't hesitate to use the **Key**. It is there to guide you in your efforts to construct the Puzzle. If you need a quick reference on a particular character and the compounds it forms, you can find it in the **Alphabetical Index** or the **Radical Index** which uses the number of strokes in the radical to look up characters.

Your job as a self-paced learner is to focus on each character as you write it. The character should be written stroke by stroke, following the stroke order. You need to follow the stroke order and remember the number of strokes as you practice writing each character. There's also a short note to remind you how to write the character. Unlike English, Chinese characters are written in squarish forms, and each of the components conforms to rules of symmetry and balance. Writing them in a rectangular or round shape destroys the visual integrity of the character. You can't simply write them in any shape or size, because the visual images of your own handwriting will help you remember the characters. This is why there are model characters and proper squares in this book. Writing each character in the squares teaches you to copy the model character provided. If you take your time, referring to the model character, the correct stroke order and the character components that make up each character, you will get twice the result with half the effort.

Students' Guide

Chinese Characters

One of the great fascinations of learning Chinese lies in the Chinese writing system. Each character looks like a square-shaped box written in various strokes. Learners who are used to the alphabetical writing system find characters difficult to recognize, time consuming to write and near impossible to remember. In this book we teach 250 characters with a view to demonstrate how the large number of components you are learning both as visual and phonetical elements can be recycled and used in different combinations to form new characters. Through remembering the configuration, meaning and pronunication of these components, you will gain a basic knowledge of the compositions of Chinese characters — the radical and the phonetic. This will establish a relationship between form, pronunciation and meaning in characters and will enable you to transfer what you already know when you learn new characters.

Structurally there are two types of characters: those that exist as an integral unit, and those that can be divided into radical and phonetic components. Integral characters are often radicals themselves. Thus some basic knowledge of a radical is desirable not just for learning a certain character but for using the radical index when looking up a character in a Chinese dictionary.

It is often said that radicals are categories of thought which the ancient Chinese used to describe the world around them. A combination of a radical and a sound element gives specific meaning. As you come across radicals in this book you will learn to classify characters under these categories or radicals. *The Chinese-English Dictionary* (published in 1995 by the Foreign Language Teaching and Research Press in Beijing) uses 189 radicals to organize the characters contained in the dictionary. That dictionary is probably the most widely used Chinese-English Dictionary in the world and is deemed likely to be the dictionary most often consulted by users of this book. You will learn 103 radicals in this book. Of these about 50 are the most common radicals. We believe that the knowledge you gained from these radicals will enable you to guess the meaning of many common Chinese characters.

The Basic Strokes

Chinese characters are written in various strokes. Although we can identify over 30 different strokes, only 8 are basic ones and all the others are their variants. Certain arrangements of strokes form components or the building blocks for characters.

The strokes that make up a component of a character and by extension the whole character are given names. Below are the 8 basic strokes:

[—] The *héng* or 'horizontal' stroke is written from left to right.

[|] The *shù* or 'vertical' stroke is written from top to bottom.

[）] The *piě* or 'downward-left' stroke is written from top-right to bottom-left.

[＼] The *nà* or 'downward-right' stroke is written from top-left to bottom-right.

[丶] The *diǎn* or 'dot' stroke is written from top to bottom-right, finishing firmly. It can also be finished from top to bottom-left, depending on how the dot is written.

[ㄱ] The *zhé* or 'turning' stroke can be a horizontal stroke with a downward turn, or it can be a vertical stroke with a horizontal turn to the right.

[亅] The *gōu* or 'hook' stroke is written by a quick flick of the pen or a Chinese brush. There are five types of *gōu* 'hook' strokes. They are:

[→]   the *hénggōu* or 'horizontal hook',

[亅]   the *shùgōu* or 'vertical hook',

[乚]   the *wān'gōu* or 'bending hook',

[乀]   the *xiégōu* or 'slanting hook',

[⌣]   the *pínggōu* or 'level hook',

[✓] The *tí* or 'upward stroke to the right' is written from bottom-left to top-right.

Stroke Order

It is important to remember that the components in a character are written according to some fixed rules or stroke order. The same stroke order should be used every time you write a character. If you write a character according to the prescribed order, you will find it easier to remember as repetition will develop muscular cues in your fingers which will assist in the recall of the character, much like remembering a figure in dancing. Thus, when writing a character, the following rules should be observed:

1. From top to bottom:

三		一	二	三	
学		丶	⺌	㗊	学
是		日	旦	早	是

2. From left to right:

你		亻	𠂆	伫	你
好		女	奵	好	
她		女	她		

3. The horizontal before the vertical:

十		一	十	
七		一	七	
天		二	于	天

4. The horizontal before the downward stroke to the left:

大		一	ナ	大
有		一	ナ	冇	有
在		一	ナ	才	在

5. The downward stroke to the left before that to the right:

人		丿	人	
八		丿	八	
文		亠	亣	文

6. The enclosing strokes first, then the enclosed and finally the sealing stroke:

四		丨	冂	四	四
国		冂	囯	囯	国
回		冂	囘	囘	回

7. The middle stroke before those on both sides:

小		亅	小	小	
你		仴	竹	你	你
水		亅	氺	水	水

8.   Inside stroke before side stroke:

这		宀	丆	文	这
过		寸	寸	讨	过
道		丷	艹	首	道

Explanatory Notes for Character Entries

Below is an annotated character entry. It has been reduced to show the full range of information:

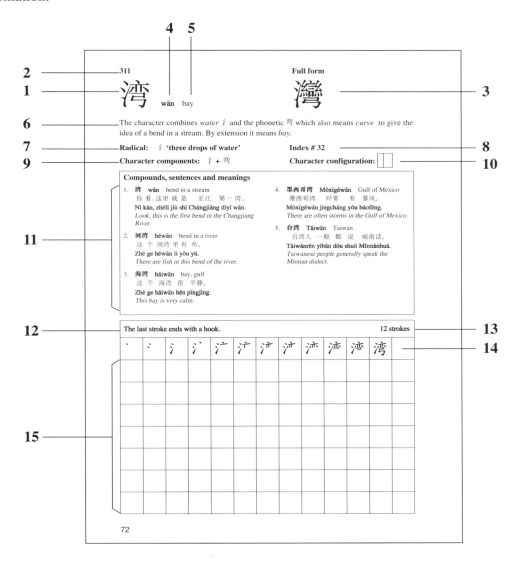

KEY:

  1. the character
  2. character serial number as sequenced in this book
  3. full form of the character
  4. pronunciation and tone
  5. character definition
  6. character explanation and points to note on the use of the character.
  7. radical information
  8. radical index number (based on *The Chinese-English Dictionary 1995*)
  9. character components
  10. character configuration
  11. character combinations and example sentences with pronunciation and meaning
  12. points to note when writing out the character.
  13. total number of strokes of the character
  14. stroke order
  15. space to practice writing out the character

Simplified characters versus full characters

Out of the 250 characters studied in this book, 84 are simplified. This is just one-third which is generally the number of characters simplified for common usage. Where a simplified form exists, the full form is given as a reference. It is useful to know how the full form looks like as it is often used to illustrate how the character came to evolve to its present form.

Simplified characters have existed long before the Communist Chinese Government sanctioned their use with an official list in 1986. For example, the characters *cóng* 从 (from), *wàn* 万 (ten thousand) and *bǐ* 笔 (writing brush) existed side by side with their full forms 從, 萬 and 筆 in classical Chinese. The official sanction only means the abolition of the complex forms.

Several techniques were employed to create simplified characters. One was to replace the original component of a character with a component of fewer strokes but which had the same sound as the given character. For example, the simplified character for 'remember' is *jì* 记 . The component 己 is pronounced as *jǐ* by itself but when it is combined with the radical 讠, it takes on the pronunciation of *jì*. Other examples are *fǔ* 辅, *wān* 湾, *jī* 机, *jí* 极 and *yōu* 优 .

Another technique used was simply to take one section of a complex character and used it as the simplified one. Compare the full form for *kāi* 開 'open' and its simplified form 开 which uses only the inside component in simplification. Other examples in this collection are *shēng* 聲 'sound', *fēi* 飛 'to fly', *yàn* 厭 'to loathe', *suī* 雖 'although' and *qì* 氣 (gas, vapor) with their respective simplified forms 声, 飞, 厌, 虽 and 气.

Some characters are simplified on the basis of having adopted the cursive forms and in the process lost some of their strokes. For example, the radical 言 (speech) is simplified to 讠 by the adoption of its cursive form when used as a radical. Other radicals in this collection simplified on the same basis are 纟, 钅, 饣 and 页. This manner of simplification is responsible for many simplified forms being created. Examples are *huà* 话, *diào/tiáo* 调, *tán* 谈, *yì* 议, *sù* 诉, *jiǎng* 讲, *gāi* 该; *gěi* 给, *jí* 级, *hóng* 红, *lǜ* 绿; *cuò* 错, *yín* 银; *yǐn* 饮, *guǎn* 馆; and *xū* 须, *shùn* 顺, *yù* 预, *tí* 题, *yán* 颜. In addition, there are cursive forms adopted as simplified characters. Examples are *wéi/wèi* 为, *lè/yuè* 乐, *zhāng* 张, *yīng* 应, *yàn* 验, *cháng* 尝, *jiān* 坚, *jǐn* 紧, *wān* 弯, *guàn* 惯, *lán* 蓝, *xìng* 兴, *gāng* 刚, *dān* 单, *fēng* 风 and *jī* 鸡.

Some cursive forms are arbitrary created for the sake of fast writing of a character. They are used to replace some complicated phonetic components. One common stereotype is *yòu* 又 made up of only two strokes. It is used in the characters *nán* 难, *jī* 鸡, and *shuāng* 双 replacing 難, 雞, and 雙 respectively. Another such stereotype is *yún* 云 made up of only four strokes. It is used in the characters *yún* 云, *yùn* 运, and *dòng* 动 replacing 雲, 運, and 動 respectively.

Finally, it is worth mentioning that some simplified forms are quite unlike their traditional forms and thus will give you some problems. The ones found in this collection are *tīng* 听, *yè* 叶, *fā* 发, *jié* 节, *dǎo* 导 and *jiù* 旧, replacing 聽, 葉, 發, 節, 導 and 舊 respectively.

The Pinyin System of Romanization

The system used in this book to write Chinese with Roman letters is the *Hanyu Pinyin* system which is the standard in mainland China and is now used almost everywhere else in the world. The imitated pronunciation should be read as if it were English, bearing in mind the following main points:

Consonants

b, d, f, g, h, k, l, m, n, p, s, t, w, y as in English

c	like English **ts** in i**ts**
j	like English **j** in **j**eep
q	like English **ch** in **ch**eer, with a strong puff of air
r	like English **ur** in leis**ur**e, with the tongue rolled back
x	like English **see** (whole word)
z	like English **ds** in ki**ds**
ch	like English **ch** in **ch**urch, with the tongue rolled back and a strong puff of air
sh	like English **sh** in **sh**e, with the tongue rolled back
zh	like English **j**, with the tongue rolled back

Vowels

a	like English **ar** in f**ar**
e	like English **ur** in f**ur**
i	like English **ee** in f**ee**
o	like English **or** in f**or**
u	like English **ue** in s**ue**
ü	like French **u**

Tones

A tone is a variation in pitch by which a syllable can be pronounced. In Chinese, a variation of pitch or tone changes the meaning of the word. There are four tones each marked by a diacritic or tone mark. In addition there is a neutral tone which does not carry any tone marks. Below is a tone chart which describes tones using the 5-degree notation. It divides the range of pitches from lowest (1) to highest (5). Note that the neutral tone is not shown on the chart as it is affected by the tone that precedes it.

Tone chart

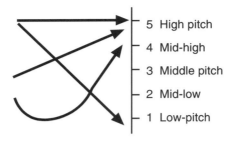

The first tone is a high-level tone represented by a level tone mark (–).

The second tone is a high-rising tone represented by a rising tone mark (´).

The third tone is a low-dipping tone represented by a dish-like tone mark (ˇ).

The fourth tone is a high-falling tone represented by a falling tone mark (`).

In addition to the above tones, there is a neutral tone which is pronounced light and soft in comparison to other tones. A neutral tone is not marked by any tone mark. A syllable is said to take on a neutral tone when it forms part of a word or is placed in various parts of a sentence.

How to use the Alphabetical Index

The words and phrases collected in the Chinese-English Glossary (approximately 1200 items) are arranged alphabetically according to the *Hanyu Pinyin* system of romanization. In this system each syllable (represented by a character) is a unit. The first character in a word or phrase is the head character. Each word or phrase is ordered in the first instance according to the phonetic value of this character. In a succession of entries having the same head character, alphabetical order is then determined by the phonetic value of the second character. This arrangement has the advantage of enhancing meaning by grouping together words which share a common character root, even though it is done at the expense of a straight alphabetical ordering.

The ordering of characters is affected by two other considerations. Firstly, in the case of characters represented by the same Roman letters, alphabetization is determined by the tone of each character (represented in *Hanyu Pinyin* by diacritics or tone marks), in the order first, second, third, fourth and neutral tone. Secondly, in the case of characters represented by the same Roman letters which also have the same tone, alphabetization follows the principle that simpler characters (those composed of fewer strokes) are listed before more complex characters (those composed of more strokes).

For example, the first 38 entries under "J" have as their head character variations of the syllable 'ji'. These entries are *jī* — first tone (4 instances of a 6-stroke character, 5 of another 6-stroke character, 1 of a 10-stroke character, and 5 of a 11-stroke character); *jí* — second tone (2 instances of a 6-stroke character, 4 of a 7-stroke character); *jǐ* — third tone (1 instance of a 3-stroke character; 1 of a 9-stroke character); *jì* — fourth tone (6 instances of a 4-stroke character, 4 of a 5-stroke character, 1 instance of a 6-stroke character and 4 instances of an 8-stroke character). The neutral tone *ji*, written without any tone mark, is absent in this collection.

How to use the Radical Index

The radical index is based on the 189 radicals used by *The Chinese-English Dictionary 1995*, published by the Foreign Language Teaching and Research Press in Beijing. When you look up a character, first determine which part of the character constitutes the radical and then count the remaining number of strokes to locate the character under that radical. Where a character is made up of two components which can function as radicals, it is sometimes classified under both radicals. For example, the character #255, *xiāng* 香 'fragrant', is classified under both components which are treated as radicals: *rì* 日 'sun' and *hé* 禾 'grain', in the same way as found in the *Chinese-English Dictionary 1995*.

huà speech

Full form

The character combines *word* 讠 and *tongue* 舌 to give the meaning of *speak*.

Radical: 讠 'word'

Index # 9

Character components: 讠 + 舌

Character configuration:

Compounds, sentences and meanings

1. **话** **huà** word, talk
   话 不能 这么 说。
   Huà bùnéng zhème shuō.
   I wouldn't say that.

2. **大话** **dàhuà** brag, talk big
   他 常常 说 大话。
   Tā chángcháng shuō dàhuà.
   He often brags.

3. **电话** **diànhuà** telephone
   今晚 请给 我 回 个 电话。
   Jīnwǎn qǐng gěi wǒ huí ge diànhuà.
   Please give me a call tonight.

4. **好话** **hǎohuà** word of praise
   请 给 我 说 句 好话。
   Qǐng gěi wǒ shuō jù hǎohuà.
   Please put in a good word for me.

5. **听话** **tīnghuà** obedient
   这 个 孩子 很 听话。
   Zhè ge háizi hěn tīnghuà.
   This child is very obedient.

The top stroke of 舌 sweeps from right to left.   8 strokes

、	讠	讠	讠	话	话	话	话				

yòu also, again

The character represents the figure of the right hand which when extended, can be used for self-protection. It came to mean *again*.

Radical: 又 'again'

Index # 24

Character components: 又

Character configuration: ☐

Compounds, sentences and meanings

1. 又 **yòu** again
   她 把 信 看 了 又 看。
   Tā bǎ xìn kànle yòu kàn.
   She read the letter over and over again.

2. 又 **yòu** in addition to
   跳舞 是 一 种 娱乐，又 是 一 种
   Tiàowǔ shì yì zhǒng yúlè, yòu shì yì zhǒng
   运动。
   yùndòng.
   Dancing is a form of entertainment and a sport.

3. 又···又 **yòu ... yòu** both ... and
   这 种 汽车 又 便宜 又 好。
   Zhè zhǒng qìchē yòu piányi yòu hǎo.
   This type of automobile is cheap and good.

4. 又 **yòu** but
   我 想 去，又 怕 没 时间。
   Wǒ xiǎng qù, yòu pà méi shíjiān.
   I'd like to go, but I'm not sure if I can find the time.

The last stroke comes down firmly and then tapers off. 2 strokes

乃	又								

普 **pǔ** general

The character combines *sun* 日 and 並. In ancient form, 並 means 'two people standing abreast,' which carries the idea of co-existing with the sun and came to mean *universal*.

Radical: 日 'sun'　　　　　　　　　**Index # 90**

Character components: ˋ + 亚 + 日

Character configuration:

Compounds, sentences and meanings

1. **普 pǔ** general
   今天 阳光 普照。
   Jīntiān yángguāng pǔ zhào.
   Today, the sun is shining everywhere.

2. **普通 pǔtōng** ordinary
   这 件 衣服 很 普通。
   Zhè jiàn yīfu hěn pǔtōng.
   This garment is nothing special.

3. **普通话 Pǔtōnghuà** Mandarin
   他的 普通话 带 南方 腔调。
   Tāde Pǔtōnghuà dài nánfāng qiāngdiào.
   His Mandarin has a southern accent.

4. **普及 pǔjí** be made popular among
   中国 正普及法律 常识。
   Zhōngguó zhèng pǔjí fǎlǜ chángshí.
   China is making basic legal principles widely known.

5. **普洱茶 Pǔ'ěrchá** Pu'er tea (red tea from Yunnan province)
   普洱茶 能 帮助 消化。
   Pǔ'ěrchá néng bāngzhù xiāohuà.
   Pu'er tea is a digestive aid.

The vertical strokes do not cross through the second horizontal stroke.　　12 strokes

`	ˊ	˙	ㄧ	ㅛ	ㅛ	ㅛ	並	普	普	普	普

 **tōng** through

The character combines *movement* 辶 and *fence* 甬 to give the idea of *passing through*.

Radical: 辶 'movement'

Index # 38

Character components: 甬 + 辶

Character configuration:

Compounds, sentences and meanings

1. 通 **tōng** go to
   这 趟 列车 直通 西安。
   Zhè tàng lièchē zhítōng Xī'ān.
   This train goes straight to Xian.

2. 通常 **tōngcháng** usually
   我 通常 七点 起床。
   Wǒ tōngcháng qīdiǎn qǐchuáng.
   I usually get up at 7:00.

3. 通过 **tōngguò** by means of
   通过 姐姐 介绍，我 认识了 她。
   Tōngguò jiějie jièshào, wǒ rènshile tā.
   I got to know her through my older sister.

4. 通知 **tōngzhī** notify
   请 马上 通知 他。
   Qǐng mǎshàng tōngzhī tā.
   Please notify him immediately.

5. 交通 **jiāotōng** transport
   北京 的 交通 很 方便。
   Běijīng de jiāotōng hěn fāngbiàn.
   The transport system in Beijing is very convenient.

The second stroke of 甬 is a dot.   10 strokes

フ	マ	ア	甬	甬	甬	甬	甬	诵	通			

xiāng   fragrant

The character combines *rice plants* 禾 and *sun* 日 to suggest that the sun is shining on the ripening rice plants, emitting the *fragrance* of the harvest.

Radical: 日 'sun'   **Index # 90**
or   禾 'grain'   **Index # 124**
Character component: 禾 + 日   **Character configuration:**

Compounds, sentences and meanings

1. 香 **xiāng** fragrant
   茉莉花 香。
   Mòlǐhuā xiāng.
   Jasmine has a fragrant perfume.

2. 香蕉 **xiāngjiāo** banana
   香蕉 很 有 营养。
   Xiāngjiāo hěn yǒu yíngyǎng.
   Bananas are very nutritious.

3. 香水 **xiāngshuǐ** perfume
   这 是 法国 香水。
   Zhè shì Fǎguó xiāngshuǐ.
   This is French perfume.

4. 香甜 **xiāngtián** sound (of sleep)
   你 昨晚 睡得 香甜 吗?
   Nǐ zuówǎn shuìde xiāngtián ma?
   Did you sleep well last night?

5. 吃香 **chīxiāng** popular
   这 种 自行车 在 中国 很
   Zhè zhǒng zìxíngchē zài Zhōngguó hěn
   吃香。
   chīxiāng.
   This type of bicycle is popular in China.

The top stroke sweeps from right to left.   9 strokes

一 二 千 禾 禾 禾 香 香 香

256

港 gǎng harbor

The character combines *water* 氵 and the phonetic 巷 to suggest the idea of *harbor*.

Radical: 氵 '3 drops of water'   **Index # 32**

Character components: 氵 + 巷   **Character configuration:** ▢

Compounds, sentences and meanings

1. 港 **gǎng** harbor
   悉尼 是 一个 天然 港。
   Xīní shì yí ge tiānrán gǎng.
   Sydney is a natural harbor.

2. 港口 **gǎngkǒu** port
   三藩市 是 一个 港口。
   Sānfānshì shì yí ge gǎngkǒu.
   San Francisco is a port.

3. 海港 **hǎigǎng** harbor
   上海 的 海港 不太 深。
   Shànghǎi de hǎigǎng bú tài shēn.
   Shanghai Harbor is not very deep.

4. 香港 **Xiānggǎng** Hong Kong (Literally, fragrant harbor)
   香港 的 夜景 很 美。
   Xiānggǎng de yèjǐng hěn měi.
   Hong Kong is very pretty at night.

5. 港币 **Gǎngbì** Hong Kong dollars
   港币 比 人民币 高。
   Gǎngbì bǐ Rénmínbì gāo.
   The Hong Kong dollar is higher than the Chinese dollar.

The last stroke is a vertical bend ending with a hook.   12 strokes

丶 冫 氵 氵 汢 汢 洪 洰 洪 洪 港 港

6

 **chū** come out

The character represents the foot protruding past a certain line. It came to suggest the idea of *appear* or *start*.

Radical: 凵 '3-sided frame, open top'　　**Index # 29**

Character components: 凵 + 山　　**Character configuration:**

Compounds, sentences and meanings

1. 出　**chū**　put up
   你 给 我 出 个 主意, 好 吗?
   Nǐ gěi wǒ chū ge zhǔyi, hǎo ma?
   How about giving me a suggestion?

2. 出差　**chūchāi**　to go on a business trip
   我 这次 去 北京 是 出差。
   Wǒ zhè cì qù Běijīng shì chūchāi.
   I'm going to Beijing on business.

3. 出错　**chūcuò**　make mistakes
   她 做事 很少 出错。
   Tā zuòshì hěnshǎo chūcuò.
   She seldom makes a mistake.

4. 出发　**chūfā**　start off
   我们 明天 几 点 出发?
   Wǒmen míngtiān jǐ diǎn chūfā?
   When do we set out tomorrow?

5. 出去　**chūqu**　go out
   我们 出去 走走, 好 不 好?
   Wǒmen chūqu zǒuzou, hǎo bù hǎo?
   Why don't we go for a walk?

The vertical stroke in the middle does not cross the lower horizontal stroke.　　5 strokes

㇄	凵	屮	出	出								

定 dìng calm

The character combines *roof* 宀 and 疋 which is derived from 正 meaning 'right.' Thus, 定 represents the idea of keeping a house in order and hence means *fix*.

Radical: 宀 'roof'

Character component: 宀 + 疋

Index # 34

Character configuration:

Compounds, sentences and meanings

1. **定　dìng**　fix, establish
   开会 时间 定 在 后天　上午
   Kāihuì shíjiān dìng zài hòutiān shàngwǔ
   十点。
   shídiǎn.
   The meeting is fixed for the day after tomorrow at 10 a.m.

2. **定做　dìngzuò**　have something made to order
   我 这 双　跳舞鞋 是 定做 的。
   Wǒ zhè shuāng tiàowǔxié shì dìngzuò de.
   My dancing shoes were made to order.

3. **定期　dìngqī**　regular
   我 定期 检查 身体。
   Wǒ dìngqī jiǎnchá shēntǐ.
   I have a regular medical checkup.

4. **一定　yídìng**　certainly
   七点 以前 我 一定 能 回家。
   Qīdiǎn yǐqián wǒ yídìng néng huíjiā.
   I'll certainly be home before 7:00.

5. **约定　yuēdìng**　arrange
   我们 约定 在 火车站　见面。
   Wǒmen yuēdìng zài huǒchēzhàn jiànmiàn.
   We've arranged to meet at the station.

The last stroke curves, then levels off.　　　　　　　8 strokes

丶	丷	宀	宀	宁	宇	定	定				

tīng   listen

The full form of the character combines *ear* 耳, *king* 王, *essential* 十, *eyes* 四, *one* 一 and *heart* 心 to suggest that concentration is essential for effective listening.

Radical: 口 'mouth'

Index # 50

Character components: 口 + 斤

Character configuration:

Compounds, sentences and meanings

1. **听** **tīng** listen
   请 听 一下 电话。
   Qǐng tīng yíxià diànhuà.
   Please answer the phone.

2. **听不懂** **tīngbudǒng** not understand (by listening)
   我 听不懂 你 说 什么。
   Wǒ tīngbudǒng nǐ shuō shénme.
   I don't understand what you said.

3. **听得懂** **tīngdedǒng** understand (by listening)
   我 听得懂 法语。
   Wǒ tīngdedǒng Fǎyǔ.
   I can understand French.

4. **听见** **tīngjiàn** hear
   我 听见 有 人 敲门。
   Wǒ tīngjiàn yǒu rén qiāomén.
   I heard a knock at the door.

5. **听说** **tīngshuō** be told
   听说 她 到 上海 工作 去了。
   Tīngshuō tā dào Shànghǎi gōngzuò qù le.
   I hear that she went to work in Shanghai.

The left side of 斤 is made up of two strokes.   **7 strokes**

丶	冂	口	叴	叿	听	听					

懂 dǒng understand

The character combines *upright heart* 忄 and the phonetic 董 which means a heavy plant needing supervision or it will droop. It came to mean *understand*.

Radical: 忄 'upright heart'　　　　　　**Index # 33**

Character components: 忄 + 董　　　　**Character configuration:**

Compounds, sentences and meanings

1. **懂 dǒng** understand
   不要 不 懂 装 懂。
   Búyào bù dǒng zhuāng dǒng.
   Don't pretend to understand when you don't.

2. **懂得 dǒngde** understand
   你 懂得 这 句 话 的 意思 吗?
   Nǐ dǒngde zhè jù huà de yìsi ma?
   Do you understand the meaning of this sentence?

3. **懂事 dǒngshì** sensible, intelligent
   她 是 一个 懂事 的 孩子。
   Tā shì yí ge dǒngshì de háizi.
   She is a sensible child.

4. **看懂 kàndǒng** understand (by reading)
   我 看不懂 中文 报。
   Wǒ kànbudǒng Zhōngwén bào.
   I can't understand Chinese newspapers.

5. **听懂 tīngdǒng** understand (by hearing)
   我 能 听懂 上海话。
   Wǒ néng tīngdǒng Shànghǎihuà.
   I can understand Shanghai dialect.

Write the two dots before the vertical stroke in the upright heart 忄.　　　　15 strokes

丶	丷	忄	忄	忭	忭	忭	忭	忭	惜	惜	惜	懂
懂	懂											

Quiz 26 (251–260)

A. Look at the 16-character grid and CIRCLE words or phrases. They can be written horizontally or vertically. (Look at the circled characters in the Key if you are unsure.) Copy the word or phrase next to the grid and write down the pinyin and meaning.

			Word or phrase			**Pinyin**	**Meaning**
出 有 能 中			(i) 中 国 话			Zhōngguóhuà	Chinese language
定 香 港 国			(ii)				
就 普 通 话			(iii)				
听 不 懂 又			(iv)				

The grid:

出	有	能	中
定	香	港	国
就	普	通	话
听	不	懂	又

B. Using the characters in the 16-character grid, convert the pinyin sentences into characters and write the English meaning.

(i)	Hànyǔ jiù shì Zhōngguóhuà.							
(ii)	Hànyǔ yòu jiào Pǔtōnghuà.							
(iii)	Zài Xiānggǎng chūshēng de rén bù yídìng néng tīngdǒng Pǔtōnghuà.							

C. Match the Chinese words with their English meaning.

(i)

普通	word of praise
普 jí	inform
通常	through
通过	common
通知	become popular
jiāo 通	lie, boast
好话	in general
大话	transport

(ii)

听见	set out
听话	make a mistake
出 cuò	definitely
出 fā	mature
定做	hear
一定	understand
懂 shì	obedient
懂得	made to order

11

言 yán word

The character depicts a *knife* pointing down at a *mouth,* referring to the clear-cut pronunciation of sounds to form words. It came to mean *word.*

Radical: 言 'whole word' **Index # 154**

Character components: 亠 + 二 + 口 **Character configuration:**

Compounds, sentences and meanings

1. 言 **yán** word
   你 为什么 一 言 不发?
   Nǐ wèishénme yì yán bù fā?
   Why don't you say something?

2. 言论 **yánlùn** opinion on public affairs
   西方 社会 有 言论 自由。
   Xīfāng shèhuì yǒu yánlùn zìyóu.
   There is freedom of speech in Western societies.

3. 言谈 **yántán** the way one speaks
   言谈 之间 可以 看出 他 很 懂事。
   Yántán zhījiān kěyǐ kànchū tā hěn dǒngshì.
   It's clear from the way he talks that he is very mature.

4. 言行 **yánxíng** words and deeds
   这 个 人 言行 不一。
   Zhè ge rén yánxíng bù yī.
   This man's words don't match his deeds.

5. 言语 **yányǔ** speech
   这 个 人 言语 粗鲁。
   Zhè ge rén yányǔ cūlǔ.
   This man speaks crudely.

The top horizontal is the longest. **7 strokes**

丶 一 二 三 言 言 言

yào want

The character is a pictograph of a man standing with his hands on his waist. Perhaps because the waist is an important part of the body, it came to mean *important*.

Radical: 西 'west'   **Index # 139**

or   女 'female'   **Index # 65**

Character components: 西 + 女   **Character configuration:**

Compounds, sentences and meanings

1. **要 yào** want
   您 要 买 什么?
   Nín yào mǎi shénme?
   What would you like to buy?

2. **要不 yàobù** otherwise
   你 可 以 坐 船 去, 要 不 坐 火 车 也
   Nǐ kěyi zuò chuán qù, yàobù zuò huǒchē yě
   行。
   xíng.
   You can go there by boat or by train.

3. **要好 yàohǎo** be close friends
   他们 从小 就 很 要好。
   Tāmen cóngxiǎo jiù hěn yàohǎo.
   They have been close friends since childhood.

4. **要紧 yàojǐn** important
   我 有 件 要紧 的 事儿 跟 他 商量。
   Wǒ yǒu jiàn yàojǐn de shìr gēn tā shāngliang.
   I have an important matter to discuss with him.

5. **首要 shǒuyào** of the first importance
   首要 的 事 先 办。
   Shǒuyào de shì xiān bàn.
   First things first.

The two vertical strokes are parallel.   **9 strokes**

一	厂	二	两	西	西	要	要	要			

 **xiān** first

The character combines *to do* 生 and *people* 儿 to represent the act of going before other people, and means *ahead* or *before*.

Radical: 儿 'child'   **Index # 21**

Character components: 生 + 儿   **Character configuration:**

Compounds, sentences and meanings

1. **先** **xiān** first
   他 比 我 先 到。
   Tā bǐ wǒ xiān dào.
   He arrived before me.

2. **先后** **xiānhòu** priority
   这些 事 都 该办, 不过 得 有 个 先后。
   Zhèxiē shì dōu gāi bàn, búguò děi yǒu ge xiānhòu.
   All these matters should be tackled, but they should be taken up in order of priority.

3. **先前** **xiānqián** previously
   这 孩子 比 先前 高 多了。
   Zhè háizi bǐ xiānqián gāo duō le.
   This child is much taller than before.

4. **先生** **xiānsheng** mister, gentleman
   女士们, 先生们。
   Nǚshìmen, xiānshengmen.
   Ladies and gentlemen.

5. **先头** **xiāntóu** formerly
   你 先头 没 说过 这 件 事。
   Nǐ xiāntóu méi shuōguo zhè jiàn shì.
   You didn't mention this before.

The last stroke is a vertical-bend-hook. **6 strokes**

ノ	㇒	卅	生	歩	先						

发 fā develop

發

The full form of the character combines *speed of a person's legs* 癶 and the sketch of a *bow* with *legs apart* 殳. It suggests the shooting of an arrow while standing with legs spread and the word now means *start*. It is not clear how the simplified form was derived.

Radical: 又 'again'

Index # 24

Character components: 屮 + 又 + 、

Character configuration:

Compounds, sentences and meanings

1. 发 **fā** develop
   她 从来 没 发过 脾气。
   Tā cónglái méi fāguo píqi.
   She has never lost her temper.

2. 发火 **fāhuǒ** loses one's temper
   你 别 发火, 咱们 慢慢儿 谈。
   Nǐ bié fāhuǒ, zánmen mànmānr tán.
   Don't get angry. Let's talk it over calmly.

3. 发热 **fārè** runs a temperature
   你 好像 有点儿 发热。
   Nǐ hǎoxiàng yǒudiǎnr fārè.
   You look as if you are running a temperature.

4. 发生 **fāshēng** happen
   前面 发生了 事故。
   Qiánmiàn fāshēngle shìgù.
   There's an accident ahead of us.

5. 发言 **fāyán** make a statement
   他 在 会 上 发言 了 吗?
   Tā zài huì shàng fāyán le ma?
   Did he speak at the meeting?

The first stroke is a slanting-horizontal-bend.											5 strokes
㇀	少	岁	发	发							

 **yīn** sound

The character is a derivation of *speak* 立, with a line 一 in the *mouth* 口 to represent the tongue making a *sound*.

Radical: 音 'sound'　　　　　　　　**Index # 178**

Character components: 立 + 日　　　**Character configuration:**

Compounds, sentences and meanings

1. 音 **yīn** sound
   美国 之 音。
   Měiguó Zhī Yīn.
   The Voice of America.

2. 音响 **yīnxiǎng** hi-fi set
   这 套 音响 设备 比较 贵。
   Zhè tào yīnxiǎng shèbèi bǐjiào guì.
   This hi-fi set is rather expensive.

3. 音乐 **yīnyuè** music
   你 喜欢 什么 音乐?
   Nǐ xǐhuan shénme yīnyuè?
   What kind of music do you like?

4. 声音 **shēngyīn** sound
   她的 声音 很 高。
   Tāde shēngyīn hěn gāo.
   She has a high-pitched voice.

5. 噪音 **zàoyīn** noise
   城市 里 噪音 污染 是 一个 严重
   Chéngshì lǐ zàoyīn wūrǎn shì yí ge yánzhòng
   问题。
   wèntí.
   Noise pollution in the city is a serious problem.

The second horizontal stroke is longer.　　　　　　　**9 strokes**

丶	亠	六	立	立	音	音	音	音			

声

shēng sound

Full form

The full form of the character was derived from a pictograph of an *instrument* made of suspended stones. It means *sound*. The simplified form takes only the top left component of the full form.

Radical: 士 'scholar'

Index # 41

Character components: 士 + 尸

Character configuration:

Compounds, sentences and meanings

1. 声 **shēng** sound
   你 听见 脚步 声 了 没有?
   Nǐ tīngjiàn jiǎobù shēng le méiyǒu?
   Did you hear the sound of footsteps?

2. 声调 **shēngdiào** tones
   学 汉语 一定 要 学好 声调。
   Xué Hànyǔ yídìng yào xuéhǎo shēngdiào.
   In learning Chinese, one must learn the tones properly.

3. 小声 **xiǎoshēng** in a low voice
   请 小声 说话。
   Qǐng xiǎoshēng shuōhuà.
   Please speak softly.

4. 声旁 **shēngpáng** phonetic element of a character
   "请" 的 声旁 是 "青"。
   "Qǐng" de shēngpáng shì "qīng".
   The phonetic element for the character "qīng" is "qīng."

5. 大声 **dàshēng** loudly
   请 你 说 大声 点儿。
   Qǐng nǐ shuō dàshēng diǎnr.
   Please speak up a little.

The second horizontal stroke of 士 is shorter.   7 strokes

一	十	士	声	声	声	声					

调

diào/tiáo   tone/adjust

調

The character combines *word* 讠 and the phonetic 周 to give two meanings: *tone* and *adjust*.

Radical: 讠 'word'

Character components: 讠 + 周

Index # 9

Character configuration:

Compounds, sentences and meanings

1. **调 diào** tone
   这 人 说 英语 带 美国 调。
   Zhè rén shuō Yīngyǔ dài Měiguó diào.
   This person speaks English with an American accent.

2. **调查 diàochá** investigate
   人口 调查 一般 是 十 年 一次。
   Rénkǒu diàochá yìbān shì shí nián yí cì.
   A census is usually carried out every ten years.

3. **调子 diàozi** tune
   这 个 调子 倒 挺 熟 的。
   Zhè ge diàozi dào tǐng shóu de.
   The tune is quite familiar.

4. **调 tiáo** adjust
   请 把 声音 调 低 一点儿。
   Qǐng bǎ shēngyīn tiáo dī yìdiǎnr.
   Please turn the volume down a little.

5. **调皮 tiáopí** mischievous
   小冬 是 个 调皮 的 孩子。
   Xiǎodōng shì ge tiáopí de háizi.
   Xiaodong is a mischievous child.

The second horizontal stroke of 土 is longer.   10 strokes

`	讠	讠	讠	讠	调	调	调	调	调			

pīn put together

The character is made up of *hand* 扌 and *merge* 并 to suggest the idea of *putting together*.

Radical: 扌 'hand'　　　　　　　**Index # 48**

Character components: 扌 + 丷 + 开　　**Character configuration:**

Compounds, sentences and meanings

1. 拼　**pīn**　put together
把 两 块 木板 拼起来。
Bǎ liǎng kuāi mùbǎn pīnqǐlai.
Put two boards together side by side.

2. 拼命　**pīnmìng**　exerting the utmost strength
他 工作 很 认真，老 是 拼命地 干。
Tā gōngzuò hěn rènzhēn, lǎo shì pīnmìngde gàn.
He works conscientiously, often pushing himself to the limit.

3. 拼盘　**pīnpán**　assorted cold dishes
这 是 乳猪 拼盘。
Zhè shì rǔzhū pīnpán.
This cold dish assortment features suckling pig.

4. 拼写　**pīnxiě**　transliterate, spell
请 你 用 拼音 把 这 个 汉字
Qǐng nǐ yòng pīnyīn bǎ zhè ge Hànzì
拼写出来。
pīnxiěchūlai.
Please transliterate this character into pinyin romanization.

5. 拼音　**pīnyīn**　pinyin romanization
拼音 的 全名 是 汉语 拼音。
Pīnyīn de quánmíng shì Hànyǔ Pīnyīn.
The full term for pinyin is Hanyu Pinyin.

The second horizontal on the right-hand side is longer.	9 strokes

一	扌	扌	扌	扩	扩	扞	抴	拼				

cái   only then, just

The character combines *land* 一 and the pictograph of *sprout* 入 to suggest the idea that the sprout will grow into a tree. Thus, it means *ability* or *talent*.

Radical: 一 'horizontal stroke'   **Index # 2**

Character components: 一 + 亅 + 丿   **Character configuration:** ⬚

Compounds, sentences and meanings

1. 才 **cái**   only then (late occurrence)
   下雪 路滑，汽车 晚了 半个 小时 才
   Xiàxuě lù huá, qìchē wǎnle bàn ge xiǎoshí cái
   到。
   dào.
   It was snowing and the road was slippery so the bus was half an hour late.

2. 才华 **cáihuá**   literary or artistic talent
   他 是 一 位 很 有 才华 的 作家。
   Tā shì yí wèi hěn yǒu cáihuá de zuòjiā.
   He is a gifted writer.

3. 才识 **cáishí**   ability and insight
   我 觉得 你 哥哥 才识 过 人。
   Wǒ juéde nǐ gēge cáishí guò rén.
   I think your older brother is extraordinarily talented.

4. 人才 **réncái**   talent
   她 是 个 难得 的 人才。
   Tā shì ge nándé de réncái.
   She is a person of extraordinary ability.

5. 刚才 **gāngcái**   just now
   他 刚才 还 说 要 去 呢。
   Tā gāngcái hái shuō yào qù ne.
   He was saying only a moment ago that he wanted to go.

The final sweeping stroke comes down from the intersection of the first two strokes.						3 strokes
一	十	才				

第

dì ordinal number

The character combines *bamboo* ⺮ and the phonetic 弟 to express the idea of putting bamboo slats in order of height. It means *order* or *grade*.

Radical: ⺮ 'bamboo'   **Index # 145**

Character components: ⺮ + 弟   **Character configuration:** ▭

Compounds, sentences and meanings

1. **第** **dì** ordinal number
   我 是 第二次 世界 大战 后 出生 的。
   Wǒ shì Dì'èrcì Shìjiè Dàzhàn hòu chūshēng de.
   I was born after the Second World War.

2. **第一声** **dìyīshēng** first tone
   第一声
   dìyīshēng
   First tone in Mandarin (high-level tone)

3. **第二声** **dì'èrshēng** second tone
   第二声
   dì'èrshēng
   Second tone in Mandarin (high-rising tone)

4. **第三声** **dìsānshēng** third tone
   第三声
   dìsānshēng
   Third tone in Mandarin (low-dipping tone)

5. **第四声** **dìsìshēng** fourth tone
   第四声
   dìsìshēng
   Fourth tone in Mandarin (high-falling tone)

The ninth stroke ends with a hook.   **11 strokes**

ノ	⺈	⺅	⺉	𥫗	𥫗	笁	笘	笋	第	第	

Quiz 27 (261–270)

A. Look at the 16-character grid and CIRCLE words or phrases. They can be written horizontally or vertically. (Look at the circled characters in the Key if you are unsure.) Copy the word or phrase next to the grid and write down the pinyin and meaning.

					Word or phrase			Pinyin	Meaning
学	拼	音	声	(i)	学	拼	音	xué pīnyīn	learn pinyin
进	语	拼	调	(ii)					
要	言	认	发	(iii)					
先	助	读	才	(iv)					

B. Using the characters in the 16-character grid, convert the pinyin sentences into characters and write the English meaning.

(i)	Pǔtōnghuà yǒu sì ge shēngdiào.								
(ii)	Xué Hànyǔ yào xiān xué fāyīn,								
	xué fāyīn yào xué Hànyǔ Pīnyīn								
	hái yào duō shuō cái huì yǒu jìnbù.								

C. Match the Chinese words with their English meaning.

(i)

言 lùn — make a speech
发言 — occur
发生 — otherwise
先生 — comment
先前 — important
先后 — previously
要 jǐn — Mister
要不 — priority

(ii)

口音 — sound
声音 — just now
小声 — accent
调 chá — spell
调 pí — talent
拼写 — mischievous
gāng 才 — softly
人才 — investigate

22

感 gǎn feel

The character combines *heart* 心 and the phonetic 咸 to suggest the idea of *feeling*. The phonetic value of the top component is lost in this instance.

Radical: 心 'heart'　　　　　　　**Index # 76**

Character components: 咸 + 心

Character configuration:

Compounds, sentences and meanings

1. **感　gǎn**　feel, sense
   他 感到 自己 错了。
   Tā gǎndào zìjǐ cuòle.
   He sensed that he was wrong.

2. **感觉　gǎnjué**　feel, perceive
   你 感觉 怎么样?
   Nǐ gǎnjué zěnmeyàng?
   How do you feel now?

3. **感冒　gǎnmào**　common cold, flu
   医生 说 我 得了 感冒。
   Yīshēng shuō wǒ déle gǎnmào.
   The doctor said that I've got the flu.

4. **感情　gǎnqíng**　feeling, emotion
   这 两 年 来, 我 对 她 产生了
   Zhè liǎng nián lái, wǒ duì tā chǎnshēngle
   感情。
   gǎnqíng.
   I've grown very close to her these past two years.

5. **感谢　gǎnxiè**　thank
   非常 感谢 你的 帮助。
   Fēicháng gǎnxiè nǐde bāngzhù.
   Thanks very much for your help.

The seventh stroke ends with a hook.												13 strokes
一	厂	厂	斤	后	后	咸	咸	咸	咸	感	感	感

兴

xīng/xìng prosper/interest

The full form of the character can be thought of as people gathering together to have *fun*.

Radical: 八 'eight'   **Index # 17**

Character components: ⭢ + 八

Character configuration: ▭

Compounds, sentences and meanings

1. 兴 **xīng** mood, desire
   兴 高 采 烈。
   Xīng gāo cǎi liè.
   In high spirits.

2. 兴奋 **xīngfèn** be excited
   我 兴奋得 睡不着 觉。
   Wǒ xīngfènde shuìbuzháo jiào.
   I'm so excited I can't sleep.

3. 兴趣 **xìngqù** interest
   我 对 下棋 很 感 兴趣。
   Wǒ duì xiàqí hěn gǎn xìngqù.
   I'm very interested in chess.

4. 兴头 **xīngtóu** enthusiasm
   我的 朋友 对体育 活动 兴头 很
   Wǒde péngyou duì tǐyù huódòng xīngtóu hěn
   大。
   dà.
   My friends are very keen on sport.

5. 高兴 **gāoxìng** happy
   认识 你 很 高兴。
   Rènshi nǐ hěn gāoxìng.
   I'm pleased to meet you.

The third stroke sweeps down from right to left.   6 strokes

丶	丷	⭢	⭢	兴	兴					

273

趣 **qù** delight

The character combines *walk* 走 and the phonetic 取 which suggests *fetch* or *aim at*. It came to mean *interest* or *delight*.

Radical: 走 'walk'

Index # 156

Character components: 走 + 取

Character configuration:

Compounds, sentences and meanings

1. **趣** **qù** interest, delight
   我 觉得 他 表演得 很 有趣。
   Wǒ juéde tā biǎoyǎnde hěn yǒuqù.
   I found his performance quite delightful.

2. **趣味** **qùwèi** taste
   这 种 电影 迎合 低级 趣味。
   Zhè zhǒng diànyǐng yínghé dījí qùwèi.
   This type of movies caters for vulgar tastes.

3. **乐趣** **lèqù** interest, delight
   我 觉得 跳舞 的乐趣 无穷。
   Wǒ juéde tiàowǔ de lèqù wúqióng.
   I think dancing is truly wonderful.

4. **兴趣** **xìngqù** interest
   我 对 下棋 很 感 兴趣。
   Wǒ duì xiàqí hěn gǎn xìngqù.
   I'm very interested in chess.

5. **有趣** **yǒuqù** interesting
   这 是 个 有趣 的 游戏。
   Zhè shì ge yǒuqù de yóuxì.
   This is an interesting game.

End the last stroke firmly.

15 strokes

一	十	土	走	走	走	走	走	走	起	起	起	起
趣	趣											

tán talk

Full form

The character combines *word* 讠 and the phonetic 炎 which refers to *the shape of flames*. It suggests the idea of *talking in a quiet manner like the movement of a small flame*.

Radical: 讠 'word'

Index # 9

Character components: 讠 + 炎

Character configuration:

Compounds, sentences and meanings

1. **谈** **tán** talk
   我 跟 他 很 谈得来。
   Wǒ gēn tā hěn tándelái.
   I get along with him very well.

2. **谈话** **tánhuà** talk
   我们 进行了 友好 的 谈话。
   Wǒmen jìnxíngle yǒuhǎo de tánhuà.
   We had a friendly talk.

3. **谈判** **tánpàn** negotiate
   两 国 进行了 贸易 谈判。
   Liǎng guó jìnxíngle màoyì tánpàn.
   The two countries held trade negotiations.

4. **谈天** **tántiān** chat
   有空儿 到 我 这里 谈天。
   Yǒukòngr dào wǒ zhèlǐ tántiān.
   Come for a chat when you're free.

5. **谈吐** **tántù** style of conversation
   从 她的 谈吐 看得出 她 是 有 教养
   Cóng tāde tántù kàndechū tā shì yǒu jiàoyǎng
   的 人。
   de rén.
   From her style of speech, I can see that she's well educated.

The second stroke lifts at the end.									10 strokes
丶	讠	讠	讠	诮	诶	诶	谈	谈	谈

yàn experience

Full form

The character combines *horse* 马 and the phonetic 金 to suggest the idea of *examine*. The simplified form was derived from the cursive form of the full character.

Radical: 马 'horse'

Index # 69

Character components: 马 + 金

Character configuration:

Compounds, sentences and meanings

1. 验 **yàn** examine
   请 把 护照 给 我 验一验。
   Qǐng bǎ hùzhào gěi wǒ yànyiyàn.
   Please let me check your passport.

2. 验血 **yànxiě** blood test
   医生 让 我 去 验血。
   Yīshēng ràng wǒ qù yànxiě.
   The doctor told me to get a blood test.

3. 经验 **jīngyàn** experience
   你 学 汉语 的 经验 对 我 很 有用。
   Nǐ xué Hànyǔ de jīngyàn duì wǒ hěn yǒuyòng.
   Your experience in learning Chinese is very useful to me.

4. 实验 **shíyàn** experiment
   念 理科 经常 要 做 实验。
   Niàn lǐkē jīngcháng yào zuò shíyàn.
   If you study Science you have to do experiements regularly.

5. 体验 **tǐyàn** to experience
   年轻人 应该 去 社会 体验
   Niánqīngrén yīnggāi qù shèhuì tǐyàn
   生活。
   shēnghuó.
   Young people should experience life in the real world.

The bottom horizontal stroke is longer.									10 strokes
フ	马	马	驭	驵	验	验	验	验	

jiāo exchange

The character combines the components 亠 and 父 to suggest the sense of criss-crossing. The original pattern describes a person sitting with crossed legs. By extension it means *exchange*.

Radical: 亠 'top of 六'　　　　　　**Index # 6**

Character components: 亠 + 父　　　　**Character configuration:**

Compounds, sentences and meanings

1. **交　jiāo**　deliver
   我们 什么 时候 交钱？
   Wǒmen shénme shíhou jiāoqián?
   When do we pay?

2. **交换　jiāohuàn**　exchange
   我们 在 会 上 交换了 意见。
   Wǒmen zài huì shàng jiāohuànle yìjiàn.
   We exchanged views at the meeting.

3. **交际　jiāojì**　social intercourse
   她 不 善于 交际。
   Tā bú shànyú jiāojì.
   She's not a good mixer.

4. **交流　jiāoliú**　exchange
   以后 我们 要 多 交流 经验。
   Yǐhòu wǒmen yào duō jiāoliú jīngyàn.
   We should exchange our experiences more often in the future.

5. **交通　jiāotōng**　transport
   这里 交通 很 方便。
   Zhèlǐ jiāotōng hěn fāngbiàn.
   The transport is very convenient here.

The last two strokes taper off.　　　　　　　　　　　　**6 strokes**

丶	亠	宀	六	交	交				

 **liú** flow

The character combines water 氵 and the phonetic 㐬 to suggest the idea of water flowing from a river. It means *flow*.

Radical: 氵 'three drops of water'　　　　**Index # 32**

Character component: 氵 + 亠 + 厶 + 儿　　　**Character configuration:**

Compounds, sentences and meanings

1. **流 liú** flow
   中国 的 河大 都 向 东 流。
   Zhōngguó de hé dà dōu xiàng dōng liú.
   Most of the rivers in China flow to the east.

2. **流传 liúchuán** hand down
   这 是 个 古代 流传下来 的 寓言。
   Zhè shì ge gǔdài liúchuánxiàlai de yùyán.
   This is a fable handed down from ancient times.

3. **流动 liúdòng** on the move
   中国 有 很多 流动 人口。
   Zhōngguó yǒu hěnduō liúdòng rénkǒu.
   China has a large floating population.

4. **流利 liúlì** fluent
   他 说 一 口 流利的 法语。
   Tā shuō yì kǒu liúlì de Fǎyǔ.
   He speaks fluent French.

5. **流行 liúxíng** popular
   这 首 歌 在 台湾 很 流行。
   Zhè shǒu gē zài Táiwān hěn liúxíng.
   This song is very popular in Taiwan.

The last stroke is a vertical-bend-hook.　　　　　　　　　　　10 strokes

丶	冫	氵	氵	汸	浐	浐	浐	浐	流			

 **jiàn** build

The phonetic 建 is used as a character. It takes on the meaning of *build*.

Radical: 廴 'move on'   **Index # 25**

Character components: 聿 + 廴   **Character configuration:**

Compounds, sentences and meanings

1. **建 jiàn** build
   这 个 学校 是 新 建 的。
   Zhè ge xuéxiào shì xīn jiàn de.
   This school was recently built.

2. **建立 jiànlì** build, establish
   多 去 表演 就 能 建立 信心。
   Duō qù biǎoyǎn jiù néng jiànlì xìnxīn.
   Giving more performances builds up your confidence.

3. **建设性 jiànshèxìng** constructive
   我们 欢迎 建设性 的 意见。
   Wǒmen huānyíng jiànshèxìng de yìjiàn.
   We welcome constructive suggestions.

4. **建议 jiànyì** suggest
   这 是 个 很 好 的 建议。
   Zhè shì ge hěn hǎo de jiànyì.
   This is a good suggestion.

5. **修建 xiūjiàn** build
   这里 将 要 修建 一 个 国际 机场。
   Zhèlǐ jiāng yào xiūjiàn yí ge guójì jīchǎng.
   They are going to build an international airport here.

The middle section is written before the radical.   8 strokes

フ	フ	ヨ	彐	彐	聿	律	建			

yì discuss

Full form

議

The full character combines *word* 言, and the phonetic 義, which means righteousness to suggest constructive *discussion*. In simplfication, 义 replaces 義.

Radical: 讠 'word'

Index # 9

Character components: 讠 + 义

Character configuration:

Compounds, sentences and meanings

1. **议 yì** discuss
   我们 对 各种 方案 都 议了议。
   Wǒmen duì gèzhǒng fāng'àn dōu yìleyì.
   We exchanged views on each of the different proposals.

2. **议程 yìchéng** agenda
   我们 可以 把 这 件 事 列入 议程。
   Wǒmen kěyǐ bǎ zhè jiàn shì lièrù yìchéng.
   We can place this matter on the agenda.

3. **议论 yìlùn** comment, talk
   人们 对 这 件 事 议论 纷纷。
   Rénmen duì zhè jiàn shì yìlùn fēnfēn.
   Everyone is talking about it.

4. **下议院 Xiàyìyuàn** Lower House of Parliament
   在 美国 下议院 叫 众议院。
   Zài Měiguó, Xiàyìyuàn jiào Zhòngyìyuàn.
   In the United States, the Lower House is called the Congress.

5. **议题 yìtí** topic for discussion
   今天 的议题是 什么?
   Jīntiān de yìtí shì shénme?
   What are the topics for discussion today?

End the last stroke firmly.   5 strokes

`	讠	议	议	议							

跟

gēn follow

The character combines *foot* 足 and the phonetic 艮 to represent the image of a person who stops walking and looks back. It suggests the idea of *being followed*.

Radical: 𧾷 'foot'　　　　　　　　　　**Index # 164**

Character components: 𧾷 + 艮　　　　**Character configuration:**

Compounds, sentences and meanings

1. **跟 gēn** with
   她 跟 父母 住 在 一起。
   Tā gēn fùmǔ zhù zài yìqǐ.
   She lives with her parents.

2. **跟⋯一样 gēn ... yíyàng** the same as
   弟弟 长得 跟 我 一样 高。
   Dìdi zhǎngde gēn wǒ yíyàng gāo.
   My younger brother is as tall as me.

3. **跟上 gēnshàng** keep pace with
   你 走得 太 快，我 跟不上。
   Nǐ zǒude tài kuài, wǒ gēnbúshàng.
   You walk too fast, I can't keep up with you.

4. **跟着 gēnzhe** follow
   请 跟着 我 念。
   Qǐng gēnzhe wǒ niàn
   Please read after me.

5. **高跟鞋 gāogēnxié** high-heel shoes
   她 喜欢 穿 高跟鞋。
   Tā xǐhuan chuān gāogēnxié.
   She likes to wear high-heel shoes.

The last two strokes of 𧾷 are vertical and lift, respectively.　　　　　**13 strokes**

丶	口	口	甼	甼	𧾷	足	𧾷⁷	𧾷⁷	𧾷⁷	跟	跟	跟

A. Look at the 16-character grid and CIRCLE words or phrases. They can be written horizontally or vertically. (Look at the circled characters in the Key if you are unsure.) Copy the word or phrase next to the grid and write down the pinyin and meaning.

对	感	跟	下
谈	兴	经	验
可	趣	本	建
交	流	书	议

	Word or phrase			Pinyin	Meaning
(i)	感	兴	趣	gǎn xìngqù	be interested in something
(ii)					
(iii)					
(iv)					

B. Using the characters in the 16-character grid, convert the pinyin sentences into characters and write the English meaning.

(i)	Wǒ duì Hànzì hěn gǎn xìngqù.								
(ii)	Kěyǐ tántan nǐde jīngyàn ma?								
(iii)	Wǒmen kěyǐ jiāoliú yíxiàr.								
(iv)	Wǒ jiànyì gēnzhe zhè běn shū xué.								

C. Match the Chinese words with their English meaning.

(i)

感动	be excited
感觉	interest, delight
感谢	feeling
高兴	be touched by
兴 fèn	pleasure
趣 wèi	talk, conversation
lè 趣	happy
谈话	thanks

(ii)

验 xiě	exchange ideas
shí 验	popular
交流	blood test
流 chuán	build
流 lì	establish
流 xíng	hand down
建 lì	experiment
xiū 建	fluent

gào tell

In ancient script, the character is similar to *tongue* 舌 and suggests the idea of words coming from the tongue. The *mouth* 口 makes it quite clear that the meaning is *to tell*.

Radical: 口 'mouth'   **Index # 50**

Character components: 牛 + 口   **Character configuration:**

Compounds, sentences and meanings

1. 告 **gào** tell
   什么 时候 离开, 盼 告。
   Shénme shíhou líkāi, pàn gào.
   Please tell me when you are leaving.

2. 告别 **gàobié** bid farewell to
   我 向 你 告别 来了。
   Wǒ xiàng nǐ gàobié lái le.
   I've come to say good-bye.

3. 告假 **gàojià** take leave
   我 身体 不舒服, 明天 告假。
   Wǒ shēntǐ bù shūfu, míngtiān gàojià.
   I don't feel well, I won't come in tomorrow.

4. 告诉 **gàosu** tell
   告诉 他们 别 等 了。
   Gàosu tāmen bié děng le.
   Tell them not to wait.

5. 报告 **bàogào** report
   报告 大家 一个 好 消息。
   Bàogào dàjiā yí ge hǎo xiāoxi.
   Here's a piece of good news for us all.

The second horizontal stroke is longer than the first.   7 strokes

丿 ㇒ 牛 生 告 告 告

 **sù** tell

The character combines *word* 讠 and the phonetic 斥 which means *scold* to suggest the idea of *extension by words*.

Radical: 讠 'word'

Index # 9

Character components: 讠 + 斥

Character configuration:

Compounds, sentences and meanings

1. **诉** sù tell
   他 常常 向 我 诉苦。
   Tā chángcháng xiàng wǒ sù kǔ.
   He often tells me his troubles.

2. **诉说** sùshuō relate, recount
   她 向 我 诉说 苦衷。
   Tā xiàng wǒ sùshuō kǔzhōng.
   She tells me her troubles.

3. **诉讼** sùsòng litigation
   他 提出 离婚 诉讼。
   Tā tíchū líhūn sùsòng.
   He has started divorce proceedings.

4. **控诉** kòngsù accuse, denounce
   她 控诉 社会 对她的 歧视。
   Tā kòngsù shèhuì duì tā de qíshì.
   She spoke out against the way society had discriminated against her.

5. **倾诉** qīngsù pour out one's heart
   我 是你的 好 朋友， 有 什么 事可以
   Wǒ shì nǐde hǎo péngyou, yǒu shénme shì kěyǐ
   向 我 倾诉。
   xiàng wǒ qīngsù.
   I'm your good friend, you can pour your heart out to me.

Don't forget to end 斥 firmly with a dot.

7 strokes

丶	讠	讠	讠	讠	诉	诉					

想

xiǎng think

The character combines *heart* 心 and the phonetic 相 to suggest visualizing something. Thus, it means *think*.

Radical: 心 'heart'

Index # 76

Character components: 相 + 心

Character configuration:

Compounds, sentences and meanings

1. **想** **xiǎng** think
   你 想得 很 周到。
   Nǐ xiǎngde hěn zhōudào.
   You have thought of everything.

2. **想到** **xiǎngdào** think of
   我们 没 想到 你 会 来。
   Wǒmen méi xiǎngdào nǐ huì lái.
   We didn't expect you to come.

3. **想法** **xiǎngfa** idea, opinion
   把 你的 想法 给 大家 说说。
   Bǎ nǐde xiǎngfa gěi dàjiā shuōshuo.
   Tell us what you have in mind.

4. **想念** **xiǎngniàn** remember with longing
   我们 都 很 想念 你。
   Wǒmen dōu hěn xiǎngniàn nǐ.
   We all miss you very much.

5. **想象力** **xiǎngxiànglì** imagination
   这 孩子 很 有 想象力。
   Zhè háizi hěn yǒu xiǎngxiànglì.
   This child is full of imagination.

The horizontal hook in 心 curves to the left.												13 strokes
一	十	才	木	利	初	相	相	相	相	想	想	想

讲　**jiǎng**　speak/explain

Full form

講

The full character combines *words* 言 and *piled up* 冓 to suggest the idea that when people put words together, they are *talking*. In simplification, the stereotype 井 replaces 冓.

Radical: 讠 'word'　　　　　　　　　　**Index # 9**

Character components: 讠 + 井

Character configuration:

Compounds, sentences and meanings

1. 讲　**jiǎng**　speak
   我们 讲 英语，好 不 好?
   Wǒmen jiǎng Yīngyǔ, hǎo bu hǎo?
   Can we speak English, please?

2. 讲话　**jiǎnghuà**　speak, talk
   他 在 会 上 讲了 话。
   Tā zài huì shàng jiǎngle huà.
   He spoke at the meeting.

3. 讲价　**jiǎngjià**　bargain
   在 中国 买 东西 一般 要 讲价。
   Zài Zhōngguó mǎi dōngxi yībān yào jiǎngjià.
   In China, people usually bargain when they buy things.

4. 讲究　**jiǎngjiu**　be particular about
   他 不 讲究 吃穿。
   Tā bù jiǎngjiu chīchuān.
   He is not too fastidious about food or clothing.

5. 讲理　**jiǎnglǐ**　reason with someone
   我们 跟 他 讲理 去。
   Wǒmen gēn tā jiǎnglǐ qù.
   Let's go and talk it over with him.

The left vertical stroke of 井 ends with a sweep.　　　　　**6 strokes**

丶	讠	讠	讠	讲	讲						

利 lì sharp

The character combines *rice plant* 禾 and *sword* 刂 to represent an edged tool used for reaping rice. From this it came to mean *cut well* or *sharp*.

Radical: 禾 'grain' **Index # 124**

or 刂 'upright knife' **Index # 15**

Character components: 禾 + 刂 **Character configuration:**

Compounds, sentences and meanings

1. 利 **lì** favorable
   文化 交流 对 两 国 都 有利。
   Wénhuà jiāoliú duì liǎng guó dōu yǒu lì.
   Cultural exchange benefits both countries.

2. 利害 **lìhai** terrible, formidable
   这 几 天 热得 很 利害。
   Zhè jǐ tiān rède hěn lìhai.
   It's been terribly hot these last few days.

3. 利落 **lìluo** neat, orderly
   他 做事 干净 利落。
   Tā zuòshì gānjìng lìluo.
   He is a neat worker.

4. 利益 **lìyì** benefit
   我 这样 做 是 为 你的 利益 着想。
   Wǒ zhèyàng zuò shì wèi nǐde lìyì zháoxiǎng.
   I did it out of consideration for your interests.

5. 利用 **lìyòng** make use of
   我们 应该 好好儿地 利用 空余 的
   Wǒmen yīnggāi hǎohāorde lìyòng kōngyú de
   时间。
   shíjiān
   We should utilize our spare time properly.

The vertical stroke of 禾 has no hook. 7 strokes

一	二	千	禾	禾	利	利					

开 **kāi** open

Full form

開

The full form of the character combines *door* 門, *bolt* 一 and *both hands* 廾 to represent the lifting of the bar of a gate with both hands. Thus, the character means *open*.

Radical: 一 'horizontal stroke'

or 廾 'bottom of 开'

Character components: 一 + 廾

Index # 2

Index # 44

Character configuration: ☐

Compounds, sentences and meanings

1. 开 **kāi** open
   这 把 钥匙 开不了 这 个 锁。
   Zhè bǎ yàoshi kāibuliǎo zhè ge suǒ.
   This key doesn't open this lock.

2. 开车 **kāichē** drive or start a vehicle
   快 开车 了,大家 上车 吧。
   Kuài kāichē le , dàjiā shàngchē ba.
   The bus is going to start. Hurry up, everybody.

3. 开放 **kāifàng** open to public use
   星期天 图书馆 照常 开放。
   Xīngqītiān túshūguǎn zhàocháng kāifàng.
   The library is always open on Sundays.

4. 开口 **kāikǒu** start to talk
   没 等 我 开口,他 就 抢先 替我
   Méi děng wǒ kāikǒu, tā jiù qiǎngxiān tì wǒ
   说 了。
   shuō le.
   Before I could open my mouth, he jumped in and spoke on my behalf.

5. 开始 **kāishǐ** begin
   舞会 什么 时候 开始?
   Wǔhuì shénme shíhou kāishǐ?
   What time does the dance start?

The left vertical stroke of 开 ends with a sweep to the left.

4 strokes

一	二	于	开						

 **pà** afraid

The character combines *upright heart* 忄 and *white* 白 to suggest the idea of being scared of something. It means *afraid*.

Radical: 忄 'upright heart'   **Index # 33**

Character components: 忄 + 白   **Character configuration:** ▭▭

Compounds, sentences and meanings

1. 怕 **pà** be afraid of
   我 怕 黑。
   Wǒ pà hēi.
   I'm afraid of the dark.

2. 怕事 **pàshì** be afraid of getting into trouble
   她 胆小 怕事。
   Tā dǎnxiǎo pàshì.
   She's timid and overcautious.

3. 怕冷 **pàlěng** be afraid of the cold
   我 从小 就 不 怕冷。
   Wǒ cóngxiǎo jiù bú pàlěng.
   Since young, I do not fear the cold.

4. 怕羞 **pàxiū** bashful
   我 小 时候 很 怕羞。
   Wǒ xiǎo shíhou hěn pàxiū.
   I was very shy when I was small.

5. 恐怕 **kǒngpà** be afraid of
   这样 做, 恐怕 不行。
   Zhèyàng zuò, kǒngpà bùxíng.
   I'm afraid this won't work.

The first stroke of 白 tapers down from right to left.   **8 strokes**

丶	忄	忄	忄	忄	怕	怕	怕					

cuò   wrong

Full form

錯

The character combines *metal* 钅 and *the past* 昔 to suggest the idea of a *mistake*. In simplification, the radical 金 changes to 钅.

Radical: 钅 'metal'

Index # 122

Character component: 钅 + 昔

Character configuration:

Compounds, sentences and meanings

1. **错 cuò** wrong
   他 弄错 了。
   Tā nòngcuò le.
   He has got it wrong.

2. **错别字 cuòbiézì** wrongly written or mispronounced characters
   我 经常 会 写 错别字。
   Wǒ jīngcháng huì xiě cuòbiézì.
   I often write characters wrongly.

3. **错误 cuòwù** mistake
   这 是 一个 严重 的 错误。
   Zhè shì yí ge yánzhòng de cuòwù.
   This is a serious mistake.

4. **错过 cuòguò** miss, let slip
   错过 这 趟 汽车 就要 等 一 个
   Cuòguò zhè tàng qìchē jiù yào děng yí ge
   小时。
   xiǎoshí
   If we miss this bus, we have to wait an hour (for the next one).

5. **不错 búcuò** not bad, pretty good
   这 个 电影 不错。
   Zhè ge diànyǐng búcuò.
   This movie is quite good.

The last stroke of 钅 is a vertical lift to the right.   13 strokes

ノ	ト	ヒ	ヒ	钅	钅	针	钔	铒	错	错	错	错

gǎi change

The character combines *self* 己 and *movement with deep thinking* 攵. From self-correction, it is extended to mean *to correct others*.

Radical: 攵 'tap'　　　　　　　　　**Index # 99**

Character components: 己 + 攵　　　　**Character configuration:**

Compounds, sentences and meanings

1. 改 **gǎi** change
   几 年 没 来,这里 完全 改 样 了。
   Jǐ nián méi lái, zhèlǐ wánquán gǎi yàng le.
   I've only been away for only a few years, but the place has changed completely.

2. 改变 **gǎibiàn** change
   我 可以 改变 主意 吗?
   Wǒ kěyǐ gǎibiàn zhǔyi ma?
   Can I change my mind?

3. 改掉 **gǎidiào** give up, drop
   他 决定 改掉 坏 习惯。
   Tā juédìng gǎidiào huài xíguàn.
   He has decided to give up his bad habits.

4. 改革 **gǎigé** reform
   中国 还是 坚持 改革 开放。
   Zhōngguó háishì jiānchí gǎigé kāifàng.
   China is still continuing its reform and open-door policy.

5. 改正 **gǎizhèng** correct
   老师 让 我们 在 课 上 改正
   Lǎoshī ràng wǒmen zài kè shàng gǎizhèng
   错误。
   cuòwù.
   The teacher asks us to correct our mistakes in class.

The last stroke of 己 is written as a vertical lift.						7 strokes					
一	丁	己	己'	己"	改	改					

zhèng right, correct

The character combines *line* 一 and *stop* 止 to refer to the idea that *something stops where it should*. Thus, it came to mean *right, correct* or *just*.

Radical: 一 'horizontal stroke'	**Index # 2**	
or 止 'stop'	**Index # 88**	
Character components: 一 + 止	**Character configuration:**	

Compounds, sentences and meanings

1. 正 **zhèng** precisely
   这 双 鞋 大小 正 合适。
   Zhè shuāng xié dàxiǎo zhèng héshì.
   This pair of shoes is just the right size.

2. 正常 **zhèngcháng** normal
   这 几 天 天气 不 太 正常。
   Zhè jǐ tiān tiānqì bù tài zhèngcháng.
   The weather in the past few days has been quite abnormal.

3. 正好 **zhènghǎo** just in time
   你 来得 正好。
   Nǐ láide zhènghǎo.
   You've come just in time.

4. 正确 **zhèngquè** correct
   你 这样 做 是 正确 的。
   Nǐ zhèyàng zuò shì zhèngquè de.
   What you are doing is right.

5. 正在 **zhèngzài** right at the moment
   他们 正在 吃 晚饭。
   Tāmen zhèngzài chī wǎnfàn.
   They are having their dinner right now.

The bottom horizontal stroke is slightly longer.	5 strokes

一	丁	下	正	正							

Quiz 29 (281–290)

A. Look at the 16-character grid and CIRCLE words or phrases. They can be written horizontally or vertically. (Look at the circled characters in the Key if you are unsure.) Copy the word or phrase next to the grid and write down the pinyin and meaning.

	Word or phrase		Pinyin	Meaning
练 (告 诉) 习	(i) 告 诉		gàosu	tell
讲 改 流 怕	(ii)			
想 正 利 就	(iii)			
多 得 开 口	(iv)			

B. Using the characters in the 16-character grid, convert the pinyin sentences into characters and write the English meaning.

(i)	Wǒ gàosu nǐ zěnyàng liànxí ba.								
(ii)	Xiǎng jiǎngde liúlì jiù yào duō jiǎng.								
(iii)	Yào duō kāikǒu, búyào pà shuōcuò.								
(iv)	Cuòle jiù zhīdao zěnyàng gǎizhèng.								

C. Match the Chinese words with their English meaning.

(i)

想 fa	talk, speak
想 niàn	fluent
讲话	open to public use
讲 jià	way of thinking
讲 jiu	miss (someone)
流利	bargain
开 fàng	begin
开 shǐ	be particular about

(ii)

怕 lěng	change, correct
错过	normal
错 wù	dislike the cold
改 gé	miss
改 biàn	accurate
正 cháng	mistake
正 què	reform
正在	right this moment

44

yīng/yìng ought to/answer

Full form

The full form of the character combines *heart* 心 and the phonetic 雁 to suggest the idea of something responding to one's heart. By extension, it means *what ought to be*.

Radical: 广 'broad'

Index # 36

Character components: 广 + ㅛ + 一

Character configuration:

Compounds, sentences and meanings

1. 应 **yīng** ought to
   发现 错误 应 马上 纠正。
   Fāxiàn cuòwù yīng mǎshàng jiūzhèng.
   When a mistake is discovered, it should be corrected at once.

2. 应该 **yīnggāi** ought to
   不用 谢, 这 是 我们 应该 做 的。
   Búyòng xiè, zhè shì wǒmen yīnggāi zuò de.
   Don't mention it, it's the least we could do.

3. 应酬 **yìngchóu** social engagement
   今天 晚上 有 个 应酬。
   Jīntiān wǎnshang yǒu ge yìngchóu.
   I've been invited to a social event this evening.

4. 应当 **yīngdāng** ought to
   我们 是 朋友, 应当 互相
   Wǒmen shì péngyou, yīngdāng hùxiāng
   帮助。
   bāngzhù.
   We are friends, we ought to help each other.

5. 应付 **yìngfu** deal with, cope with
   定单 过多, 难 与 应付。
   Dìngdān guòduō, nán yǔ yìngfu.
   We cannot cope with such a flood of orders.

The third stroke tapers down to the left.　　　　7 strokes

丶	亠	广	广	応	应	应							

Full form

该 **gāi** ought to

該

The character combines *word* 讠 and the phonetic 亥 to suggest the idea of *what ought to be* or *should be*.

Radical: 讠 'word'　　　　　　　　　**Index # 9**

Character components: 讠 + 亥　　　**Character configuration:**

Compounds, sentences and meanings

1. **该　gāi** ought to
   我 该 走 了。
   Wǒ gāi zǒu le.
   I must be off now.

2. **该当　gāidāng** deserve
   你 晚来了 一个 小时，该当 何罪？
   Nǐ wǎnláile yī ge xiǎoshí, gāidāng hé zuì?
   You are an hour late. What punishment do you think you deserve?

3. **该死　gāisǐ** exclamation (showing anger)
   该死! 我 又 忘了 带 钥匙 了。
   Gāisǐ, wǒ yòu wàngle dài yàoshi le.
   Oh no! I've forgotten my key again.

4. **活该　huógāi** exclamation (it serves someone right)
   活该，谁 叫你 不听 我的 话。
   Huógāi, shéi jiào nǐ bùtīng wǒde huà.
   It serves you right for not listening to me.

5. **应该　yīnggāi** ought to
   不用 谢，这 是 我们 应该 做 的。
   Búyòng xiè, zhè shì wǒmen yīnggāi zuò de.
   Don't mention it, it's the least we could do.

The last stroke ends firmly.　　　　　　　　　　　　　　8 strokes

丶	讠	讠	讠	讠	该	该	该				

zhǎo look for

The character combines *hand* 扌 and *spear* 戈 to suggest the idea of holding a weapon in one hand when searching for lost property. It means *to look for.*

Radical: 扌 'hand'　　　　　　　　　　**Index # 48**

Character components: 扌 + 戈　　　　**Character configuration:**

Compounds, sentences and meanings

1. **找　zhǎo** look for
我 到处 在 找 你。
Wǒ dàochù zài zhǎo nǐ.
I've been looking for you all over the place.

2. **找对象　zhǎo duìxiàng** look for a partner in marriage
她 念 大学 为的是 找 对象。
Tā niàn dàxué wèi de shì zhǎo duìxiàng.
She's only going to university to find a husband.

3. **找麻烦　zhǎo máfan** look for trouble
对不起，我 给 你们 找 麻烦 了。
Duìbuqǐ, wǒ gěi nǐmen zhǎo máfan le.
I'm sorry to have caused you so much trouble.

4. **找不开　zhǎobukāi** have no small change for
对不起,你 这 张 五十 元 票子 我
Duìbuqǐ, nǐ zhè zhāng wǔshí yuán piàozi wǒ
找不开。
zhǎobukāi.
Sorry, I can't change a fifty.

5. **找钱　zhǎoqián** give change
这 是 找 给你 的 钱。
Zhè shì zhǎo gěi nǐ de qián.
Here's your change.

The two components do not join in the middle.　　　**7 strokes**

一	十	扌	扌	找	找	找							

Full form

辅 **fǔ** assist

The character combines *vehicle* 车 and the phonetic 甫 to suggest the idea of *assisting*.

Radical: 车 'vehicle'

Index # 84

Character components: 车 + 甫

Character configuration:

Compounds, sentences and meanings

1. 辅 **fǔ** supplement
   北方菜 以 面食 为 主，肉食 为 辅。
   Běifāngcài yǐ miànshí wéi zhǔ, ròushí wéi fǔ.
   The main ingredient of Northern Chinese food is wheat; meat is less important.

2. 辅导 **fǔdǎo** coach, tutor
   周末 我 辅导 孩子们 练 游泳。
   Zhōumò wǒ fǔdǎo háizimen liàn yóuyǒng.
   On weekends, I give swimming lessons to children.

3. 辅导员 **fǔdǎoyuán** tutor
   他 在 大学 当 辅导员。
   Tā zài dàxué dāng fǔdǎoyuán.
   He works as a university tutor.

4. 辅音 **fǔyīn** consonants
   汉语 辅音 用 在 韵母 的 不 多。
   Hànyǔ fǔyīn yòng zài yùnmǔ de bù duō.
   Consonants are rarely used at the end of syllables in Mandarin.

5. 辅助 **fǔzhù** assist
   请 你 给 我 多 加 辅助。
   Qǐng nǐ gěi wǒ duō jiā fǔzhù.
   Please give me some more help.

The bottom stroke lifts slightly in 车 when used as a radical.   11 strokes

一	𠂉	𰀁	车	车	𨊰	𨋀	𨋉	𨋨	辅	辅			

Full form

导 **dǎo** guide

The full form of the character combines *inch* 寸 and the phonetic 道 to suggest the idea that knowledge is gained by slow *guidance*. In simplification, the stereotype 巳 replaces 道.

Radical: 巳 '9 a.m. –11 a.m'　　　　**Index # 62**

Or　　　寸 'inch'　　　　　　　　**Index # 46**

Character components: 巳 + 寸　　　**Character configuration:**

Compounds, sentences and meanings

1. **导 dǎo** guide, lead
   前方　有个牌子导引　来宾　去
   Qiánfāng yǒu ge páizi dǎoyǐn láibīn qù
   参观。
   cān'guān.
   There is a sign at the front to guide visitors.

2. **导师 dǎoshī** teacher, tutor
   他是　我们的　英语　导师。
   Tā shì wǒmende Yīngyǔ dǎoshī.
   He is our English tutor.

3. **导演 dǎoyǎn** director
   张　艺谋 是 一位　有名　的 导演。
   Zhāng Yìmóu shì yí wèi yǒumíng de dǎoyǎn.
   Zhang Yimou is a famous director.

4. **导游 dǎoyóu** tourist guide
   去 旅行　最好　有　导游　讲解。
   Qù lǚxíng zuìhǎo yǒu dǎoyóu jiǎngjiě.
   When traveling, it's a good idea to have a tour guide to explain things.

5. **领导人 lǐngdǎorén** leader
   中国　的　领导人　一般 年纪 都　很大。
   Zhōngguó de lǐngdǎorén yìbān niánjì dōu hěn dà.
   In general, Chinese leaders are quite old.

The third stroke finishes with a vertical-bend-hook.　　　　**6 strokes**

㇇	㇆	巳	巳	导	导						

qiú   beg, seek

The character is a phonetic used as a character. It came to mean *seek*.

Radical: 一 'horizontal stroke'   **Index # 2**

Character components: 一 + 亅 + 氺 + 丶   **Character configuration:**

Compounds, sentences and meanings

1. **求**   **qiú**   beg, request
我 求 你 帮 个 忙, 行 吗?
Wǒ qiú nǐ bāng ge máng, xíng ma?
May I ask you a favor?

2. **求教**   **qiújiào**   come to seek advice
不懂 的 事 要 向 别人 求教。
Bùdǒng de shì yào xiàng biéren qiújiào.
If you don't understand, you should ask someone.

3. **求情**   **qiúqíng**   plead
他 父母 来 学校 为 儿子 求情。
Tā fùmǔ lái xuéxiào wèi érzi qiúqíng.
His parents came to the school to plead for their son.

4. **求之不得**   **qiú zhī bù dé**   all one could wish for
这 是 个 求 之 不 得 的 好 机会。
Zhè shì ge qiú zhī bù dé de hǎo jīhuì.
This is a most welcome opportunity.

5. **要求**   **yāoqiú**   requirement
父母 不要 对 孩子 要求 过 高。
Fùmǔ bùyào duì háizi yāoqiú guò gāo.
Parents should not ask too much of their children.

The vertical stroke ends with a hook.   7 strokes

一	丁	寸	寸	才	求	求				

确

què accurate

確

The full form of the character combines *stone* 石 and the phonetic 隺 to suggest the idea of being *definite* or *accurate*. In simplification, 角 is used to replace 隺.

Radical: 石 'rock'　　　　　　　　　　　　**Index # 115**

Character components: 石 + 角　　　　　　　**Character configuration:**

Compounds, sentences and meanings

1. **确 què** true, authentic
   确 有 其 事。
   Què yǒu qí shì.
   It really happened.

2. **确定 quèdìng** fix, determine
   请 确定 开会 的 日期和 地点。
   Qǐng quèdìng kāihuì de rìqī hé dìdiǎn.
   Please fix the time and place for the meeting.

3. **确认 quèrèn** confirm
   我 想 确认 机票。
   Wǒ xiǎng quèrèn jīpiào.
   I'd like to confirm my plane ticket.

4. **确实 quèshí** really
   他 最近 确实 有些 进步。
   Tā zuìjìn quèshí yǒuxiē jìnbù.
   He's really made some progress recently.

5. **正确 zhèngquè** correct
   你 这样 做 是 正确 的。
   Nǐ zhèyàng zuò shì zhèngquè de.
   What you are doing is right.

The left vertical stroke in 角 tapers while the right vertical ends with a hook.　　　　**12 strokes**

一	丆	石	石	石	石	矿	矿	硝	硝	确	确

fǎ law, method

The character combines *water* 氵 and *go* 去 to suggest dykes around a body of water to prevent it overflowing. By extension, it means *the rules and regulations in handling people.*

Radical: 氵 '3 drops of water'   **Index # 32**

Character components: 氵 + 去   **Character configuration:** ▢

Compounds, sentences and meanings

1. **法　fǎ**　law
   国家 不能 无法。
   Guójiā bùnéng wú fǎ.
   All countries need laws.

2. **法国　Fǎguó**　France
   法国 大革命 对 美国 独立 战争
   Fǎguó Dàgémìng duì Měiguó Dúlì Zhànzhēng
   影响 很 大。
   yǐngxiǎng hěn dà.
   The French Revolution greatly influenced the American War of Independence.

3. **法定人数　fǎdìng rénshù**　quorum
   法定 人数 不足。
   Fǎdìng rénshù bùzú.
   We haven't got a quorum.

4. **法律　fǎlǜ**　law
   法律 面前 人人 平等。
   Fǎlǜ miànqián rénrén píngděng.
   Everyone is equal before the law.

5. **法子　fǎzi**　way, method
   我们 要 想 个法子解决 这 个 问题。
   Wǒmen yào xiǎng ge fǎzi jiějué zhè ge wèntí.
   We have to think of a way to solve this problem.

The second horizontal stroke is longer.								8 strokes
丶	丷	氵	汇	汁	泔	法	法	

最 zuì most

The character combines *at any cost* 曰 and *gather* 取 to suggest the idea of 'taking at any cost'. By extension, it means *the maximum*.

Radical: 曰 'speech'   **Index # 91**

Character components: 曰 + 取   **Character configuration:** ▭

Compounds, sentences and meanings

1. **最 zuì** most
   同学 之 中 可算 小王 最为
   Tóngxué zhī zhōng kě suàn Xiǎowáng zuì wéi
   积极。
   jījí.
   Of all our classmates, Xiaowang's the most active.

2. **最多 zuìduō** at most, maximum
   我 最多 只 能 等 半 个 小时。
   Wǒ zuìduō zhǐ néng děng bàn ge xiǎoshí.
   I can wait half an hour at the most.

3. **最好 zuìhǎo** best, first rate
   这 是 最好 的 办法。
   Zhè shì zuìhǎo de bànfǎ.
   This is the best way.

4. **最后 zuìhòu** last, final
   我 坐 在 最后 一 排。
   Wǒ zuò zài zuìhòu yī pái.
   I sat in the last row.

5. **最近 zuìjìn** recently, of late
   我 最近 很 忙。
   Wǒ zuìjìn hěn máng.
   I've been very busy lately.

The top horizontal line of 取 extends to cover 又.											12 strokes
丶	冂	冂	曰	旦	昌	昌	昻	昻	晜	最	最

理

lǐ reason

The character combines *king* 王 or *jade* 玉 and the phonetic 里 to suggest the act of polishing a jewel or to find out the essentials. It means *methodical* or *logic*.

Radical: 王 'king'

Index # 79

Character components: 王 + 里

Character configuration:

Compounds, sentences and meanings

1. **理** lǐ reason
   他 讲 的 句句 是 理。
   Tā jiǎng de jùjù shì lǐ.
   There is truth in everything he says.

2. **理发** lǐfà haircut
   她 去 理发。
   Tā qù lǐfà.
   She's going to have her hair done.

3. **理解** lǐjiě understand
   你的 意思 我 完全 理解。
   Nǐde yìsi wǒ wánquán lǐjiě.
   I understand you completely.

4. **理想** lǐxiǎng ideal
   这 天气 出去 郊游 太 理想 了。
   Zhè tiānqì chūqu jiāoyóu tài lǐxiǎng le.
   This weather is ideal for an outing.

5. **理由** lǐyóu reason
   他 没有 理由 抱怨。
   Tā méiyǒu lǐyóu bàoyuàn.
   He has no grounds for complaint.

The bottom horizontal stroke is longer.										11 strokes
一	二	干	王	王	玑	玑	珇	理	理	理

A. Look at the 16-character grid and CIRCLE words or phrases. They can be written horizontally or vertically. (Look at the circled characters in the Key if you are unsure.) Copy the word or phrase next to the grid and write down the pinyin and meaning.

						Word or phrase			Pinyin	Meaning
找	辅	应	该		(i)	辅	导		fǔdǎo	tutor, to give tuition
语	导	理	音		(ii)					
要	发	正	确		(iii)					
求	想	法	最		(iv)					

B. Using the characters in the 16-character grid, convert the pinyin sentences into characters and write the English meaning.

(i)	Nǐ yīnggāi zhǎo ge Hànyǔ fǔdǎo.								
(ii)	Yāoqiú tāde fāyīn zhèngquè.								
(iii)	Hái yào néng jiǎng Hànyǔ yǔfǎ.								
(iv)	Zhǎo ge Zhōngguórén zuì lǐxiǎng.								

C. Match the Chinese words with their English meaning.

(i)

应 dāng — ought to
应 fù — plead
辅 zhù — seek advice
导游 — confirm
求 qíng — determine
求 jiào — assistance
确定 — tourist guide
确认 — deal with

(ii)

法 lǜ — best
法子 — recently
最多 — law
最好 — way, method
最后 — ideal
最近 — reason
理想 — at most
理 yóu — last

CHARACTER BUILDING 6 (251–300)

A. Memorize the following radicals and their English names. As a review exercise, write the pinyin and the English meaning of the examples under each radical:

1. ［一］ 'horizontal stroke'
   才 (＿＿＿＿) ＿＿＿＿＿＿ ; 开 (＿＿＿＿) ＿＿＿＿＿＿ ;
   正 (＿＿＿＿) ＿＿＿＿＿＿ ; 求 (＿＿＿＿) ＿＿＿＿＿＿ .

2. ［讠］ 'word'
   话 (＿＿＿＿) ＿＿＿＿＿＿ ; 调 (＿＿＿＿) ＿＿＿＿＿＿ .
   议 (＿＿＿＿) ＿＿＿＿＿＿ ; 诉 (＿＿＿＿) ＿＿＿＿＿＿ .
   谈 (＿＿＿＿) ＿＿＿＿＿＿ ; 讲 (＿＿＿＿) ＿＿＿＿＿＿ .
   该 (＿＿＿＿) ＿＿＿＿＿＿ .

3. ［八］ 'eight'
   兴 (＿＿＿＿) ＿＿＿＿＿＿ ; 典 (＿＿＿＿) ＿＿＿＿＿＿ .

4. ［儿］ 'son'
   儿 (＿＿＿＿) ＿＿＿＿＿＿ ; 先 (＿＿＿＿) ＿＿＿＿＿＿ ;
   元 (＿＿＿＿) ＿＿＿＿＿＿ ; 兄 (＿＿＿＿) ＿＿＿＿＿＿ .

5. ［又］ 'again'
   又 (＿＿＿＿) ＿＿＿＿＿＿ ; 发 (＿＿＿＿) ＿＿＿＿＿＿ .

6. ［氵］ 'three drops of water'
   港 (＿＿＿＿) ＿＿＿＿＿＿ ; 流 (＿＿＿＿) ＿＿＿＿＿＿ .
   法 (＿＿＿＿) ＿＿＿＿＿＿ .

7. ［忄］ 'upright heart'
   怕 (＿＿＿＿) ＿＿＿＿＿＿ ; 懂 (＿＿＿＿) ＿＿＿＿＿＿ .

8. ［宀］ 'roof'
   定 (＿＿＿＿) ＿＿＿＿＿＿ ; 家 (＿＿＿＿) ＿＿＿＿＿＿ .

9. ［广］ 'broad'
   应 (＿＿＿＿) ＿＿＿＿＿＿ ; 床 (＿＿＿＿) ＿＿＿＿＿＿ .

10. ［辶］ 'movement'
    通 (＿＿＿＿) ＿＿＿＿＿＿ ; 道 (＿＿＿＿) ＿＿＿＿＿＿ .

11. ［士］ 'scholar'
    声 (＿＿＿＿) ＿＿＿＿＿＿ ; 喜 (＿＿＿＿) ＿＿＿＿＿＿ .

12. ［寸］ 'inch'
    导 (＿＿＿＿) ＿＿＿＿＿＿ ; 对 (＿＿＿＿) ＿＿＿＿＿＿ .

13. ［扌］ 'hand'
    找 (＿＿＿＿) ＿＿＿＿＿＿ ; 拼 (＿＿＿＿) ＿＿＿＿＿＿ .

14. ［口］ 'mouth'
    听 (＿＿＿＿) ＿＿＿＿＿＿ ; 唱 (＿＿＿＿) ＿＿＿＿＿＿ .

15. ［女］ 'female'
要 (＿＿＿＿) ＿＿＿＿＿＿ ； 她 (＿＿＿＿) ＿＿＿＿＿＿ ．

16. ［心］ 'heart'
想 (＿＿＿＿) ＿＿＿＿＿＿ ； 感 (＿＿＿＿) ＿＿＿＿＿＿ ．

17. ［车］ 'vehicle'
车 (＿＿＿＿) ＿＿＿＿＿＿ ； 辅 (＿＿＿＿) ＿＿＿＿＿＿ ．

18. ［日］ 'sun'
普 (＿＿＿＿) ＿＿＿＿＿＿ ； 香 (＿＿＿＿) ＿＿＿＿＿＿ ．

19. ［曰］ 'speech'
最 (＿＿＿＿) ＿＿＿＿＿＿ ； 者 (＿＿＿＿) ＿＿＿＿＿＿ ．

20. ［钅］ 'metal'
错 (＿＿＿＿) ＿＿＿＿＿＿ ； 钟 (＿＿＿＿) ＿＿＿＿＿＿ ．

21. ［西］ 'west'
要 (＿＿＿＿) ＿＿＿＿＿＿ ； 西 (＿＿＿＿) ＿＿＿＿＿＿ ．

22. ［竹］ 'bamboo'
第 (＿＿＿＿) ＿＿＿＿＿＿ ； 算 (＿＿＿＿) ＿＿＿＿＿＿ ．

23. ［走］ 'walk'
趣 (＿＿＿＿) ＿＿＿＿＿＿ ； 起 (＿＿＿＿) ＿＿＿＿＿＿ ．

24. ［足］ 'foot'
跟 (＿＿＿＿) ＿＿＿＿＿＿ ； 跑 (＿＿＿＿) ＿＿＿＿＿＿ ．

B. Write the pinyin and meaning against the characters classified under the following radicals.

1. ［刂］ 'upright knife' 利 (＿＿＿＿) ＿＿＿＿＿

2. ［廴］ 'move on' 建 (＿＿＿＿) ＿＿＿＿＿

3. ［凵］ '3-sided frame, top open' 出 (＿＿＿＿) ＿＿＿＿＿

4. ［巳］ '9.00 a.m. -11.00 a.m.' 导 (＿＿＿＿) ＿＿＿＿＿

5. ［王］ 'king' 理 (＿＿＿＿) ＿＿＿＿＿

6. ［攵］ 'tap' 改 (＿＿＿＿) ＿＿＿＿＿

7. ［石］ 'stone' 确 (＿＿＿＿) ＿＿＿＿＿

8. ［言］ 'full word' 言 (＿＿＿＿) ＿＿＿＿＿

9. ［音］ 'sound' 音 (＿＿＿＿) ＿＿＿＿＿

C. Write the pinyin and meaning against the characters which share the following components.
(Note that these components are not necessarily used as radicals.)

1. ［舌］ 活 (＿＿＿＿) ＿＿＿＿＿＿ ； 话 (＿＿＿＿) ＿＿＿＿＿＿ ．

2. ［日］　音 (_____) _____ ; 普 (_____) _____ .

3. ［斤］　听 (_____) _____ ; 近 (_____) _____ .

4. ［禾］　香 (_____) _____ ; 利 (_____) _____ .

5. ［白］　怕 (_____) _____ ; 百 (_____) _____ .

6. ［亥］　该 (_____) _____ ; 孩 (_____) _____ .

7. ［取］　趣 (_____) _____ ; 最 (_____) _____ .

8. ［艮］　跟 (_____) _____ ; 很 (_____) _____ .

9. ［业］　兴 (_____) _____ ; 应 (_____) _____ .

REVIEW 6 (251–300)

The following words and phrases are classified under parts of speech. Write their pinyin and meaning.

Nouns
普通话 (_____) _____ ; 话 (_____) _____ ;
电话 (_____) _____ ; 好话 (_____) _____ ;
语言 (_____) _____ ; 外语 (_____) _____ ;
声调 (_____) _____ ; 发音 (_____) _____ ;
拼音 (_____) _____ ; 兴趣 (_____) _____ ;
经验 (_____) _____ ; 建议 (_____) _____ ;
辅导 (_____) _____ ; 要求 (_____) _____ .

Ordinal no.　第 (_____) _____ .

Verbs
说话 (_____) _____ ; 讲话 (_____) _____ ;
通知 (_____) _____ ; 交流 (_____) _____ ;
交谈 (_____) _____ ; 建议 (_____) _____ ;
听　(_____) _____ ; 听见 (_____) _____ ;
听说 (_____) _____ ; 告诉 (_____) _____ ;
懂　(_____) _____ ; 懂得 (_____) _____ ;
看懂 (_____) _____ ; 听懂 (_____) _____ ;
想　(_____) _____ ; 讲　(_____) _____ ;
谈　(_____) _____ ; 怕　(_____) _____ ;
错　(_____) _____ ; 改正 (_____) _____ ;
找　(_____) _____ ; 辅导 (_____) _____ .

Auxiliary　想　(_____) _____ ; 要　(_____) _____ .
Verbs　应该 (_____) _____ .

Adjectives	普通 (_____) _____ ;	香 (_____) _____ ;
	理想 (_____) _____ ;	流利 (_____) _____ .

Adverbs	一定 (_____) _____ ;	正 (_____) _____ ;
	正在 (_____) _____ ;	要不 (_____) _____ ;
	才 (_____) _____ ;	最 (_____) _____ .

Preposition 跟 (_____) _____ .

WORD/SENTENCE PUZZLE 6

Find and CIRCLE the words, phrases and sentences hidden in the puzzle. They can be found horizontally from left to right or vertically. The lines across and down are indicated by numbers. Write their meaning next to the pinyin. The first one is done for you.

ACROSS

2. Wǒ hái tīngbudǒng Pǔtōnghuà.   *I still can't understand Mandarin.*
4. jiāoliú   _____
5. Shēngdiào yǒu sì ge.   _____
6. Xué yǔyán yào xiān xué fāyīn.   _____
9. yāoqiú   _____
10. yǒuqù   _____
11. Wǒ yǒu ge Hànyǔ fǔdǎo.   _____
12. yǔfǎ   _____
14. zhèngquè fāyīn   _____

DOWN

2. Wǒ duì jiāoliú yǔyán gǎn xìngqù.   _____
4 (i) tīngshuō   _____
   (ii) Nǐ yào duō shuō cái huì yǒu jìnbù.   _____
6 (i) kàndǒng   _____
   (ii) Xué fāyīn yào xué Hànyǔ Pīnyīn.   _____
7. yǔfǎ   _____
8 (i) Shēngyīn hěn dà.   _____
   (ii) quèdìng   _____
9. tánhuà   _____
12. Nǐ yīnggāi zhǎo ge Yīngyǔ fǔdǎo.   _____

	1	2	3	4	5	6	7	8	9	10	11	12	13
1	块	书	台	万	旁	看	到	雨	谈	可	院	你	只
2	喜	我	还	听	不	懂	普	通	话	猫	亲	应	再
3	还	对	本	说	母	工	通	早	饭	睡	爱	该	前
4	欢	交	流	千	知	公	站	道	远	手	火	找	在
5	就	流	久	你	两	语	经	声	调	有	四	个	用
6	学	语	言	要	先	学	发	音	贵	词	或	英	西
7	时	言	也	多	城	发	走	很	园	男	汉	语	太
8	间	感	进	说	后	音	昨	大	妹	北	经	辅	习
9	见	兴	认	才	写	要	求	爸	已	面	觉	导	能
10	有	趣	会	会	候	学	样	分	步	难	生	忙	脑
11	长	请	我	有	个	汉	语	辅	导	南	星	冷	买
12	问	常	老	进	谢	语	法	东	动	识	地	岁	练
13	街	家	身	步	午	拼	右	游	弟	离	医	方	卖
14	姓	帮	做	体	发	音	正	确	身	问	泳	校	书
15	女	较	比	住	这	助	晚	定	零	边	便	小	钱

301

民 **mín** people

The character is a phonetic used as a character. It means *people.*

Radical: 乛 **'horizontal-bend'** **Index # 5**

Character component: 民 **Character configuration:** □

Compounds, sentences and meanings

1. **民 mín** people
   连 年 内战，民 不 聊 生。
   Lián nián nèizhàn mín bù liáo shēng.
   Years of civil war made life impossible for the people.

2. **人民 rénmín** people
   中华 人民 共和国。
   Zhōnghuá Rénmín Gònghéguó.
   The People's Republic of China.

3. **民歌 mín'gē** folk songs
   〈茉莉花〉是 一 首 民歌。
   <Mòlìhuā> shì yì shǒu mín'gē.
   Jasmine *is a folk song.*

4. **民主 mínzhǔ** democratic
   美国 是 一个 民主 国家。
   Měiguó shì yí ge mínzhǔ guójiā.
   The United States is a democratic country.

5. **民族 mínzú** nation, ethnic group
   中国 是一个 多 民族 国家。
   Zhōngguó shì yí ge duō mínzú guójiā.
   China is a multi-ethnic country.

The last stroke is a slanting hook. **5 strokes**

歌  gē song

The character combines *open mouth* 欠 , 可 and 可 which might suggest the sound of *singing*. It came to mean *song*.

Radical: 欠 'owe'

Index # 104

Character components: 可 + 可 + 欠

Character configuration:

Compounds, sentences and meanings

1. **歌** **gē** song
   唱 首 歌 给 我们 听听， 怎么样?
   Chàng shǒu gē gěi wǒmen tīngting, zěnmeyàng?
   How about singing us a song?

2. **歌星** **gēxīng** singer (star)
   宋 祖英 是 中国 有名 的 歌星。
   Sòng Zǔyīng shì Zhōngguó yǒumíng de gēxīng.
   Song Zuying is a famous Chinese singer.

3. **歌剧院** **gējùyuàn** opera house
   悉尼 歌剧院 世界 有名。
   Xīní Gējùyuàn shìjiè yǒumíng.
   Sydney Opera House is world-famous.

4. **歌迷** **gēmí** fan (of singer)
   他 是 宋 祖英 的 忠实 歌迷。
   Tā shì Sòng Zǔyīng de zhōngshí gēmí.
   He is a fan of Song Zuying.

5. **歌声** **gēshēng** sound of singing
   她的 歌声 很 清晰。
   Tāde gēshēng hěn qīngxī.
   Her (singing) voice is very clear.

The fifth stroke is a vertical stroke.													14 strokes
一	丆	丆	㕩	可	피	哥	哥	哥	哥	哥	歌	歌	歌
歌													

dàn   but, yet

The phonetic part of the character 旦 suggests that the sun is coming up from the horizon. It is unclear how the character came to mean *but* when combined with the radical *person* 亻.

Radical: 亻 'person'

Character components: 亻 + 旦

Index # 19

Character configuration:

Compounds, sentences and meanings

1. **但 dàn** but
   他 早 已 年 过 六十, 但 毫 不 见 老。
   Tā zǎo yǐ nián guò liùshí, dàn háo bú jiàn lǎo.
   Although he is well over sixty, he doesn't look at all old.

2. **但是 dànshì** but
   他 很 聪明, 但是 不 喜欢 学习。
   Tā hěn cōngmíng, dànshì bù xǐhuan xuéxí.
   Although he is clever, he doesn't like studying.

3. **但愿 dànyuàn** if only
   但愿 天气 赶快 下雨。
   Dànyuàn tiānqì gǎnkuài xiàyǔ.
   If only it would rain soon.

4. **但凡 dànfán** in every case
   但凡 认识 她 的 人, 没有 一 个 不 说 她 好。
   Dànfán rénshi tā de rén , méiyǒu yí ge bù shuō tā hǎo.
   Everyone who meets her says she is nice.

5. **不但 búdàn** not only
   这里 的 东西 不但 好吃, 而且 便宜。
   Zhèlǐ de dōngxi búdàn hǎochī, érqiě piányi.
   The food here is not only delicious, it's also inexpensive.

The last stroke is longer than the ones above.   **7 strokes**

ノ	亻	介	佃	佃	但	但					

Full form

难 **nán** difficult

難

The full form of the character combines *clay and fire* 堇 with *bird* 隹 to give the idea of a bird having difficulty in surviving. It means *difficult*.

Radical: 又 'again'

Index # 24

Character components: 又 + 隹

Character configuration: ⊟

Compounds, sentences and meanings

1. 难 **nán** difficult
   说起来 容易，做起来 难。
   Shuōqǐlai róngyì, zuòqǐlai nán.
   It is easier said than done.

2. 难得 **nándé** rare
   像 他 这样 的 人 很 难得。
   Xiàng tā zhèyàng de rén hěn nándé.
   It's rare to find a person like him.

3. 难说 **nánshuō** it's hard to say
   很 难说 谁 对 谁 不对。
   Hěn nánshuō shéi duì shéi búduì.
   It's hard to say who's right and who's wrong.

4. 难过 **nán'guò** sad
   他 听到 朋友 去世的 消息 非常
   Tā tīngdào péngyou qùshì de xiāoxi fēicháng
   难过。
   nán'guò.
   He was deeply saddened by the death of his friend.

5. 难为 **nánwei** press, embarrass
   他 不会 唱歌 就别 难为 他 了。
   Tā búhuì chànggē jiù bié nánwéi tā le.
   He can't sing, so don't press him to.

There is equal spacing between the horizontal strokes. | 10 strokes

| 丆 | 又 | 対 | 邓 | 邓 | 邓 | 邓 | 邓 | 难 | 难 | | | |

chàng sing

The character combines *mouth* 口 and *excites attention* 昌 to suggest that sound coming out of the mouth can attract attention. It means *sing*.

Radical: 口 'mouth'

Index # 50

Character components: 口 + 昌

Character configuration:

Compounds, sentences and meanings

1. **唱 chàng** sing
   他 唱 得 很 难听。
   Tā chàngde hěn nántīng.
   He sings badly.

2. **唱歌 chànggē** sing
   他 就 喜欢 人 听 他 唱歌。
   Tā jiù xǐhuan rén tīng tā chànggē.
   He likes people to listen when he sings.

3. **唱片 chàngpiàn** phonograph record
   现在 不 用 唱片 了。
   Xiànzài bú yòng chàngpiàn le.
   Nowadays (people) don't play phonograph records.

4. **歌唱家 gēchàngjiā** singer, vocalist
   他 是 个 有名 的 歌唱家。
   Tā shì ge yǒumíng de gēchàngjiā.
   He is a famous singer.

5. **合唱团 héchàngtuán** choir
   我 最近 参加 了 一 个 合唱团。
   Wǒ zuìjìn cānjiāle yí ge héchàngtuán.
   Recently I joined a choir.

The bottom 日 component is wider than the one above.											11 strokes	
丶	𠃌	口	叩	叩	叩	唱	唱	唱	唱	唱		

sú custom

The character combines *person* 亻 and the phonetic 谷 to suggest the idea of *popular*.

Radical: 亻 'upright person'

Index # 19

Character components: 亻 + 谷

Character configuration:

Compounds, sentences and meanings

1. 俗 **sú** vulgar
   他 这 个 人 俗 不 可 耐。
   Tā zhè ge rén sú bù kě nài.
   He is unbearably vulgar.

2. 俗气 **súqì** in poor taste
   她 穿得 很 俗气。
   Tā chuānde hěn súqì.
   The clothes she wears are in poor taste.

3. 俗话 **súhuà** common saying, proverb
   俗话 说: "男 大 当 婚, 女 大 当 嫁。"
   Súhuà shuō: "Nán dà dāng hūn, nǚ dà dāng jià."
   As the saying goes: "Men and women should marry when they reach adulthood."

4. 通俗 **tōngsú** popular
   《甜蜜蜜》 是 一 首 通俗 歌曲。
   <Tiánmìmì> shì yì shǒu tōngsú gēqǔ.
   Sweet as Honey is a pop song.

5. 习俗 **xísú** custom, convention
   中国人 过 春节 的习俗 很多。
   Zhōngguórén guò Chūnjié de xísú hěnduō.
   When Chinese people celebrate the Lunar New Year, they observe many customs.

The fifth and sixth strokes are written like 人. 9 strokes

丿	亻	亻	𤼈	伙	伙	伀	俗	俗			

qū/qǔ mistake/song

The character is a phonetic used as a character. It has two pronunciations: **qū** means *winding* or *mistake* and **qǔ** means *song*.

Radical: 曰 'speech'　　　　　　　　　　**Index # 91**

Character component: 曰 + 丨 + 丨

Character configuration: ☐

Compounds, sentences and meanings

1. **曲 qū** wrong
   你 不能 是非曲直。
   Nǐ bùnéng shìfēi-qūzhí.
   You cannot twist the right and wrong of it.

2. **曲解 qūjiě** misinterpret
   你曲解了他的意思。
   Nǐ qǔjiěle tāde yìsi.
   You've twisted his meaning.

3. **曲子 qǔzi** song, tune
   这 首 曲子我 好像 听过。
   Zhè shǒu qǔzi wǒ hǎoxiàng tīngguo.
   I seem to have heard this song before.

4. **作曲 zuòqǔ** write music
   莫扎特 五岁就 开始 作曲了。
   Mòzhātè wǔ suì jiù kāishǐ zuòqǔ le.
   Mozart began to compose when he was five years old.

5. **作曲家 zuòqǔjiā** composer
   贝多芬 是 有名 的 作曲家。
   Bèiduōfēn shì yǒumíng de zuòqǔjiā.
   Beethoven is a famous composer.

There is equal spacing between all the lines.											6 strokes
丨	冂	日	内	曲	曲						

gāo tall

The character represents a building and thus depicts a *high* outlook.

Radical: 亠 'top of 六'　　　　　　**Index # 6**

Character components: 亠 + 口 + 冂 + 口　　**Character configuration:**

Compounds, sentences and meanings

1. **高　gāo** high, tall
   他比　小王　高一头。
   Tā bǐ Xiǎowáng gāo yì tóu.
   He is a head taller than Xiaowang.

2. **高矮　gāo'ǎi** height
   这　两　棵　树　高矮　差不多。
   Zhè liǎng kē shù gāo'ǎi chàbuduō.
   These two trees are nearly the same height.

3. **高低　gāodī** high and low
   每个人的　声音　高低　不同。
   Měi ge rén de shēngyīn gāodī bùtóng.
   Everyone's voice has a different pitch.

4. **高大　gāodà** tall and big
   那　栋　建筑物　很　高大。
   Nà dòng jiànzhùwù hěn gāodà.
   That building is huge.

5. **高兴　gāoxìng** happy, pleased
   很　高兴　看见　你。
   Hěn gāoxìng kànjiàn nǐ.
   It's nice to see you.

The first 口 above is larger than the one below.									10 strokes

`丶　亠　六　方　亢　肖　高　高　高　高`

róng　contain

The character combines *cave* 穴, *person* 人 and 口 to suggest the idea of *contain*. It also means *easy*.

Radical: 穴 '**cave**'

Character components: 穴 + 人 + 口

Index # 110

Character configuration:

Compounds, sentences and meanings

1. 容　**róng**　hold, contain
   这 个 礼堂 能 容 五百 人。
   Zhè ge lǐtáng néng róng wǔbǎi rén.
   This room can hold 500 people.

2. 容纳　**róngnà**　have a capacity of
   这 个 体育馆 能 容纳 一万 观众。
   Zhè ge tǐyùguǎn néng róngnà yīwàn guānzhòng.
   This stadium has a seating capacity of 10,000.

3. 容忍　**róngrěn**　put up with
   你 怎么 能 容忍 他的 脾气?
   Nǐ zěnme néng róngrěn tāde píqi?
   How can you put up with his temper?

4. 容许　**róngxǔ**　tolerate, permit
   请 容许 别人 把 话 说完。
   Qǐng róngxǔ biéren bǎ huà shuōwán.
   Please allow others to finish speaking.

5. 笑容　**xiàoróng**　smiling face
   他 常常 满面 笑容。
   Tā chángcháng mǎnmiàn xiàoróng.
   He often has a grin on his face.

Note the difference between 容 and 客.　　　10 strokes

丶	丷	宀	宀	穴	宊	突	突	容	容			

310

易 **yì** change/easy

The character is a pictograph of a lizard. The three left sliding strokes denoted color which changed easily. The character means both *change* and *easy.*

Radical: 日 **'sun'** **Index # 90**

Character components: 日 **+** 勿 **Character configuration:** 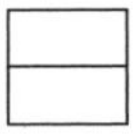

Compounds, sentences and meanings

1. **易 yì** easy
   冬天 易 患 感冒。
   Dōngtiān yì huàn gǎnmào.
   It is easy to catch a cold in winter.

2. **易经 Yìjīng** the Book of Changes
   易经 这 本 书 很 难 懂。
   Yìjīng zhè běn shū hěn nán dǒng.
   It is difficult to understand the Book of Changes.

3. **交易 jiāoyì** transaction
   对不起，这里 现款 交易。
   Duìbuqǐ, zhèlǐ xiànkuǎn jiāoyì.
   I'm sorry, it's cash transactions here only.

4. **轻易 qīngyì** easily
   不要 轻易地 下 结论。
   Búyào qīngyìde xià jiélùn.
   Don't jump to conclusions.

5. **容易 róngyì** easy
   在 美国 生活 不太 容易。
   Zài Měiguó shēnghuó bú tài róngyì.
   Life is not easy in America.

The bottom section is 勿. **8 strokes**

Quiz 31 (301–310)

A. Look at the 16-character grid and CIRCLE words or phrases. They can be written horizontally or vertically. (Look at the circled characters in the Key if you are unsure.) Copy the word or phrase next to the grid and write down the pinyin and meaning.

						Word or phrase			Pinyin	Meaning
高	民	歌	容	(i)		民	歌		mín'gē	folk song
喜	首	曲	易	(ii)						
通	俗	唱	较	(iii)						
难	比	调	懂	(iv)						

B. Using the characters in the 16-character grid, convert the pinyin sentences into characters and write the English meaning.

(i)	Nǐ xǐhuan tīng Zhōngguó mín'gē ma?								
(ii)	Xǐhuan, dànshì mín'gē hěn nán chàng.								
(iii)	Wǒ bǐjiào xǐhuan tōngsú gēqǔ.								
(iv)	Diàozi bú tài gāo, róngyì chàng.								

C. Match the Chinese words with their English meaning.

(i)

民 zhǔ — sad
人民 — but
唱歌 — sing
但是 — people
不但 — democracy
难得 — transaction
难过 — rare
交易 — not only

(ii)

俗气 — happy
习俗 — misinterpret
高大 — in poor taste
高兴 — custom
歌曲 — put up with
曲 jiě — song
xiào 容 — tall and big
容 rěn — smile

wān bay

The character combines *water* 氵 and the phonetic 弯 which also means *curve* to give the idea of a bend in a stream. By extension it means *bay*.

Radical: 氵 'three drops of water'

Index # 32

Character components: 氵 + 弯

Character configuration:

Compounds, sentences and meanings

1. **湾 wān** bend in a stream
   你 看, 这里 就 是 长江 第一 湾。
   Nǐ kàn, zhèlǐ jiù shì Chángjiāng dīyī wān.
   Look, this is the first bend in the Changjiang River.

2. **河湾 héwān** bend in a river
   这 个 河湾 里 有 鱼。
   Zhè ge héwān li yǒu yú.
   There are fish in this bend of the river.

3. **海湾 hǎiwān** bay, gulf
   这 个 海湾 很 平静。
   Zhè ge hǎiwān hěn píngjìng.
   This bay is very calm.

4. **墨西哥湾 Mòxīgēwān** Gulf of Mexico
   墨西哥湾 经常 有 暴风。
   Mòxīgēwān jīngcháng yǒu bàofēng.
   There are often storms in the Gulf of Mexico.

5. **台湾 Táiwān** Taiwan
   台湾人 一般 都 说 闽南话。
   Táiwānrén yībān dōu shuō Mǐnnánhuà.
   Taiwanese people generally speak the Minnan dialect.

The last stroke ends with a hook.

12 strokes

丶	丶	氵	氵	汀	汀	浐	浐	浐	湾	湾	湾

jiāo/jiào teach

The character combines *stick* 攵, *adult* 耂 and *child* 子 to represent a person holding a stick and teaching a child. It is pronounced **jiāo** as a verb and **jiào** when used as part of a noun phrase.

Radical: 攵 'tap'　　　　　　　　　　　**Index # 99**

Character components: 耂 + 子 + 攵　　　**Character configuration:** ⊟

Compounds, sentences and meanings

1. 教 **jiāo** teach
   我 教 汉语 已经 三十 年 了。
   Wǒ jiāo Hànyǔ yǐjīng sānshí nián le.
   I've taught Chinese for thirty years.

2. 教书 **jiāoshū** teach
   我 哥哥 在 小学 教书。
   Wǒ gēge zài xiǎoxué jiāoshū.
   My older brother teaches in a primary school.

3. 教师 **jiàoshī** teacher
   当 教师 要 有 耐心。
   Dāng jiàoshī yào yǒu nàixīn.
   You need patience to be a teacher.

4. 教堂 **jiàotáng** church
   我 每 个 星期天 都 去 教堂。
   Wǒ měi ge xīngqītiān dōu qù jiàotáng.
   I go to church every Sunday.

5. 教育 **jiàoyù** education
   我 母亲 受过 高等 教育。
   Wǒ mǔqin shòuguo gāoděng jiàoyù.
   My mother had tertiary education.

Note the difference between 攵 and 欠.　　　　　　　　　11 strokes

一	十	土	耂	耂	孝	孝	孝	教	教	教		

Full form

给 **gěi/jǐ** give/supply

給

The character combines *silk* 纟 and *a meeting of two hands* 合 to refer to the idea of giving silk as a gift. It means to *give*.

Radical: 纟 'silk'

Index # 68

Character components: 纟 + 合

Character configuration: ⊟

Compounds, sentences and meanings

1. **给** **gěi** for
   我 给 你 当 翻译。
   Wǒ gěi nǐ dāng fānyì.
   I'll act as interpreter for you.

2. **给了** **gěile** gave
   他 给 了 我 一 本 书 作为 礼物。
   Tā gěile wǒ yì běn shū zuòwéi lǐwù.
   He gave me a book as a present.

3. **供给** **gōngjǐ** supply
   教材 由 学校 供给。
   Jiàocái yóu xuéxiào gōngjǐ.
   Teaching materials are provided by the school.

4. **自给** **zìjǐ** self-sufficient
   现在 很少 国家 是 经济自给。
   Xiànzài hěnshǎo guójiā shì jīngjì zìjǐ.
   Nowadays very few countries are economically self-sufficient.

5. **给予** **jǐyǔ** (formal) give, render
   给予 难民 适当 的 法律 保护。
   Jǐyǔ nànmín shìdàng de fǎlǜ bǎohù.
   Give appropriate legal protection to asylum seekers.

The third stroke rises.								9 strokes
乙	纟	纟	纠	纵	纵	给	给	给

shǒu main, number one

The character is made up of the *inverted eight* `丷`, *one* 一 and *self* 自. It is the last component which derives the meaning of *main* or *number one*.

Radical: `丷` 'eight'　　　　　　　　　　**Index # 17**

Character components: `丷` + 一 + 自

Character configuration:

Compounds, sentences and meanings

1. **首　shǒu** classifier
   这 首 中国 民歌 很 好听。
   Zhè shǒu Zhōngguó mín'gē hěn hǎotīng.
   This Chinese folk song is nice.

2. **首次　shǒucì** for the first time
   今天 是 这 个 电影 的 首次 公演。
   Jīntiān shì zhè ge diànyǐng de shǒucì gōngyǎn.
   Today is the premiere of this film.

3. **首都　shǒudū** capital
   北京 是 中国 的 首都。
   Běijīng shì Zhōngguó de shǒudū.
   Beijing is the capital of China.

4. **首先　shǒuxiān** first of all
   首先, 我 要 问 你 一个 问题。
   Shǒuxiān, wǒ yào wèn nǐ yí ge wèntí.
   Firstly, I'd like to ask you a question.

5. **部首　bùshǒu** radical (part of character which carries meaning)
   "请" 的 部首 是 "讠字旁。"
   "Qǐng" de bùshǒu shì "yánzìpáng."
   The radical for the character "qǐng" is "yán (word)."

The strokes in the middle are equally spaced.											9 strokes
丶	丷	丷	丷	产	产	首	首	首			

題　**tí**　topic

題

The character combines *to be* 是 and *page* 页 to suggest the idea of something put up in front, a *subject* or *topic*.

Radical: 页 'page'

Index # 140

Character components: 是 + 页

Character configuration: ⊔

Compounds, sentences and meanings

1. **题 tí** problem
   这 道 题 我 没 回答 对。
   Zhè dào tí wǒ méi huídá duì.
   I didn't give the correct answer to the problem.

2. **问题 wèntí** question
   我 提个 问题, 可以 吗?
   Wǒ tí ge wèntí, kěyǐ ma?
   Can I ask a question?

3. **题材 tícái** subject matter
   这 是 写 小说 的 好 题材。
   Zhè shì xiě xiǎoshuō de hǎo tícái.
   This is good material for a novel.

4. **题目 tímù** topic
   你 刚 发表 的 那篇 文章 叫
   Nǐ gāng fābiǎo de nà biān wénzhāng jiào
   什么 题目?
   shénme tímù?
   What's the topic of the article you just published?

5. **话题 huàtí** topic of conversation
   我们 换 个 话题 好 不 好?
   Wǒmen huàn ge huàtí hǎo bù hǎo?
   Why don't we change the topic of conversation?

The last stroke of 页 ends firmly.　　　　　　　　　　　　**15 strokes**

| 丶 | 丨冂 | 日 | 日 | 旦 | 早 | 早 | 昇 | 是 | 是 | 是 | 昰 | 題 |
| 題 | 題 | | | | | | | | | | | |

金 jīn gold

The character combines *treasure* `丷`, *in the ground* 土 and *cover* 人 to suggest *hidden treasure, namely gold.*

Radical: 金 'gold'

Index # 175

Character component: 金

Character configuration:

Compounds, sentences and meanings

1. **金 jīn** gold
   金 银 财 宝
   Jīn yín cái bǎo
   Gold, silver and other treasures

2. **金不换 jīnbuhuàn** not to be exchanged
   even for gold
   浪子 回头 金不换。
   Làngzi huítóu jīnbuhuàn.
   A prodigal son who returns is more precious than gold.

3. **金融 jīnróng** finance, banking
   上海 是 中国 的 金融 中心。
   Shànghǎi shì Zhōngguó de jīnróng zhōngxīn.
   Shanghai is the financial center of China.

4. **五金店 wǔjīndiàn** hardware store
   附近哪儿有 五金店?
   Fùjìn nǎr yǒu wǔjīndiàn?
   Where can I find a hardware store nearby?

5. **现金 xiànjīn** ready money
   对不起,这里 现金 付款。
   Duìbuqǐ, zhèlǐ xiànjīn fùkuǎn.
   Sorry, we accept only cash payments here.

The two small slanted strokes do not touch the final bottom horizontal stroke.

8 strokes

ノ	人	人	今	仐	全	金	金				

 **liàng** bright

The character contains four components: 亠, 口, 冖 and 几. It means *bright*.

Radical: 亠 'top of 六' **Index # 6**

Character components: 亠 + 口 + 冖 + 几 **Character configuration:**

Compounds, sentences and meanings

1. 亮 **liàng** bright
   那个 灯泡 很 亮。
   Nà ge dēngpào hěn liàng.
   That lightbulb is very bright.

2. 亮晶晶 **liàngjīngjīng** glittering
   今晚 可以 看到 亮晶晶 的 星星。
   Jīnwǎn kěyǐ kàndào liàngjīngjīng de xīngxīng.
   You can see the stars shining tonight.

3. 亮堂 **liàngtang** light, bright
   这 屋子 又 宽敞 又 亮堂。
   Zhè wūzi yòu kuānchang yòu liàngtang.
   The room is spacious and bright.

4. 明亮 **míngliàng** bright, shining
   我 喜欢 赵 薇 那 双 明亮 的
   Wǒ xǐhuan Zhào Wēi nà shuāng míngliàng de
   眼睛。
   yǎnjing.
   I like Zhao Wei's bright eyes.

5. 月亮 **yuèliang** the moon
   中秋节 的 月亮 最 圆。
   Zhōngqiūjié de yuèliang zuì yuán.
   The moon is at its fullest at Mid-autumn Festival.

The last stroke is a horizontal-bend ending with a hook. **9 strokes**

丶	一	亠	亠	古	亨	亨	亭	亮			

318

dài represent

The character combines 亻 and the non-character component 弋 to form the phonetic 代. It means *to take the place of*.

Radical: 亻 'upright person'

Character components: 亻 + 弋

Index # 19

Character configuration:

Compounds, sentences and meanings

1. 代 **dài** take the place of
   请 代 我 向 您 父母 问候。
   Qǐng dài wǒ xiàng nín fùmǔ wènhòu.
   Please give my regards to your parents.

2. 代办 **dàibàn** do something for somebody
   这 件 事 请 你 代办 吧。
   Zhè jiàn shì qǐng nǐ dàibàn ba.
   Could you do this for me?

3. 代表 **dàibiǎo** represent
   老师 让 她 代表 我们 班 同学 讲话。
   Lǎoshī ràng tā dàibiǎo wǒmen bān tóngxué jiǎnghuà.
   The teacher asked her to speak on behalf of the class.

4. 代价 **dàijià** price, cost
   我们 不惜 任何 代价 也 要
   Wǒmen bùxī rènhé dàijià yě yào
   完成 任务。
   wánchéng rènwù.
   We have to finish the job at any cost.

5. 代替 **dàitì** replace
   将来 很多 工作 都 能 用
   Jiānglái hěnduō gōngzuò dōu néng yòng
   机器人 代替。
   jīqìrén dàitì.
   In the future, robots will replace people in many jobs.

The second last stroke is a slanting hook.   5 strokes

ノ	亻	仁	代	代							

biǎo   show, express

The character is a phonetic used as character. It means *surface* or *to show*.

Radical: 一 'horizontal stroke'   **Index # 2**

Character components: 一 + 土 + 衣   **Character configuration:**

Compounds, sentences and meanings

1. 表 **biǎo** show, express
   我们 对 你的 遭遇 深 表 同情。
   Wǒmen duì nǐde zāoyù shēn biǎo tóngqíng.
   We would like to express our deep sympathy for what you went through.

2. 表达 **biǎodá** express
   我 激动 的 心情 难 以 用 语言
   Wǒ jīdòng de xīnqíng nán yǐ yòng yǔyán
   来 表达。
   lái biǎodá.
   Words can hardly express my excitement.

3. 表面 **biǎomiàn** surface
   你 不能 只 看 事情 的 表面。
   Nǐ bùnéng zhǐ kàn shìqing de biǎomiàn.
   Don't judge a book by its cover.

4. 表情 **biǎoqíng** expression
   他的 面部 没有 表情。
   Tāde miànbù méiyǒu biǎoqíng.
   He doesn't have any expression on his face.

5. 表演 **biǎoyǎn** perform
   他 表演得 很 好。
   Tā biǎoyǎnde hěn hǎo.
   He performed very well.

The middle horizontal stroke is shorter.								8 strokes
一	二	丰	主	声	耒	表	表	

 **xīn** heart

The character is a pictograph of the heart. In ancient times, the heart was considered as the seat of man's mental activities. Thus, it means *heart* and the *mind*.

Radical: 心 'heart'

Character component: 心

Index # 76

Character configuration:

Compounds, sentences and meanings

1. **心 xīn** heart
   他 人 在 这儿, 心 不 在。
   Tā rén zài zhèr, xīn bú zài.
   He is physically present, but his thoughts are elsewhere.

2. **心理 xīnlǐ** psychology, mentality
   这 是 一般 人 的 心理。
   Zhè shì yìbān rén de xīnlǐ.
   This is how ordinary people feel about it.

3. **心情 xīnqíng** mood
   她 今天 的 心情 不 好。
   Tā jīntiān de xīnqíng bù hǎo.
   She is in a bad mood today.

4. **心疼 xīnténg** be distressed
   这么 浪费, 叫 人 看了 心疼。
   Zhème làngfèi, jiào rén kànle xīnténg.
   It makes your heart ache to see such waste.

5. **小心 xiǎoxīn** be careful
   过 马路 要 小心。
   Guò mǎlù yào xiǎoxīn.
   Be careful when crossing the street.

The second stroke ends with a hook.										4 strokes
丶	心	心	心							

Quiz 32 (311–320)

A. Look at the 16-character grid and CIRCLE words or phrases. They can be written horizontally or vertically. (Look at the circled characters in the Key if you are unsure.) Copy the word or phrase next to the grid and write down the pinyin and meaning.

					Word or phrase			Pinyin	Meaning
台	月	亮	叫	(i)	台	湾		Táiwān	Taiwan
湾	首	教	题	(ii)					
通	给	金	曲	(iii)					
代	表	歌	心	(iv)					

B. Using the characters in the 16-character grid, convert the pinyin sentences into characters and write the English meaning.

(i)	Wǒ xiǎng xué Táiwān tōngsú gēqǔ.								
(ii)	Nǐ néng jiāo gěi wǒ yì shǒu ma?								
(iii)	Méi wèntí. Zhè shì jīnqǔ lǎogē.								
(iv)	Jiào <Yuèliang Dàibiǎo Wǒde Xīn>.								

C. Match the Chinese words with their English meaning.

(i)
教师	first of all
教 táng	question
教 yù	finance, banking
首先	teacher
问题	church
话题	ready cash
金 róng	education
现金	topic of conversation

(ii)
明亮	perform
月亮	express
代 jià	bright, shining
代 tì	mood
表 dá	the moon
表 yǎn	psychology
心 lǐ	replace
心 qíng	price, cost

82

fàng release, put

The character combines *holding a stick* 攵 and the phonetic 方, which means *direction*, to suggest the idea of *putting out to pasture*. It came to mean *let go* or *set free*.

Radical: 攵 'tap'   **Index # 99**

or   方 'direction'   **Index # 74**

Character components: 方 + 攵   **Character configuration:**

Compounds, sentences and meanings

1. 放 **fàng** put
   把 书 放 在 桌子 上。
   Bǎ shū fàng zài zhuōzi shàng.
   Put the book on the table.

2. 放大 **fàngdà** enlarge
   我 想 把 这 几 张 照片 放大。
   Wǒ xiǎng bǎ zhè jǐ zhāng zhàopiàn fàngdà.
   I'd like to enlarge these photographs.

3. 放过 **fàngguò** let off, let slip
   这 是 好 机会, 不要 放过。
   Zhè shì hǎo jīhuì, búyào fàngguò.
   This is a good opportunity. Don't let it slip.

4. 放假 **fàngjià** have a holiday
   你 什么 时候 放假。
   Nǐ shénme shíhou fàngjià?
   When do you go on holidays?

5. 放心 **fàngxīn** be at ease
   你 放心 吧, 一切 都 安排好了。
   Nǐ fàngxīn ba, yíqiè dōu ānpáihǎole.
   Don't worry, everything has been arranged.

攵 has 4 strokes. The first two strokes do not meet.   8 strokes

`	二	亠	方	方	方	放	放						

jiǎ/jiā   false/holiday

The character combines *upright person* 亻 and the phonetic 叚 to refer to two meanings: *false* (pronounced **jiǎ**) and *holiday* (pronounced **jià**).

Radical: 亻 'upright person'   **Index # 19**

Character components: 亻 + 叚   **Character configuration:**

Compounds, sentences and meanings

1. **假** **jiǎ** fake
   以 假 乱 真。
   Yǐ jiǎ luàn zhēn
   Create confusion by passing off the fake as genuine.

2. **假造** **jiǎzào** counterfeit
   这 张 钞票 是 假造 的。
   Zhè zhāng chāopiào shì jiǎzào de.
   This is a forged banknote.

3. **假如** **jiǎrú** if, supposing
   假如 我 忘 了，请 提醒 我。
   Jiǎrú wǒ wàng le, qǐng tíxǐng wǒ.
   Please remind me if I forget.

4. **假期** **jiàqī** holiday
   假期你 想 到 哪儿去 玩儿?
   Jiàqī nǐ xiǎng dào nǎr qù wánr?
   Where would you like to go for your holidays?

5. **请假** **qǐngjià** ask for leave
   她 请 病假 回家 了。
   Tā qǐng bìngjià huíjiā le.
   She's gone home sick.

The eighth and ninth strokes don't form a closed box.										11 strokes
丿	亻	亻	伫	伊	作	作	假	假	假	假

 **dǎ** hit

The character combines *hand* 扌 and *nail* 丁 to represent the idea of driving a nail with the hand. Thus, it means *hit* or *strike*.

Radical: 扌 'hand'   **Index # 48**

Character components: 扌 + 丁   **Character configuration:** ▯▯

Compounds, sentences and meanings

1. **打** **dǎ** hit, strike
   现在 父母 也 不能 打孩子 了。
   Xiànzài fùmǔ yě bùnéng dǎ háizi le.
   Nowadays parents can't hit their children.

2. **打电话** **dǎ diànhuà** phone someone
   你 应该 先 给 他打个 电话。
   Nǐ yīnggāi xiān gěi tā dǎ ge diànhuà.
   You should ring him first.

3. **打扫** **dǎsǎo** sweep, clean
   请 打扫 一下 房间。
   Qǐng dǎsǎo yíxià fángjiān.
   Please clean my room.

4. **打听** **dǎtīng** find out
   跟 您 打听 一件 事。
   Gēn nín dǎtīng yí jiàn shì.
   I'd like to ask you about something.

5. **打字** **dǎzì** type
   她打字比 我 打得 快。
   Tā dǎzì bǐ wǒ dǎde kuài.
   She types faster than me.

The last stroke ends with a hook.   **5 strokes**

一	十	扌	扌	打							

算   **suàn**   calculate

The character originated as a pictograph of *two hands* 廾 holding a *bamboo* ⺮ abacus 目, a reference to *calculating*.

Radical: ⺮ 'bamboo'   **Index # 145**

Character components: ⺮ + 目 + 廾   **Character configuration:**

Compounds, sentences and meanings

1. 算 **suàn** calculate
   请 算一算 我 该 付 多少 钱。
   Qǐng suànyisuàn wǒ gāi fù duōshao qián.
   Please work out how much I have to pay.

2. 算盘 **suànpán** abacus
   有 人 说 算盘 比 计算器 快。
   Yǒu rén shuō suànpán bǐ jìsuànqì kuài.
   It is said that the abacus is faster than a calculator.

3. 算帐 **suànzhàng** do accounts
   她 算帐 算得 很 快。
   Tā suànzhàng suànde hěn kuài.
   She's quick at accounts.

4. 打算 **dǎsuàn** plan
   你 打算 什么 时候 去 西安?
   Nǐ dǎsuàn shénme shíhou qù Xī'ān?
   When do you plan to visit Xian?

5. 计算机 **jìsuànjī** computer
   计算机 又 叫 电脑。
   Jìsuànjī yòu jiào diànnǎo.
   Another name for computer is 'electronic brain.'

The second last stroke sweeps to the left.													14 strokes
ノ	⺅	⺮	⺮	竹	竹	竹	筥	筥	笡	筥	筸	算	
算													

huáng yellow

The character was derived from a pictograph of a burning oil-tipped arrow whose flames were *yellow*.

Radical: 艹 'grass'   **Index # 42**

Character components: 艹 + 一 + 由 + 八   **Character configuration:**

Compounds, sentences and meanings

1. 黄 **huáng** yellow
   树叶 开始 发黄 了。
   Shùyè kāishǐ fāhuáng le.
   The leaves are beginning to turn yellow.

2. 黄河 **Huánghé** the Yellow River
   黄河 是 中国 文化 的 摇篮。
   Huánghé shì Zhōngguó wénhuà de yáolán.
   The Yellow River is the cradle of Chinese civilization.

3. 黄金 **huángjīn** gold
   最近 黄金 价格 涨 了。
   Zuìjìn huángjīn jiàgé zhǎng le.
   The price of gold has risen recently.

4. 黄色 **huángsè** yellow, pornographic
   中国 严禁 黄色 书刊。
   Zhōngguó yánjìn huángsè shūkān.
   China strictly forbids pornographic books and magazines.

5. 黄油 **huángyóu** butter
   请 递 给 我 黄油。
   Qǐng dì gěi wǒ huángyóu.
   Please pass me the butter.

The central vertical stroke crosses through the line above.											11 strokes
一	十	艹	共	芇	苜	昔	苗	苗	黄	黄	

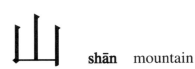

shān   mountain

The character represents the shape of a mountain.

Radical: 山 'mountain'

Index # 53

Character components: 丨 + 凵

Character configuration:

Compounds, sentences and meanings

1. 山 **shān** mountain
   中国 有 很多 山。
   Zhōngguó yǒu hěnduō shān.
   There are many mountains in China.

2. 山城 **shānchéng** mountain city
   重庆 是 一 座 山城。
   Chóngqìng shì yī zuò shānchéng.
   Chongqing is a mountain city.

3. 山顶 **shāndǐng** hilltop
   从 山顶 往 下 看, 风景 美极了。
   Cóng shāndǐng wǎng xià kàn, fēngjǐng měijíle.
   Looking down from the peak, the scenery is really beautiful.

4. 山区 **shānqū** mountain area
   很多 农民 住 在 山区。
   Hěnduō nóngmín zhù zài shānqū.
   Many peasants live in the mountains.

5. 黄山 **Huángshān** the Yellow Mountain
   黄山 风景 美极了。
   Huángshān fēngjǐng měijíle.
   The Yellow Mountain is a really beautiful spot.

The center vertical stroke is slightly higher.											3 strokes
丨	凵	山									

Full form

 fēng wind

The full form of the character combines *sail* 几 and *insect* 虫, suggesting insects blown against a sail by the wind. The simplified form uses ㄨ to replace the inside component.

Radical: 风 'wind'

Index # 105

Character components: 几 + ㄨ

Character configuration: ☐

Compounds, sentences and meanings

1. 风 **fēng** wind
   今天 很 大 风。
   Jīntiān hěn dà fēng.
   Today is very windy.

2. 风口 **fēngkǒu** a drafty place
   别 站 在 风口 上, 小心 着凉。
   Bié zhàn zài fēngkǒu shàng, xiǎoxīn zháoliáng.
   Don't stand in the draft. You may catch a cold.

3. 风趣 **fēngqù** humor, wit
   他 是 一个 很 有 风趣 的 人。
   Tā shì yí ge hěn yǒu fēngqù de rén.
   He is a man of charm and wit.

4. 风俗 **fēngsú** custom
   中国 很 大,各地 风俗 不同。
   Zhōngguó hěn dà, gèdì fēngsú bùtóng.
   China is very big: different places have different customs.

5. 风味 **fēngwèi** special flavor
   这 是 广东 风味菜。
   Zhè shì Guǎngdōng fēngwèicài.
   This is a typical Cantonese dish.

The second stroke ends with a hook.   4 strokes

丿	几	风	风						

景 jǐng scenery

The character combines *sun* 日 and *capital* 京 to represent the idea that it is good scenery when the sun shines on the capital. It means *scenery*.

Radical: 日 'sun'

Index # 90

Character components: 日 + 京

Character configuration:

Compounds, sentences and meanings

1. **景** **jǐng** scenery
   这 首 诗 描写 西湖 美 景。
   Zhè shǒu shī miáoxiě Xīhú měi jǐng.
   This poem describes the beautiful scenery around West Lake.

2. **景况** **jǐngkuàng** situation, circumstances
   她 家 的 景况 越 来 越 好 了。
   Tā jiā de jǐngkuàng yuè lái yuè hǎo le.
   Things are getting better and better for her family.

3. **不景气** **bùjǐngqì** economically depressed
   这 几 年 的 经济 不 景气。
   Zhè jǐ nián de jīngjì bù jǐngqì.
   The economy has been poor in the last few years.

4. **景色** **jǐngsè** scenery, view
   在 黄山 看 日出，景色 特别 美丽。
   Zài Huángshān kàn rìchū, jǐngsè tèbié měilì.
   The sunrise on the Yellow Mountain is spectacular.

5. **风景** **fēngjǐng** scenery
   桂林 风景 如画。
   Guìlín fēngjǐng rú huà.
   Guilin is as beautiful as a painting.

日 is written squarish.   12 strokes

| 丶 | 冂 | 冂 | 日 | 旦 | 昷 | 昗 | 昌 | 昌 | 景 | 景 | 景 | |

照 zhào   shine

The character combines *clear* 昭 and *four dots of fire* 灬 to refer to a fire illuminating an object so that it is clear. It came to mean *to shine on*.

Radical: 灬 **'four dots of fire'**

Character components: 昭 + 灬

Index # 71

Character configuration:

Compounds, sentences and meanings

1. **照** **zhào** light up
   车灯 把 大路 照得 通亮。
   Chēdēng bǎ dàlù zhàode tōngliàng.
   The headlights lit up the road.

2. **照常** **zhàocháng** as usual
   足球 比赛 遇 雨 也 照常 进行。
   Zúqiú bǐsài yù yǔ yě zhàocháng jìnxíng.
   The soccer match will be played as scheduled in the event of rain.

3. **照相** **zhàoxiàng** take a picture
   我们 星期天 照相 去。
   Wǒmen Xīngqītiān zhàoxiàng qù.
   Let's go and take photographs this Sunday.

4. **照旧** **zhàojiù** as before
   演唱会 改期, 入场券 照旧
   Yǎnchànghuì gǎiqī, rùchǎngquàn zhàojiù
   有效。
   yǒuxiào.
   The concert has been postponed, but the tickets remain valid.

5. **照片** **zhàopiàn** photograph
   我 想 加印 照片。
   Wǒ xiǎng jiāyìn zhàopiàn.
   I want to print off copies from a negative.

Note the direction of the four dots of fire.												13 strokes
丨	冂	冃	日	日	昭	昭	照	昭	照	照	照	照

相 xiāng   looks, appearance

The character combines *eyes* 目 and *tree* 木 to suggest the idea of looking carefully from the top of a tree. Thus it means *looks* or *appearance*.

Radical: 木 'tree'   **Index # 81**

Character components: 木 + 目   **Character configuration:**

Compounds, sentences and meanings

1. **相** **xiāng** appearance
   他 坐 在 那儿, 一副 可怜 相。
   Tā zuò zài nàr, yí fù kělián xiāng.
   He sat there with a pitiful appearance.

2. **相貌** **xiàngmào** facial features
   那 小伙子 好 相貌!
   Nà xiǎohuǒzi hǎo xiàngmào!
   That young man is really handsome!

3. **相片** **xiàngpiàn** photograph
   我 喜欢 这 张 相片。
   Wǒ xǐhuan zhè zhāng xiàngpiàn.
   I like this snapshot.

4. **相声** **xiàngshēng** comic dialogue/cross-talk
   我 觉得 相声 很 有 意思。
   Wǒ juéde xiàngshēng hěn yǒu yìsi.
   I enjoy comic dialogue.

5. **长相** **zhǎngxiàng** looks, features
   看 他们 的 长相 好像 是 兄弟。
   Kàn tāmen de zhǎngxiàng hǎoxiàng shì xiōngdi.
   They look like brothers.

There are two horizontal strokes inside the box.									9 strokes
一	十	才	木	朾	机	相	相	相	

Quiz 33 (321–330)

A. Look at the 16-character grid and CIRCLE words or phrases. They can be written horizontally or vertically. (Look at the circled characters in the Key if you are unsure.) Copy the word or phrase next to the grid and write down the pinyin and meaning.

假	美	黄	山
可	玩	照	相
打	算	风	时
以	放	景	想

Word or phrase

(i)	黄	山	
(ii)			
(iii)			
(iv)			

Pinyin | **Meaning**

Pinyin	Meaning
Huángshān	the Yellow Mountain

B. Using the characters in the 16-character grid, convert the pinyin sentences into characters and write the English meaning.

(i)	Fàngjià shí, nǐ xiǎng qù nǎr wán?							
(ii)	Wǒ dǎsuàn qù Huángshān wán.							
(iii)	Huángshān fēngjǐng hěn měi.							
(iv)	Nǐ kěyǐ zhào hěnduō xiàng.							

C. Match the Chinese words with their English meaning.

(i)

假 zāo	sweep, clean
假 rú	abacus
假期	counterfeit
请假	if
打字	holiday
打听	type
打 sǎo	find out
算 pán	take leave

(ii)

算 zhàng	as before
山 dǐng	photograph
风趣	summit
风 sú	scenery
景 sè	work out accounts
照 jiù	appearance
照 piàn	humorous
相 mào	custom

93

màn slow

The character combines *heart* 忄 and the phonetic 曼, which means *prolong*, to suggest the idea of *causing delay*. It came to mean *slow*.

Radical: 忄 'upright heart'　　　　　　　　**Index # 33**

Character components: 忄 + 曼　　　　　**Character configuration:** ⬚

Compounds, sentences and meanings

1. 慢　**màn**　slow
   我的 表 慢 一 分钟。
   Wǒde biǎo màn yī fēnzhōng.
   My watch is one minute slow.

2. 慢镜头　**mànjìngtóu**　slow motion
   我 可以 看 慢镜头 吗?
   Wǒ kěyǐ kàn mànjìngtóu ma?
   Can I see it in slow motion?

3. 慢慢　**mànmàn**　slowly
   别急, 慢慢 来。
   Bié jí, mànmàn lái.
   Calm down. Easy does it.

4. 慢腾腾　**màntēngtēng**　at a leisurely pace
   你 这么 慢腾腾 的, 什么 时候
   Nǐ zhème màntēngtēng de, shénme shíhou
   　能 做完?
   néng zuòwán?
   How will you ever finish the job at this pace?

5. 慢条斯理　**màntiáo-sīlǐ**　unhurriedly
   他 说话 做事 总是 慢条斯理 的。
   Tā shuōhuà zuòshì zǒngshì màntiáo-sīlǐ de.
   He always speaks slowly and acts unhurriedly.

The top part of 曼 is squarish, the middle section is rectangular.												14 strokes
丶	丷	忄	忄	忙	忙	忸	恒	悍	悍	慢	慢	慢
慢												

飞 fēi fly

The character combines *rise* 升 and two wing-like structures 飞 to suggest the idea of rising with two wings. The simplified form only uses one wing to represent *flying*.

Radical: 飞 **'horizontal-slanting-hook'**   **Index # 5**

Character components: 飞 + ´ + 丶   **Character configuration:** ☐

Compounds, sentences and meanings

1. 飞 fēi fly
   我 从 北京 直飞 广州。
   Wǒ cóng Běijīng zhí fēi Guǎngzhōu.
   I'm flying directly from Beijing to Guangzhou.

2. 飞机 fēijī aeroplane
   飞机 很 快 就要 着陆 了。
   Fēijī hěn kuài jiù yào zhuólù le.
   The plane will be landing soon.

3. 飞机场 fēijīchǎng airport
   最好 提前 两个 钟头 到 飞机场。
   Zuìhǎo tíqián liǎng ge zhōngtóu dào fēijīchǎng.
   It's a good idea to get to the airport two hours before the flight.

4. 飞快 fēikuài very fast
   汽车 以 飞快 的 速度 前进。
   Qìchē yǐ fēikuài de sùdù qiánjìn.
   The car is going at a breakneck speed.

5. 飞速 fēisù at full speed
   中国 的 经济 正在 飞速 发展。
   Zhōngguó de jīngjì zhèngzài fēisù fāzhǎn.
   The Chinese economy is developing rapidly.

The first stroke ends with a hook.												3 strokes
飞	飞	飞										

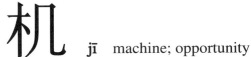 jī machine; opportunity

The full character combines *tree* 木 and the phonetic 幾 to suggest the idea of *opportunity*. The simplified form takes a simpler phonetic 几 to replace 幾.

Radical: 木 'tree'   **Index # 81**

Character components: 木 + 几   **Character configuration:**

Compounds, sentences and meanings

1. **机** jī opportunity
   机不可失, 时不再来。
   Jī bù kě shī, shí bú zài lái.
   Opportunity only knocks once.

2. **机动** jīdòng motorized
   我 买了 一 辆 机动 自行车。
   Wǒ mǎile yí liàng jīdòng zìxíngchē.
   I bought a moped.

3. **机会** jīhuì opportunity
   能 有 机会去 中国 旅行 就 好 了。
   Néng yǒu jīhuì qù Zhōngguó lǚxíng jiù hǎo le.
   It would be wonderful if I could visit China.

4. **机器** jīqì machine
   这 是 什么 机器?
   Zhè shì shénme jīqì?
   What kind of machine is this?

5. **机灵** jīlíng clever
   这 个 人 办事 挺 机灵 的。
   Zhè ge rén bànshì tǐng jīlíng de.
   This person manages things quite cleverly.

The last stroke ends with a hook.												6 strokes
一	十	才	木	朾	机							

 **kuài** fast

The character combines *upright heart* 忄 and the phonetic 夬 which also means *open*, to suggest an *open heart* or *happy*. When you're happy, all your action becomes *brisk*.

Radical: 忄 'upright heart'　　　　**Index # 33**

Character components: 忄 + 夬

Character configuration:

Compounds, sentences and meanings

1. **快 kuài** fast
   飞机 比 火车 快 得 多。
   Fēijī bǐ huǒchē kuài de duō.
   It's much faster to fly than to go by train.

2. **快餐 kuàicān** fast food
   我 喜欢 吃 快餐。
   Wǒ xǐhuan chī kuàicān.
   I like fast food.

3. **快活 kuàihuó** merry
   孩子们 快活地 打 雪仗。
   Háizimen kuàihuóde dǎ xuězhàng.
   The children were enjoying a snowball fight.

4. **快乐 kuàilè** happy
   节日 过得 很 快乐。
   Jiérì guòde hěn kuàilè.
   The festival was most enjoyable.

5. **快慢 kuàimàn** speed
   这些 按钮 是 管 快慢 的。
   Zhèxiē ànniǔ shì guǎn kuàimàn de.
   These buttons control the speed.

The second horizontal stroke is longer.									7 strokes
丶	丷	忄	忄⁻	忆	快	快			

票

piào ticket

The character combines *west* 西 and *show* 示 to form the phonetic 票. It means *ticket*.

Radical: 西 'west'　　　　　　　　　　**Index # 139**

or　　　　　　示 'show'　　　　　　　　**Index # 114**

Character components: 西 + 示　　　　**Character configuration:**

Compounds, sentences and meanings

1. 票 **piào** ticket
   你 买了 火车票 没有?
   Nǐ mǎile huǒchēpiào méiyǒu?
   Have you bought your train ticket?

2. 票房 **piàofáng** box office
   这 个 电影 打破了今年 的 票房 记录。
   Zhè ge diànyǐng dǎpòle jīnnián de piàofáng jìlù.
   This movie has smashed this year's box office record.

3. 票价 **piàojià** price of ticket
   音乐会 的 票价 是 多少?
   Yīnyuèhuì de piàojià shì duōshao?
   What's the price of a ticket to the concert?

4. 绑票 **bǎngpiào** kidnap (for ransom)
   他的儿子被 绑票了。
   Tāde érzi bèi bǎngpiàole.
   His son was held for ransom.

5. 投票 **tóupiào** vote
   这 是 无记名 投票。
   Zhè shì wújìmíng tóupiào.
   This is a secret ballot.

The second horizontal stroke of 示 is longer.　　　　　　　　**11 strokes**

一	冖	冖	两	西	西	西	覀	票	票	票		

jià price

The full form of the character combines *person* 亻 and the phonetic 賈 to suggest the idea of *value*. The simplified form uses a similar sounding phonetic 介 to convey the same concept.

Radical: 亻 'upright person'

Index # 19

Character components: 亻 + 介

Character configuration:

Compounds, sentences and meanings

1. **价** jià price
   可以 减价 吗?
   Kěyǐ jiǎnjià ma?
   Can you reduce the price?

2. **价钱** jiàqián price
   这 个 价钱 是 最 便宜 的 了。
   Zhè ge jiàqián shì zuì piányi de le.
   This is the cheapest price.

3. **价值** jiàzhí value
   这些 资料 对 我们 很 有 价值。
   Zhèxiē zīliào duì wǒmen hěn yǒu jiàzhí.
   This data is of great value to us.

4. **讲价** jiǎngjià bargain
   在 中国 买东西 要 讲价。
   Zài Zhōngguó mǎi dōngxi yào jiǎngjià.
   You have to bargain when you shop in China.

5. **涨价** zhǎngjià rise in price
   昨天 汽油 涨价 了。
   Zuótiān qìyóu zhǎngjià le.
   Yesterday the price of petrol went up.

The left vertical stroke of 介 sweeps to the left.   6 strokes

ノ	亻	仒	价	价	价						

bàn do

The full form of the character combines *exert effort* 辛, *strength* 力 and *exert effort* 辛 to suggest the idea that one needs to exert strenuous effort to do things. It means *to do*.

Radical: 力 'strength'　　　　　　**Index # 31**

Character components: ⺀ + 力 + 丶　　　　**Character configuration:** ☐

Compounds, sentences and meanings

1. **办　bàn** do, manage
   我 有 点 事 要 办。
   Wǒ yǒu diǎn shì yào bàn.
   There's something I have to do.

2. **办法　bànfǎ** way, means
   你 要 想 办法 克服 困难。
   Nǐ yào xiǎng bànfǎ kèfú kùnnàn
   You have to find a way to rise above your problems.

3. **办公室　bàngōngshì** office
   我 十 点 以后 在 办公室。
   Wǒ shí diǎn yǐhòu zài bàngōngshì.
   I'll be in my office after 10:00.

4. **办理　bànlǐ** handle, conduct
   请 到 那边 去 办理 离境 手续。
   Qǐng dào nàbiān qù bànlǐ líjìng shǒuxù.
   Please go over there to go through departure formalities.

5. **办事　bànshì** handle affairs, work
   她 办事 很 认真。
   Tā bànshì hěn rènzhēn.
   She works conscientiously.

The left dot ends firmly to the left, the right dot to the right.									4 strokes
フ	力	办	办						

 **lǚ** travel

The character combines *direction* 方, *flag* ⸃ and people 氏 which suggests the idea of people traveling in groups under a flag. It came to mean *travel*.

Radical: 方 'direction'　　　　　　　**Index # 74**

Character component: 方 + ⸃ + 氏　　　**Character configuration:**

Compounds, sentences and meanings

1. 旅　**lǚ**　travel
   这 次 北京 之 旅 愉快 吗?
   Zhè cì Běijīng zhī lǚ yúkuài ma?
   Did you enjoy your trip to Beijing?

2. 旅程　**lǚchéng**　route, itinerary
   去 中国 的 旅程 你 安排好 了 吗?
   Qù Zhōngguó de lǚchéng nǐ ānpáihǎo le ma?
   Have you arranged the itinerary for your China trip?

3. 旅馆　**lǚguǎn**　hotel
   这 家 旅馆 离市区 比较 远。
   Zhè jiā lǚguǎn lí shìqū bǐjiào yuǎn.
   This hotel is quite a distance from the city.

4. 旅途　**lǚtú**　journey
   祝 你旅途 愉快!
   Zhù nǐ lǚtú yúkuài!
   Bon voyage!

5. 旅行　**lǚxíng**　travel
   假期里你 打算 去哪儿 旅行?
   Jiàqīli nǐ dǎsuàn qù nǎr lǚxíng?
   Where do you plan to go for your holidays?

The last stroke tapers off.　　　　　　　　　　　　　**10 strokes**

丶	亠	方	方	方	方	方	旅	旅	旅			

xíng/háng travel/row

The character represents a picture of a crossroad. It came to mean *to go*.

Radical: 彳 'double person'　　　　　**Index # 54**

Character components: 彳 + 亍　　　　**Character configuration:**

Compounds, sentences and meanings

1. **行　xíng**　capable, competent
   你 看 他 干 这 个 工作　行 吗?
   Nǐ kàn tā gàn zhè ge gōngzuò xíng ma?
   Do you think he is up to it?

2. **行李　xíngli**　luggage
   这 是 我 的 手提 行李。
   Zhè shì wǒde shǒutí xíngli.
   This is my hand luggage.

3. **行驶　xíngshǐ**　travel (of a vehicle, ship etc.)
   在　中国　车辆　靠 右 行驶。
   Zài Zhōngguó chēliàng kào yòu xíngshǐ.
   In China, vehicles travel on the right side of the road.

4. **行业　hángyè**　profession
   他 是 干 什么 行业 的?
   Tā shì gàn shénme hángyè de?
   What work does he do?

5. **银行　yínháng**　bank
   中国　　银行　兑换 外币。
   Zhōngguó Yínháng duìhuàn wàibì.
   The Bank of China exchanges foreign currency.

The second horizontal stroke is longer than the one above it.								6 strokes

ノ	㇗	彳	彳	行	行			

340

 huā flower

The character combines *grass* ⁺⁺ and *change* 化 to suggest the idea of grass undergoing change, resulting in a *flower*.

Radical: ⁺⁺ 'grass'

Index # 42

Character components: ⁺⁺ + 化

Character configuration:

Compounds, sentences and meanings

1. **花** **huā** flower
春天 来了,百 花 开了。
Chūntiān lái le, bǎi huā kāi le.
Spring is here, the flowers are blossoming.

2. **花白** **huābái** grey
他的 头发 花白, 看起来 有 六十 岁。
Tāde tóufa huābái, kànqǐlai yǒu liùshí suì.
His hair is grey, he looks 60.

3. **花生** **huāshēng** peanuts
我 喜欢 吃 花生米。
Wǒ xǐhuan chī huāshēngmǐ.
I like to eat peanuts.

4. **花钱** **huāqián** spend (money)
在 中国 旅行 花不了 很多 钱。
Zài Zhōngguó lǚxíng huābuliǎo hěnduō qián.
It doesn't cost very much to travel in China.

5. **花样** **huāyàng** variety
这家 时装店 的衣服 花样 繁多。
Zhè jiā shízhuāngdiàn de yīfu huāyàng fánduō.
This boutique has a great variety of clothes.

The last stroke ends with a hook.

7 strokes

一	十	艹	艹	艿	花	花			

Quiz 34 (331–340)

A. Look at the 16-character grid and CIRCLE words or phrases. They can be written horizontally or vertically. (Look at the circled characters in the Key if you are unsure.) Copy the word or phrase next to the grid and write down the pinyin and meaning.

					Word or phrase			Pinyin	Meaning
旅	快	贵	钱	(i)	旅	行		lǚxíng	travel
行	飞	机	办	(ii)					
花	行	票	法	(iii)					
坐	怎	慢	太	(iv)					

B. Using the characters in the 16-character grid, convert the pinyin sentences into characters and write the English meaning.

(i)	Nǐ zěnme qù Huángshān? Zuò huǒchē?									
(ii)	Huǒchē tài màn, zuò fēijī kuài.									
(iii)	Fēijīpiào de jiàqián hěn guì ma?									
(iv)	Méi bànfǎ, lǚxíng yào huāqián de.									

C. Match the Chinese words with their English meaning.

(i)

机会	motorized
机动	speed
机 líng	opportunity
快 cān	value
快 lè	price
快慢	clever
价 zhí	happy
价钱	fast food

(ii)

讲价	work
办理	luggage
办 shì	handle
花样	bargain
行 li	travel
行 shǐ	bank
行 yè	variety
yín 行	profession

jì   count

The full form of the character combines *word* 言 and the number *ten* 十 to suggest the idea of *counting in tens*. By extension, it means *to measure* or *to plan*.

Radical: 讠 'word'

Index # 9

Character components: 讠 + 十

Character configuration:

Compounds, sentences and meanings

1. **计 jì** calculate, count
   现在 有 博士 学位 的 人 不 计 其 数。
   Xiànzài yǒu bóshì xuéwèi de rén bú jì qí shù.
   Nowadays there are countless people with PhD degrees.

2. **计划 jìhuà** plan
   我们 计划 下周 出发。
   Wǒmen jìhuà xiàzhōu chūfā.
   We plan to leave next week.

3. **计较 jìjiào** haggle over, fuss about
   他 不 计较 小事。
   Tā bú jìjiào xiǎoshì.
   He doesn't fuss about trifles.

4. **计时 jìshí** reckon by time
   这 是 一份 计时 工作。
   Zhè shì yī fēn jìshí gōngzuò.
   This work is paid by the time.

5. **计算 jìsuàn** planning
   做事 不能 没 个 计算。
   Zuòshì bùnéng méi ge jìsuàn.
   We shouldn't do anything without a plan.

The second stroke is a horizontal-vertical-lift.   4 strokes

丶	讠	计	计								

划   **huâ**   delimit

The full form of the character combines *draw* 畫 and *knife* 刂 to suggest that in ancient times people *made marks* or *drew* with a knife. In simplification, 戈 replaces 畫.

Radical: 刂 '**upright knife**'   **Index # 15**

or   戈 '**spear**'   **Index # 85**

Character components: 戈 + 刂   **Character configuration:**

Compounds, sentences and meanings

1. 划 **huâ**   draw, stroke (of a Chinese character)
   这 个 字 有 八 划。
   Zhè ge zì yǒu bā huâ.
   This Chinese character has eight strokes.

2. 划定 **huâdìng**   delimit, designate
   在 划定 的 区域 内 游泳。
   Zài huâdìng de qūyù nèi yóuyǒng.
   Swim within the designated areas.

3. 划分 **huâfēn**   divide
   中国 划分 为 三 种 行政 区域。
   Zhōngguó huâfēn wéi sān zhǒng xíngzhèng qūyù.
   China is divided into three types of administrative areas.

4. 划时代 **huâshídài**   epoch-making
   中国 加入 世贸 具有 划时代
   Zhōngguó jiārù Shìmào jùyǒu huâshídài
   的意义。
   de yìyì.
   China's entry into the WTO was a historic event.

5. 划一不二 **huâ yī bù èr**   fixed, rigid
   写 文章 没有 划一不二的 公式。
   Xiě wénzhāng méiyǒu huâ yī bù èr de gōngshì.
   There are no hard and fast rules for writing essays.

The last stroke ends with a hook.   **6 strokes**

一	弋	戈	戈	戋	划				

 **jué** decide

The character combines *ice* 冫 and *open* 夬 to suggest the idea of *definitely*. By extension, it means *to decide*.

Radical: 冫 'ice'

Index # 7

Character components: 冫 + 夬

Character configuration: ⊟

Compounds, sentences and meanings

1. 决 **jué** definitely
   女儿 对 她的 婚事 决 不 让步。
   Nǚ'ér duì tāde hūnshì jué bú ràngbù.
   With regard to her marriage, their daughter won't make any concessions.

2. 决不 **juébù** absolutely not
   在 这 方面 我 决不 退让。
   Zài zhè fāngmiàn wǒ juébù tuìràng.
   I will not give in under any circumstances.

3. 决定 **juédìng** decide
   我 一时 决定不了。
   Wǒ yìshí juédìngbuliǎo.
   I can't make up my mind right now.

4. 决心 **juéxīn** determination
   我 下定 决心 学好 汉字。
   Wǒ xiàdìng juéxīn xuéhǎo Hànzì.
   I'm determined to learn Chinese characters well.

5. 解决 **jiějué** resolve
   这 件 事情 不 容易 解决。
   Zhè jiàn shìqing bù róngyì jiějué.
   This matter is not easily resolved.

The last stroke firms and then tapers off.

6 strokes

丶	冫	冫	沪	决	决						

玩  wán play

The character combines *king* 王 and the phonetic 元 to suggest the idea of *having fun* or *play*.

Radical: 王 'king'

Index # 79

Character components: 王 + 元

Character configuration:

Compounds, sentences and meanings

1. 玩 **wán** play
   我 在 北京 玩了 三 天。
   Wǒ zài Běijīng wánle sān tiān.
   We spent three days enjoying ourselves in Beijing.

2. 玩具 **wánjù** toy
   现在 小孩 的 玩具 花样 多极了。
   Xiànzài xiǎohái de wánjù huāyàng duōjíle.
   Nowadays, there are lots of different toys.

3. 玩笑 **wánxiào** joke
   他 是 开 玩笑, 你 别 认真。
   Tā shì kāi wánxiào, nǐ biě rènzhēn.
   He's only joking, don't take him seriously.

4. 玩意儿 **wányìr** thing
   他 手里 拿 的 是 什么 玩意儿?
   Tā shǒulǐ ná de shì shénme wányìr?
   What's that thing in his hand?

5. 古玩 **gǔwán** antique
   这 是 古玩, 所以 这么 贵。
   Zhè shì gǔwán, suǒyǐ zhème guì.
   This is antique, that's why it's so expensive.

The last stroke is a vertical-bend-hook.   **8 strokes**

一	二	干	王	玌	玗	玕	玩				

shuǐ water

The character represents the *current* and *ripples* of a river.

Radical: 水 'water'

Index # 109

Character component: 水

Character configuration:

Compounds, sentences and meanings

1. **水** **shuǐ** water
   这里 水 平 如 镜。
   Zhèlǐ shuǐ píng rú jìng.
   The water here is as smooth as a mirror.

2. **水果** **shuǐguǒ** fruit
   多 吃 水果 对 身体 有 好处。
   Duō chī shuǐguǒ duì shēntǐ yǒu hǎochù.
   Eating fruit is good for you.

3. **水龙头** **shuǐlóngtóu** tap
   用 后 将 水龙头 关紧。
   Yòng hòu jiāng shuǐlóngtóu guānjǐn.
   Please turn off the tap tightly after use.

4. **水平** **shuǐpíng** standard, level
   中国 人民 的 生活 水平
   Zhōngguó rénmín de shēnghuó shuǐpíng
   提高了。
   tígāo le.
   The living standard of the Chinese people has improved.

5. **山水画** **shānshuǐhuà** landscape painting
   她 送 我 一 副 山水画。
   Tā sòng wǒ yī fù shānshuǐhuà.
   She gave me a landscape painting.

The vertical stroke ends with a hook. | 4 strokes

| 亅 | 刀 | 水 | 水 | | | | | | | | | |

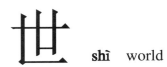

shì   world

The character is a phonetic used as a character. It came to mean *world*.

Radical: 一 'horizontal stroke'   **Index # 2**

Character components: 一 + ∟ + 凵   **Character configuration:**

Compounds, sentences and meanings

1. 世 **shì** world
   北京 烤鸭 举世 闻名。
   Běijīng kǎoyā jǔshì wénmíng.
   Beijing duck is world-famous.

2. 世故 **shìgù** ways of the world
   王 老 于 世故。
   Wáng lǎo yú shìgù.
   Wang is a man of the world.

3. 世纪 **shìjì** century
   现在 是 二十一 世纪的 开始。
   Xiànzài shì èrshíyī shìjì de kāishǐ.
   Now is the beginning of the twenty-first century.

4. 世界 **shìjiè** world
   他打破了男子 一百 米 世界 记录。
   Tā dǎpòle nánzi yībǎi mǐ shìjiè jìlù.
   He broke the men's 100 meter world record.

5. 世上 **shìshang** in the world
   世上 无 难事, 只 怕 有心人。
   Shìshang wú nánshì, zhǐ pà yǒuxīnrén.
   Nothing in the world is difficult if you set your mind to it.

The last stroke is a vertical-bend.   **5 strokes**

一	十	卅	丗	世							

jiè   boundary

The character combines *field* 田 and the phonetic 介 to suggest the idea of *boundary*.

Radical: 田 'field'

Index # 119

Character components: 田 + 介

Character configuration:

Compounds, sentences and meanings

1. **界** **jiè** boundary
   山西 和 陕西 以 黄河 为界。
   Shānxī hé Shǎnxī yǐ Huánghé wéi jiè.
   The boundary between Shanxi and Shaanxi is the Yellow River.

2. **界限** **jièxiàn** dividing line
   朋友 之 间 界限 最好 不要
   Péngyou zhī jiàn jièxiàn zuìhǎo búyào
   分得 太 清。
   fēnde tài qīng.
   Among friends, it is best that limits are not too rigid.

3. **眼界** **yǎnjiè** field of vision
   这 个 展览 使 我们 大 开 眼界。
   Zhè ge zhǎnlǎn shǐ wǒmen dà kāi yǎnjiè.
   This exhibition has been a real eye-opener.

4. **外界** **wàijiè** external world, outside
   我们 应该 向 外界 征求 意见。
   Wǒmen yīnggāi xiàng wàijiè zhēngqiú yìjiàn.
   We should seek comments and suggestions from external sources.

5. **新闻界** **xīnwénjiè** press circles
   今天 的 会议 邀请了 新闻界 人士 参加。
   Jīntiān de huìyì yāoqǐngle xīnwénjiè rénshì cānjiā.
   People from the press were invited to today's meeting.

The eighth stroke ends with a sweep to the left.   9 strokes

丶	冂	冂	田	田	甼	界	界	界					

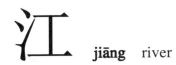 jiāng   river

The character combines *water* 氵 and *work* 工 to give the idea that it takes a great deal of work to control *a long river*.

Radical: 氵 '3 drops of water'   **Index # 32**

Character components: 氵 + 工   **Character configuration:**

Compounds, sentences and meanings

1. 江 **jiāng**   river
   我们 明天 顺流 下 江。
   Wǒmen míngtiān shùnliú xià jiāng.
   We are going downstream tomorrow.

2. 江山 **jiāngshān**   rivers and mountains
   江山 易改，本性 难移。
   Jiāngshān yì gǎi, běnxìng nán yí.
   It's easier to change rivers and mountains than to change human nature.

3. 江南 **Jiāngnán**   south of the lower reaches of the Changjiang River
   江南 是 富裕的地区。
   Jiāngnán shì fùyù de dìqū.
   Jiangnan is a rich region.

4. 长江 **Chángjiāng**   the Changjiang (Yangtze) River
   长江 是 世界 第三 大 河。
   Chángjiāng shì shìjiè dìsān dà hé.
   The Changjiang River is the third longest river in the world.

5. 珠江 **Zhūjiāng**   the Pearl River
   珠江 三角洲 是 一个 重要 的
   Zhūjiāng Sānjiǎozhōu shì yí ge zhòngyào de
   经济 发展区。
   jīngjì fāzhǎnqū.
   The Pearl River Delta is an important economic development zone.

The bottom horizontal stroke is slightly longer.   **6 strokes**

、	冫	氵	氵	汀	江					

hé river

The character combines *water* 氵 and the phonetic 可 to represent a *river*.

Radical: 氵 '3 drops of water'   **Index # 32**

Character components: 氵 + 可   **Character configuration:** ⊞

Compounds, sentences and meanings

1. 河 **hé** river
   前面 有 一 条 河。
   Qiánmiàn yǒu yī tiáo hé.
   There's a river ahead.

2. 河流 **héliú** river
   中国 有 很多 河流。
   Zhōngguó yǒu hěnduō héliú.
   There are many rivers in China.

3. 河北 **Héběi** Hebei Province
   河北 在 黄河 北边。
   Héběi zài Huánghé běibiān.
   Hebei Province is situated north of the Yellow River.

4. 河鱼 **héyú** freshwater fish
   我 不 喜欢 吃 河鱼。
   Wǒ bù xǐhuan chī héyú.
   I don't like the taste of freshwater fish.

5. 黄河 **Huánghé** the Yellow River
   黄河 是 中国 文化 的 摇篮。
   Huánghé shì Zhōngguó wénhuà de yáolán.
   The Yellow River is the cradle of the Chinese civilization.

The last stroke of 可 ends with a hook.   8 strokes

| 丶 | 冫 | 氵 | 汀 | 沔 | 沔 | 沔 | 河 | | | |

船

chuán boat, ship

The character combines *boat* 舟 and *flowing water in a ravine* 㕣, suggesting a *large boat* capable of going against a current.

Radical: 舟 'boat'　　　　　　**Index # 149**

Character components: 舟 + 几 + 口　　**Character configuration:**

Compounds, sentences and meanings

1. **船 chuán** boat, ship
   可以 坐 船 去 大连。
   Kěyǐ zuò chuán qù Dàlián.
   One can get to Dalian by ship.

2. **船票 chuánpiào** steamer ticket
   我 预订 去 大连 的 船票。
   Wǒ yùdìng qù Dàlián de chuánpiào.
   I'd like to book a passage to Dalian.

3. **帆船 fānchuán** sailing boat
   海湾 里 有 很多 帆船。
   Hǎiwān lǐ yǒu hěnduō fānchuán.
   There are lots of sailing boats in the harbor.

4. **货船 huòchuán** cargo ship
   现在 的 货船 很 大。
   Xiànzài de huòchuán hěn dà.
   Modern cargo ships are very big.

5. **客船 kèchuán** oceanliner
   这 是 六星级 的 豪华 客船。
   Zhè shì liùxīngjí de háohuá kèchuán.
   This is a 6-star luxury oceanliner.

The eighth stroke is a horizontal-bend-vertical-bend.　　**11 strokes**

丿 丆 几 肖 舟 舟 舢 舩 船 船

A. Look at the 16-character grid and CIRCLE words or phrases. They can be written horizontally or vertically. (Look at the circled characters in the Key if you are unsure.) Copy the word or phrase next to the grid and write down the pinyin and meaning.

		Word or phrase			Pinyin	Meaning
黄河	江	行	(i) 黄	河		Huánghé	The Yellow River
玩	水	世	山	(ii)			
决	定	界	长	(iii)			
名	旅	计	划	(iv)			

B. Using the characters in the 16-character grid, convert the pinyin sentences into characters and write the English meaning.

(i)	Shuōshuō nǐde lǚxíng jìhuà ba.								
(ii)	Wǒ hái méi juédìng qù nǎr wán.								
(iii)	Zhōngguó de shānshuǐ shìjiè yǒumíng.								
(iv)	Chángjiāng de fēngjǐng hěn měi.								

C. Match the Chinese words with their English meaning.

(i)

计较	epoch-making
计算	toy
划分	haggle over
划时代	divide
决心	planning
jiě 决	thing
玩 jù	determination
玩 yìr	resolve

(ii)

水 guǒ	the world
水 píng	Changjiang River
山水 huà	level
世 jì	landscape painting
世上	fruit
yǎn 界	century
界 xiàn	limits
长江	field of vision

CHARACTER BUILDING 7 (301–350)

A. Memorize the following radicals and their English names. As a review exercise, write the pinyin and the English meaning of the examples under each radical:

1. ［一］ 'horizontal stroke'
   世 (_____) _____ ; 表 (_____) _____ .

2. ［乛］ 'horizontal-bend'
   民 (_____) _____ ; 飞 (_____) _____ .

3. ［亠］ 'top of 六'
   高 (_____) _____ ; 亮 (_____) _____ .

4. ［冫］ 'ice'
   决 (_____) _____ ; 冷 (_____) _____ .

5. ［讠］ 'word'
   计 (_____) _____ ; 话 (_____) _____ .

6. ［刂］ 'upright knife'
   划 (_____) _____ ; 利 (_____) _____ .

7. ［八］ 'eight'
   首 (_____) _____ ; 兴 (_____) _____ .

8. ［亻］ 'upright person'
   但 (_____) _____ ; 代 (_____) _____ ;
   假 (_____) _____ ; 价 (_____) _____ ;
   俗 (_____) _____ .

9. ［又］ 'again'
   难 (_____) _____ ; 又 (_____) _____ .

10. ［力］ 'strength'
    办 (_____) _____ ; 助 (_____) _____ .

11. ［氵］ '3 drops of water'
    湾 (_____) _____ ; 江 (_____) _____ .

12. ［忄］ 'upright heart'
    慢 (_____) _____ ; 快 (_____) _____ .

13. ［艹］ 'grass'
    花 (_____) _____ ; 黄 (_____) _____ .

14. ［扌］ 'hand'
    打 (_____) _____ ; 找 (_____) _____ .

15. ［口］ 'mouth'
    唱 (_____) _____ ; 听 (_____) _____ .

16. ［彳］ 'double person'
    行 (_____) _____ ; 很 (_____) _____ .

17. ［纟］ 'silk'
    给 (_____) _____ ; 练 (_____) _____ .

18. ［灬］ '4 dots of fire'
    照 (_____) _____ ; 热 (_____) _____ .

19. ［方］ 'direction'
旅 (＿＿＿＿) ＿＿＿＿＿＿ ； 放 (＿＿＿＿) ＿＿＿＿＿＿ ．

20. ［心］ 'heart'
心 (＿＿＿＿) ＿＿＿＿＿＿ ； 想 (＿＿＿＿) ＿＿＿＿＿＿ ．

21. ［王］ 'king'
玩 (＿＿＿＿) ＿＿＿＿＿＿ ； 理 (＿＿＿＿) ＿＿＿＿＿＿ ．

22. ［木］ 'tree'
相 (＿＿＿＿) ＿＿＿＿＿＿ ； 机 (＿＿＿＿) ＿＿＿＿＿＿ ．

23. ［日］ 'sun'
景 (＿＿＿＿) ＿＿＿＿＿＿ ； 易 (＿＿＿＿) ＿＿＿＿＿＿ ．

24. ［曰］ 'speech'
曲 (＿＿＿＿) ＿＿＿＿＿＿ ； 最 (＿＿＿＿) ＿＿＿＿＿＿ ．

25. ［攵］ 'tap'
教 (＿＿＿＿) ＿＿＿＿＿＿ ； 放 (＿＿＿＿) ＿＿＿＿＿＿ ．

26. ［欠］ 'owe'
歌 (＿＿＿＿) ＿＿＿＿＿＿ ； 欢 (＿＿＿＿) ＿＿＿＿＿＿ ．

27. ［戈］ 'spear'
划 (＿＿＿＿) ＿＿＿＿＿＿ ； 我 (＿＿＿＿) ＿＿＿＿＿＿ ．

28. ［田］ 'field'
界 (＿＿＿＿) ＿＿＿＿＿＿ ； 男 (＿＿＿＿) ＿＿＿＿＿＿ ．

29. ［西］ 'west'
票 (＿＿＿＿) ＿＿＿＿＿＿ ； 要 (＿＿＿＿) ＿＿＿＿＿＿ ．

30. ［竹］ 'bamboo'
算 (＿＿＿＿) ＿＿＿＿＿＿ ； 第 (＿＿＿＿) ＿＿＿＿＿＿ ．

B. Write the pinyin and meaning against characters classified under the following radicals.

1. ［风］ 'wind'　　　风　　(＿＿＿＿) ＿＿＿＿＿＿
2. ［山］ 'mountain'　山　　(＿＿＿＿) ＿＿＿＿＿＿
3. ［水］ 'water'　　　水　　(＿＿＿＿) ＿＿＿＿＿＿
4. ［穴］ 'cave'　　　容　　(＿＿＿＿) ＿＿＿＿＿＿
5. ［示］ 'show'　　　票　　(＿＿＿＿) ＿＿＿＿＿＿
6. ［页］ 'page'　　　题　　(＿＿＿＿) ＿＿＿＿＿＿
7. ［金］ 'gold'　　　金　　(＿＿＿＿) ＿＿＿＿＿＿
8. ［舟］ 'boat'　　　船　　(＿＿＿＿) ＿＿＿＿＿＿

C. Write the pinyin and meaning against the characters which share the following components. (Note that these components are not necessarily used as radicals.)

1. ［口］ 哥 (＿＿＿＿) ＿＿＿＿＿＿ ； 歌 (＿＿＿＿) ＿＿＿＿＿＿ ．
2. ［谷］ 俗 (＿＿＿＿) ＿＿＿＿＿＿ ； 容 (＿＿＿＿) ＿＿＿＿＿＿ ．

3. ［方］ 放 (＿＿＿＿) ＿＿＿＿＿＿ ； 旅 (＿＿＿＿) ＿＿＿＿＿＿ ．
4. ［廾］ 开 (＿＿＿＿) ＿＿＿＿＿＿ ； 算 (＿＿＿＿) ＿＿＿＿＿＿ ．
5. ［元］ 玩 (＿＿＿＿) ＿＿＿＿＿＿ ； 远 (＿＿＿＿) ＿＿＿＿＿＿ ．
6. ［介］ 价 (＿＿＿＿) ＿＿＿＿＿＿ ； 界 (＿＿＿＿) ＿＿＿＿＿＿ ．
7. ［夬］ 快 (＿＿＿＿) ＿＿＿＿＿＿ ； 决 (＿＿＿＿) ＿＿＿＿＿＿ ．
8. ［戈］ 划 (＿＿＿＿) ＿＿＿＿＿＿ ； 找 (＿＿＿＿) ＿＿＿＿＿＿ ．
9. ［首］ 首 (＿＿＿＿) ＿＿＿＿＿＿ ； 道 (＿＿＿＿) ＿＿＿＿＿＿ ．

REVIEW 7 (301–350)

The following are words and phrases classified under parts of speech. Write their pinyin and meaning.

Nouns

人民 (＿＿＿＿) ＿＿＿＿＿ ； 民歌 (＿＿＿＿) ＿＿＿＿＿ ；
歌星 (＿＿＿＿) ＿＿＿＿＿ ； 歌声 (＿＿＿＿) ＿＿＿＿＿ ；
歌唱家 (＿＿＿＿) ＿＿＿＿＿ ； 俗话 (＿＿＿＿) ＿＿＿＿＿ ；
习俗 (＿＿＿＿) ＿＿＿＿＿ ； 作曲家 (＿＿＿＿) ＿＿＿＿＿ ；
曲子 (＿＿＿＿) ＿＿＿＿＿ ； 海湾 (＿＿＿＿) ＿＿＿＿＿ ；
台湾 (＿＿＿＿) ＿＿＿＿＿ ； 教师 (＿＿＿＿) ＿＿＿＿＿ ；
首都 (＿＿＿＿) ＿＿＿＿＿ ； 现金 (＿＿＿＿) ＿＿＿＿＿ ；
问题 (＿＿＿＿) ＿＿＿＿＿ ； 话题 (＿＿＿＿) ＿＿＿＿＿ ；
月亮 (＿＿＿＿) ＿＿＿＿＿ ； 表面 (＿＿＿＿) ＿＿＿＿＿ ；
心理 (＿＿＿＿) ＿＿＿＿＿ ； 假期 (＿＿＿＿) ＿＿＿＿＿ ；
计算机 (＿＿＿＿) ＿＿＿＿＿ ； 黄金 (＿＿＿＿) ＿＿＿＿＿ ；
黄山 (＿＿＿＿) ＿＿＿＿＿ ； 山城 (＿＿＿＿) ＿＿＿＿＿ ；
风俗 (＿＿＿＿) ＿＿＿＿＿ ； 风趣 (＿＿＿＿) ＿＿＿＿＿ ；
风景 (＿＿＿＿) ＿＿＿＿＿ ； 飞机 (＿＿＿＿) ＿＿＿＿＿ ；
机会 (＿＿＿＿) ＿＿＿＿＿ ； 快慢 (＿＿＿＿) ＿＿＿＿＿ ；
价钱 (＿＿＿＿) ＿＿＿＿＿ ； 办法 (＿＿＿＿) ＿＿＿＿＿ ；
办理 (＿＿＿＿) ＿＿＿＿＿ ； 旅行 (＿＿＿＿) ＿＿＿＿＿ ；
计算 (＿＿＿＿) ＿＿＿＿＿ ； 山水 (＿＿＿＿) ＿＿＿＿＿ ；
世界 (＿＿＿＿) ＿＿＿＿＿ ； 江山 (＿＿＿＿) ＿＿＿＿＿ ；
长江 (＿＿＿＿) ＿＿＿＿＿ ； 黄河 (＿＿＿＿) ＿＿＿＿＿ ．

Verbs

唱歌 (＿＿＿＿) ＿＿＿＿＿ ； 作曲 (＿＿＿＿) ＿＿＿＿＿ ；
交易 (＿＿＿＿) ＿＿＿＿＿ ； 教书 (＿＿＿＿) ＿＿＿＿＿ ；
代办 (＿＿＿＿) ＿＿＿＿＿ ； 代表 (＿＿＿＿) ＿＿＿＿＿ ；
放大 (＿＿＿＿) ＿＿＿＿＿ ； 放假 (＿＿＿＿) ＿＿＿＿＿ ；

放心 (_____) _____;	请假 (_____) _____;
打听 (_____) _____;	打字 (_____) _____;
打电话 (_____) _____;	打算 (_____) _____;
照相 (_____) _____;	讲价 (_____) _____;
花钱 (_____) _____;	花样 (_____) _____;
计划 (_____) _____;	划分 (_____) _____;
决心 (_____) _____;	决定 (_____) _____;

Adjectives　难过 (_____) _____;　　难得 (_____) _____;

通俗 (_____) _____;　　高大 (_____) _____;

高兴 (_____) _____;　　容易 (_____) _____;

首要 (_____) _____;　　明亮 (_____) _____;

小心 (_____) _____;　　机动 (_____) _____;

快活 (_____) _____;　　计时 (_____) _____;

Adverbs　首先 (_____) _____;　　照常 (_____) _____;

慢慢 (_____) _____;　　飞快 (_____) _____;

决不 (_____) _____;

Conjunctions 但是 (_____) _____;　　不但 (_____) _____;

WORD/SENTENCE PUZZLE 7

Find and circle words, phrases and sentences hidden in the puzzle. They can be found horizontally from left to right or vertically . The lines across and down are indicated by numbers. Write their meaning next to the pinyin. The first one is done for you.

ACROSS

1. Tā dǎsuàn qù Huángshān wán.　　　*He intends to go to the Yellow Mountain*
   for a holiday.

3. fēngsú　　　_____

4. hǎijǐng　　　_____

5. Yuèliang dàibiǎo wǒde xīn.　　　_____

8. Zhè shì hǎo jīhuì, búyào fàngguò.　　　_____

10. Táiběi　　　_____

11. hǎiwān　　　_____

12. (i)　fēijīpiào　　　_____

(ii)　lǚyóu　　　_____

14. Wǒ juédìng qǐng tā qù.　　　_____

15. Xiǎng ge hǎo de huàtí.　　　_____

DOWN

2. Tiān liàng le. _____

5 Wǒ xiǎng bǎ zhè zhāng diànyǐngpiào gěi tā. _____

7. Tā jīntiān de xīnqíng bù hǎo. _____

9. Néng yǒu jīhuì qù Táiwān lǚxíng jiù hǎo le. _____

11. Huángshān fēngjǐng hěn měi. _____

12. Nǐ fàngxīn ba, búhuì chū wèntí de. _____

	1	2	3	4	5	6	7	8	9	10	11	12	13
1	怕	价	音	建	发	容	他	打	算	去	黄	山	玩
2	开	正	改	界	该	难	今	应	调	流	山	谈	验
3	月	花	教	世	金	容	天	议	先	才	风	俗	容
4	容	天	最	高	法	跟	的	首	容	海	景	找	趣
5	月	亮	代	表	我	的	心	唱	能	曲	很	建	法
6	容	了	容	讲	想	慢	情	代	有	听	美	又	兴
7	怕	价	音	建	把	快	不	河	机	容	诉	你	港
8	的	首	容	海	这	是	好	机	会	不	要	放	过
9	识	名	没	空	张	比	做	来	去	看	半	心	美
10	子	知	妹	体	电	是	会	老	台	北	书	吧	男
11	样	昨	身	分	影	也	每	海	湾	民	十	不	亲
12	学	去	飞	机	票	口	城	年	旅	游	孩	会	练
13	星	午	身	吃	给	岁	买	父	行	好	妈	出	哥
14	我	决	定	请	她	去	母	怎	就	还	狗	问	给
15	语	再	起	在	期	明	想	个	好	的	话	题	公
16	家	这	名	跑	医	湾	汉	外	了	花	和	的	友

fù add, attach

The character combines *earth-mound* or *place* 阝 and the phonetic 付 to give the idea of *to be near a place*. The meaning of *add* or *attach* was acquired by extension.

Radical: 阝 **'left ear-lobe'**

Index # 27

Character components: 阝 + 付

Character configuration:

Compounds, sentences and meanings

1. **附 fù** attach
   附寄 两 张 照片, 请 查收。
   Fù jì liǎng zhāng zhàopiàn, qǐng cháshōu.
   Please find enclosed two photos.

2. **附带 fùdài** attach
   我 给 你的 帮助 不 附带 任何 条件。
   Wǒ gěi nǐde bāngzhu bú fùdài rènhé tiáojiàn.
   My assistance to you has no strings attached.

3. **附加税 fùjiāshuì** goods and services tax
   这 是 政府 的 附加税。
   Zhè shì zhèngfǔ de fùjiāshuì.
   This is the goods and services tax levied by the Govenment.

4. **附近 fùjìn** nearby
   附近 有 没有 邮局?
   Fùjìn yǒu méiyǒu yóujú?
   Is there a post office nearby?

5. **附上 fùshàng** be enclosed herewith
   随信 附上 商品 目录 一 份。
   Suíxìn fùshàng shāngpǐn mùlù yī fèn.
   A catalog of commodities is enclosed.

The first stroke is written like the figure 3.

7 strokes

阝	阝	阝	阝	阝一	附	附						

厕 **cè** lavatory

廁

The character combines *building* 厂 and the phonetic 则 to suggest *lavatory*.

Radical: 厂 'building'

Index # 12

Character components: 厂 + 则

Character configuration:

Compounds, sentences and meanings

1. 厕 **cè** toilet
   如厕 后 请 冲水。
   Rúcè hòu qǐng chōngshuǐ.
   Please flush the toilet after use.

2. 厕所 **cèsuǒ** toilet
   这里 的 厕所 很 干净。
   Zhèlǐ de cèsuǒ hěn gānjìng.
   The toilets here are quite clean.

3. 女厕 **nǚcè** ladies' toilet
   女厕 要 排队。
   Nǚcè yào páiduì.
   You have to queue for the women's toilet.

4. 坐厕 **zuòcè** seated toilet
   坐厕 比 蹲厕 舒服。
   Zuòcè bǐ dūncè shūfu.
   It's more comfortable to sit than to squat when on the toilet.

The first stroke is horizontal, the next is a downward sweep. | 8 strokes

| 一 | 厂 | 厂 | 斤 | 厉 | 厕 | 厕 | 厕 | | | |

suǒ   dwelling

The character combines *ax* 斤 and *household* 户 to refer to the *sound of chopping wood*. It came to mean *place*.

Radical: 户 '**household**'   **Index # 77**

or   斤 '**ax**'   **Index # 101**

Character components: 户 + 斤   Character configuration:

Compounds, sentences and meanings

1. 所 **suǒ**   measure word (for building)
   这 所 学校 的 历史 悠久。
   Zhè suǒ xuéxiào de lìshǐ yōujiǔ.
   This school has a long history.

2. 所以 **suǒyǐ**   therefore
   因为 天 太 冷，所以 我 不 去 了。
   Yīnwèi tiān tài lěng, suǒyǐ wǒ bú qù le.
   I'm not going because it's too cold.

3. 所有 **suǒyǒu**   all
   把 所有的 劲儿 都 使出来。
   Bǎ suǒyǒude jìnr dōu shǐchūlai.
   Exert all your strength.

4. 诊所 **zhěnsuǒ**   clinic, surgery
   这里 有 一 个 中医   诊所。
   Zhèlǐ yǒu yí ge zhōngyī zhěnsuǒ.
   There's a clinic for Chinese medicine here.

5. 医务所 **yīwùsuǒ**   clinic
   请问，   医务所 在 哪儿？
   Qǐngwèn, yīwùsuǒ zài nǎr?
   Excuse me, where is the clinic?

The first and fifth strokes sweep down sharply.										8 strokes
´	厂	斥	戶	斤´	所	所	所			

hóng red

Full form

紅

The character combines *silk* 纟 and 工 to represent the color *red*.

Radical: 纟 'silk'

Index # 68

Character components: 纟 + 工

Character configuration:

Compounds, sentences and meanings

1. **红 hóng** red
   他的 眼睛 都 熬红 了。
   Tāde yǎnjing dōu áohóng le.
   His eyes are bloodshot from staying up late all night.

2. **红包 hóngbāo** red envelope containing money
   小孩 喜欢 过年，因为 能 拿到
   Xiǎohái xǐhuan guònián, yīnwèi néng nádào
   很多 红包。
   hěnduō hóngbāo.
   Children love Chinese New Year because they get lots of red packages.

3. **红绿灯 hónglǜdēng** traffic lights
   在 红绿灯 右 拐弯。
   Zài hónglǜdēng yòu guǎiwān.
   Turn right at the lights.

4. **红薯 hóngshǔ** sweet potato
   烤 红薯 很 好吃。
   Kǎo hóngshǔ hěn hǎochī.
   Roasted sweet potatoes are delicious.

5. **红眼 hóngyǎn** be jealous
   他 红眼 别人 收入 比他多。
   Tā hóngyǎn biéren shōurù bǐ tā duō.
   He is jealous of people who earn more than him.

The bottom horizontal stroke is slightly longer. **6 strokes**

乡	纟	纟	纟	红	红						

Full form

绿 lǜ green

The character combines *silk* 纟 and the phonetic 录 to represent the color *green*.

Radical: 纟 'silk'

Index # 68

Character components: 纟 + 录

Character configuration:

Compounds, sentences and meanings

1. **绿 lǜ** green
   他的 毛衣 是 绿的。
   Tāde máoyī shì lǜ de.
   His woolen sweater is green.

2. **绿茶 lǜchá** green tea
   我 喜欢 喝 绿茶。
   Wǒ xǐhuan hē lǜchá.
   I like green tea.

3. **绿灯 lǜdēng** approval (literally, green light)
   他 给 我 开 绿灯。
   Tā gěi wǒ kāi lǜdēng.
   He gave me the go-ahead.

4. **绿豆芽 lǜdòuyá** mung bean sprouts
   绿豆芽 很 嫩。
   Lǜdòuyá hěn nèn.
   Mung bean sprouts are very tender.

5. **绿化 lǜhuà** greening
   市民 热烈地 参与 绿化 城市
   Shìmín rèliède cānyǔ lǜhuà chéngshì
   的 工作。
   de gōngzuò.
   The people are very positive about the greening of the city.

The last stroke slants to the right, then tapers off.

11 strokes

𠃌	纟	纟	纟	纟	纟	绉	绿	绿	绿	绿			

Full form

灯   **dēng**   light

The full form of the character combines *fire* 火 and the phonetic 登 to represent the idea of *lamp*.

Radical: 火 'fire'

Character components: 火 + 丁

Index # 75

Character configuration:

Compounds, sentences and meanings

1. **灯**   **dēng**   lamp
   突然 所有 的 灯 都 灭 了。
   Tūrán suǒyǒu de dēng dōu miè le.
   Suddenly all the lights went out.

2. **灯光**   **dēngguāng**   lamplight
   这里 灯光 很 暗。
   Zhèlǐ dēngguāng hěn àn.
   The light here is rather dim.

3. **灯火管制**   **dēnghuǒ guǎnzhì**   blackout
   这里 冬天 经常 有 灯火 管制。
   Zhèlǐ dōngtiān jīngcháng yǒu dēnghuǒ guǎnzhì.
   There are often blackouts here in winter.

4. **灯笼**   **dēnglóng**   lantern
   房子 前面 挂着 两 个 大 灯笼。
   Fángzi qiánmiàn guàzhe liǎng ge dà dēnglóng.
   In front of the house are two large lanterns.

5. **灯泡**   **dēngpào**   lightbulb
   有 没有 乳白 灯泡?
   Yǒu méiyǒu rǔbái dēngpào?
   Do you have an opaque lightbulb?

End the fourth stroke firmly.   **6 strokes**

丶	丷	少	火	灯	灯							

xiàng toward

The character was the hieroglyphic form of the back of a house facing north with a window. From this, the meaning of *direction* was derived.

Radical: 丿 'downward-left stroke'　　　**Index # 4**
or 厶 'mouth'　　　**Index # 50**
Character components: 丿 + 冂 + 口　　　Character configuration: ▯

Compounds, sentences and meanings

1. **向　xiàng**　toward
   河水　向　东流去。
   Héshuǐ xiàng dōng liú qù.
   The river flows east.

2. **向导　xiàngdǎo**　act as a guide
   我 来 给 你们 做 向导, 怎么样?
   Wǒ lái gěi nǐmen zuò xiàngdǎo, zěnmeyàng?
   Why don't I come as your guide?

3. **向来　xiànglái**　always, all along
   他 向来 做事 认真。
   Tā xiànglái zuòshì rènzhēn.
   He's always been conscientious in his work.

4. **向例　xiànglì**　usual practice
   我们 这里 向例 起得早。
   Wǒmen zhèlǐ xiànglì qǐde zǎo.
   Here, we get up early as a rule.

5. **向往　xiàngwǎng**　yearn for, look forward to
   我 终于 登上了 向往 已久
   Wǒ zhōngyú dēngshàngle xiàngwǎng yǐ jiǔ
   的 长城。
   de Chángchéng.
   I finally climbed the Great Wall, which I had wanted to do for a long time.

The first stroke sweeps down from right to left.											6 strokes
丿	亻	白	向	向	向						

guǎi turn (corner)

The character combines *hand* 扌 and *other* 另 to suggest the idea of *turning a corner*.

Radical: 扌 'hand'　　　　　　　　　　**Index # 48**

Character components: 扌 + 口 + 力　　　**Character configuration:**

Compounds, sentences and meanings

1. **拐 guǎi** turn
   拐 进 一 条 小 巷。
   Guǎi jìn yī tiáo xiǎo xiàng.
   Turn into a small lane.

2. **拐角 guǎijiǎo** corner, turning
   街 拐角 有 个 邮筒。
   Jiē guǎijiǎo yǒu ge yóutǒng.
   There is a postbox at the corner of the street.

3. **拐弯 guǎiwān** make a turn
   拐弯 要 慢 行。
   Guǎiwān yào màn xíng.
   Slow down when turning a corner.

4. **拐弯抹角 guǎiwān-mǒjiǎo** in a round-about way
   说话 不 要 拐弯抹角。
   Shuōhuà bǔ yào guǎiwān-mǒjiǎo.
   Don't beat about the bush. Get to the point.

5. **拐杖 guǎizhàng** walking stick
   我 爷爷 走路 要 用 拐杖。
   Wǒ yéye zǒulù yào yòng guǎizhàng.
   My grandfather needs a walking stick.

The seventh stroke ends with a hook.								8 strokes
一	扌	扌	扌	扩	护	拐	拐	

wān bend

The top part of the full form is made up of *words* 言 with *silk* 纟 on both sides, sitting on top of a *bow* 弓 to suggest *twists and turns*. Thus, it means *winding*.

Radical: 弓 'bow'

Index # 63

Character components: 亦 + 弓

Character configuration:

Compounds, sentences and meanings

1. 弯　**wān**　curve, bend
   这 条 路 前面 有 一个 弯。
   Zhè tiáo lù qiánmiàn yǒu yí ge wān.
   A little further down the road is a bend.

2. 弯弯　**wānwān**　curving
   弯弯 的 月亮 像 一只 船。
   Wānwān de yuèliang xiàng yì zhī chuán.
   The crescent moon is like a boat.

3. 弯路　**wānlù**　roundabout way
   应该 少 走 弯路。
   Yīnggāi shǎo zǒu wānlù.
   It's best to avoid detours.

4. 弯曲　**wānqū**　winding
   这 是 一条 弯曲 的 路。
   Zhè shì yì tiáo wānjū de lù.
   This is a winding road.

5. 弯子　**wānzi**　curve
   有 话 直 说，别 绕 弯子。
   Yǒu huà zhí shuō, bié rào wānzi.
   If you have something to say, say it.

The vertical strokes are straight with no hooks.

9 strokes

丶	亠	广	亣	亦	亦	峦	峦	弯			

 mǐ   rice

The character depicts the tip of a stalk of *rice*.

Radical: 米 'rice'

Index # 134

Character component: 米

Character configuration:

Compounds, sentences and meanings

1. **米** **mǐ** rice
   米 煮熟了 就是 米饭。
   Mǐ zhǔshóule jiù shì mǐfàn.
   When rice is cooked, it is called boiled rice.

2. **米饭** **mǐfàn** cooked rice
   我 每天 吃 两 顿 米饭。
   Wǒ měitiān chī liǎng dùn mǐfàn.
   I eat rice twice a day.

3. **米粉** **mǐfěn** rice-flour noodles
   我 妻子 喜欢 吃 米粉。
   Wǒ qīzi xǐhuan chī mǐfěn.
   My wife is fond of rice noodles.

4. **米酒** **mǐjiǔ** rice wine
   米酒 要 暖了 才 喝。
   Mǐjiǔ yào nuǎnle cái hē.
   Rice wine needs to be heated.

5. **一百米** **yībǎi mǐ** 100 meters
   我 家离 火车站 只有 一百 米。
   Wǒ jiā lí huǒchēzhàn zhǐyǒu yībǎi mǐ.
   My home is only 100 meters from the train station.

The fifth stroke sweeps left, and the last stroke firms, then tapers off.   6 strokes

丶	丷	丷	半	米	米						

Quiz 36 (351–360)

A. Look at the 16-character grid and CIRCLE words or phrases. They can be written horizontally or vertically. (Look at the circled characters in the Key if you are unsure.) Copy the word or phrase next to the grid and write down the pinyin and meaning.

				Word or phrase			Pinyin	Meaning
红	绿	灯	右	(i) 红	绿	灯	hónglǜdēng	traffic lights
路	厕	拐	弯	(ii)				
第	所	附	近	(iii)				
向	前	到	走	(iv)				

B. Using the characters in the 16-character grid, convert the pinyin sentences into characters and write the English meaning.

(i)	Qǐngwèn, fùjìn yǒu méiyǒu cèsuǒ?									
(ii)	Zài qiánmiàn hónglǜdēng, xiàng yòu guǎi.									
(iii)	Dào dì'èr ge lùkǒu, zuǒ guǎiwān.									
(iv)	Zài zǒu 50 mǐ, yǒu gōnggòng cèsuǒ.									

C. Match the Chinese words with their English meaning.

(i)

所以	lightbulb
所有	green tea
红 yǎn	greening
绿 huà	green light
绿灯	therefore
绿 chā	lighting
灯 pào	be jealous
灯 guāng	possession

(ii)

弯 qū	winding
拐 jiǎo	cooked rice
向导	yearn for
向来	bend, turning
向往	rice wine
拐弯	always
米 jiǔ	turn a corner
米饭	act as a guide

场

chǎng field

場

The full form of the character consists of *earth* 土, *sun* 日 and *shining down* 勿 to suggest a *level open space*.

Radical: 土 'earth'

Character components: 土 + 勿

Index # 40

Character configuration: ⊟

Compounds, sentences and meanings

1. **场** **chǎng** measure word
   昨晚 下了 一 场 大雨。
   Zuówǎn xiàle yì chǎng dà yǔ.
   It rained heavily last night.

2. **广场** **guǎngchǎng** public square
   天安门 广场 在 北京市 中心。
   Tiān'ānmén Guǎngchǎng zài Běijīngshì zhōngxīn.
   Tiananmen Square is in the center of Beijing.

3. **剧场** **jùchǎng** theater
   今晚 剧场 有 杂技 表演。
   Jīnwǎn jùchǎng yǒu zájì biǎoyǎn.
   There's an acrobatic performance at the theater tonight.

4. **商场** **shāngchǎng** arcade/commercial bazaar
   商场 里面 有 小吃店。
   Shāngchǎng lǐmiàn yǒu xiǎochīdiàn.
   There are snack bars in the arcade.

5. **市场** **shìchǎng** market
   他们 去 市场 买 东西 了。
   Tāmen qù shìchǎng mǎi dōngxi le.
   They went shopping at the market.

The fourth stroke has 3 bends, ending with a hook. | 6 strokes

一	十	土	圬	场	场						

yín silver

Full form

The character combines *metal* 钅 and the phonetic 艮 to suggest the idea of the precious metal *silver*.

Radical: 钅 'metal'

Index # 122

Character components: 钅 + 艮

Character configuration:

Compounds, sentences and meanings

1. **银** **yín** silver
   金 银 财 宝
   Jīn, yín, cái, bǎo.
   Gold, silver, treasures, and jewels

2. **银行** **yínháng** bank
   银行 离邮局 不 远。
   Yínháng lí yóujú bù yuǎn.
   The bank is not far from the post office.

3. **银色** **yínsè** silver color
   我 喜欢 银色。
   Wǒ xǐhuan yínsè.
   I like the color silver.

4. **银牌** **yínpái** silver medal
   她 在 2000 年 奥运会 赢过 女子
   Tā zài 2000 nián Àoyùnhuì yíngguo nǚzi
   一百米 银牌。
   yībǎimǐ yínpái.
   She won the silver medal at the 2000 Olympics for the women's 100 meters.

5. **银杏** **yínxìng** gingko tree
   秋天 来了，银杏 的 叶子 变黄了。
   Qiūtiān láile, yínxìng de yèzi biànhuángle.
   Autumn is here, the leaves on the gingko tree have turned yellow.

The tenth stroke sweeps left, pointing but not joining the ninth stroke.   11 strokes

丿	𠂉	𠂆	𠂋	钅	钅'	钅⁷	钅⁷	钅艮	钅艮	银			

清 qīng clear

The character combines *water* 氵 and *blue* 青 to represent pure water and generally means *pure*.

Radical: 氵 '3 drops of water'　　　　**Index # 32**

Character components: 氵 + 青　　　　**Character configuration:** ⊟

Compounds, sentences and meanings

1. 清　qīng　clear
   谁 是 谁 非，我 也 搞不清。
   Shéi shì shéi fēi, wǒ yě gǎobuqīng.
   I can't work out who's right and who's wrong.

2. 清楚　qīngchu　clear
   她的 发音 很 清楚。
   Tāde fāyīn hěn qīngchu.
   Her pronunciation is very clear.

3. 清理　qīnglǐ　put in order
   请 把 房间 清理 一下。
   Qǐng bǎ fángjiān qīnglǐ yíxià.
   Please tidy (my) room.

4. 清静　qīngjìng　quiet
   我们 找 个 清静 的 地方 谈谈。
   Wǒmen zhǎo ge qīngjìng de dìfang tántan.
   Let's find a quiet place to chat.

5. 清闲　qīngxián　at leisure, idle
   他 过不惯 清闲 的 退休 生活。
   Tā guòbuguàn qīngxián de tuìxiū shēnghuó.
   He can't get used to having nothing to do, now that he's retired.

The ninth stroke ends with a hook.　　　　11 strokes

丶	丶	氵	汁	汁	汁	汢	清	清	清	清		

chǔ   clear, neat

The character combines *rolls of cloth* 疋 and *forest* 林 to suggest that something is *neat*.

Radical: 疋 **'rolls of cloth'**

Character components: 林 + 疋

Index # 130

Character configuration:

Compounds, sentences and meanings

1. 楚   **Chǔ**   one of the Warring States
   楚 才 晋 用。
   Chǔ cái Jìn yōng.
   The talents of Chu used by Jìn (meaning brain drain).

2. 楚楚   **chǔchǔ**   tidy, neat
   她 今天 穿得 衣冠 楚楚 的。
   Tā jīntiān chuānde yīguān chǔchǔ de.
   She is immaculately dressed today.

3. 楚楚可怜   **chǔchǔ kělián**   (of young woman)
   delicate and charming
   她 长得 楚楚 可怜 的。
   Tā zhǎngde chǔchǔ kělián de.
   She is delicate and charming.

4. 苦楚   **kǔchǔ**   suffering
   爱滋病 给 这 个 国家 带来了 极大的
   Àizībìng gěi zhè ge guójiā dàiláile jídàde
   苦楚。
   kǔchǔ.
   AIDS has brought great misery to this country.

5. 清楚   **qīngchu**   clear
   她的发音 很 清楚。
   Tāde fāyīn hěn qīngchu.
   Her pronunciation is very clear.

The ninth stroke ends with a hook.												13 strokes
一	十	才	木	朩	村	材	林	楚	楚	楚	楚	楚

许 **xǔ** allow

The full form of the character combines *word* 言 and *nodding and agreeing* 午 to suggest *agreement* with another person. By extension, it means to *permit*.

Radical: 讠 'word'　　　　　　　　**Index # 9**

Character components: 讠 + 午　　　　**Character configuration:**

Compounds, sentences and meanings

1. 许　**xǔ**　allow
   每 组 只 许 去 一 个 人。
   Měi zǔ zhǐ xǔ qù yī ge rén.
   Only one person is allowed from each group.

2. 许多　**xǔduō**　many
   家里 有 许多 事情 要 干。
   Jiālǐ yǒu xǔduō shìqing yào gàn.
   There are lots of things to do at home.

3. 许久　**xǔjiǔ**　for a long time
   我们　商量了　许久 了。
   Wǒmen shāngliangle xǔjiǔ le.
   We talked things over for a long time.

4. 不许　**bùxǔ**　not allowed
   对不起, 这里 不许 吸烟。
   Duìbuqǐ, zhèlǐ bùxǔ xīyān.
   I'm sorry, you can't smoke here.

5. 也许　**yěxǔ**　perhaps, maybe
   也许 我 不 应该 告诉 她。
   Yěxǔ wǒ bù yīnggāi gàosu tā.
   Perhaps I shouldn't have told her.

The second horizontal stroke is longer.　　　　　　　　　**6 strokes**

丶	讠	订	讠	许	许						

如 rú *similar*

The character combines *female* 女 and *mouth* 口 to form the phonetic 如. It means *resemble*.

Radical: 女 'female'

Index # 65

Character components: 女 + 口

Character configuration: ⊟

Compounds, sentences and meanings

1. **如** **rú** resemble, as if
   事情 不如 他们 所 想 那么 简单。
   Shìqing bùrú tāmen suǒ xiǎng nàme jiǎndān.
   Things are not as simple as they think.

2. **如此** **rúcǐ** so, like that
   他的 脾气 向来 如此。
   Tāde píqi xiànglái rúcǐ.
   His temper has always been like this.

3. **如果** **rúguǒ** if
   你 如果 要 来,请 事先 告诉 我。
   Nǐ rúguǒ yào lái, qǐng shìxiān gàosu wǒ.
   Let me know in advance if you're coming.

4. **如何** **rúhé** how, what
   这 个 电影 你 觉得 如何?
   Zhè ge diànyǐng nǐ juéde rúhé?
   How did you like the film?

5. **如今** **rújīn** nowadays
   如今 很少 有 人 用 毛笔 了。
   Rújīn hěnshǎo yǒu rén yòng máobǐ le.
   Hardly anyone uses writing brushes these days.

口 is written rectangular, not a square. | 6 strokes

乚	夊	女	如	如	如						

 **guǒ** fruit

The character combines *tree* 木 and the character 田, which is taken here to mean a roundish object, to suggest the idea of a *fruit* at the end of the branch of a tree.

Radical: 木 'tree'　　　　　　　　**Index # 81**

Character components: 田 + 木　　　**Character configuration:**

Compounds, sentences and meanings

1. **果　guǒ**　really
   果 不 出 所 料。
   Guǒ bù chū suǒ liào.
   Just as you would expect.

2. **果断　guǒduàn**　decisive, resolute
   他 办事 果断。
   Tā bànshì guǒduàn.
   He works decisively.

3. **果然　guǒrán**　really, as expected
   他 说 要 下雪，果然 就 下雪 了。
   Tā shuō yào xiàxuě, guǒrán jiù xiàxuě le.
   He said it would snow, and sure enough it did.

4. **苹果　píngguǒ**　apple
   我 买 一 斤 苹果。
   Wǒ mǎi yì jīn píngguǒ.
   I'd like to buy a catty (500 grams) of apples.

5. **后果　hòuguǒ**　consequence
   后果 不堪 设想。
   Hòuguǒ bùkān shèxiǎng.
   The consequences would be too ghastly to contemplate.

The vertical stroke does not protrude at the top.								8 strokes
丶	冂	曱	曰	旦	甲	果	果	

huí   return

The character was derived from a pictograph of a whirl, which suggests the idea of *going around*.

Radical: 口 '4-sided frame'   **Index # 51**

Character components: 口 + 口   **Character configuration:** ▢

Compounds, sentences and meanings

1. 回 **huí**   return
   今天   晚上   你几点 回家?
   Jīntiān wǎnshang nǐ jǐ diǎn huíjiā?
   What time will you go home tonight?

2. 回答 **huídá**   reply
   请 你 回答 我的 问题。
   Qǐng nǐ huídá wǒde wèntí.
   Answer my question, please.

3. 回来 **huílái**   come back
   请你 稍   等, 她 马上   就回来。
   Qǐng nǐ shāo děng, tā mǎshàng jiù huílái.
   Please wait a while, she'll be back shortly.

4. 回去 **huíqù**   go back
   天 太 晚 了,你 今天 回不去 了。
   Tiān tài wǎn le, nǐ jīntiān huíbuqù le.
   It's too late; you can't go back home today.

5. 回头 **huítóu**   turn one's head
   他 回头 往 后 看。
   Tā huítóu wǎng hòu kàn.
   He turned his head and looked back.

The rectangular frame is taller than it is wide.										6 strokes
丨	冂	冂	冋	回	回					

yóu mail

The character combines *place* 阝 and the phonetic 垂 to give the idea of *sending letters* or *parcels from place to place*. In simplification, a more correct phonetic 由 is used.

Radical: 阝 'right ear-lobe'

Index # 28

Character components: 由 + 阝

Character configuration:

Compounds, sentences and meanings

1. **邮** yóu post
   我 上 月 给 家里 邮 去了 一千 元。
   Wǒ shàng yuè gěi jiālǐ yóu qù le yīqiān yuán.
   I sent 1000 yuan home last month.

2. **邮包** yóubāo postal parcel
   你 觉得 需要 买 邮包 保险 吗?
   Nǐ juéde xūyào mǎi yóubāo bǎoxiǎn ma?
   Do you think postal insurance is necessary?

3. **邮递员** yóudìyuán postman
   今天 邮递员 来过 没有?
   Jīntiān yóudìyuán láiguo méiyǒu?
   Has the postman been today?

4. **邮寄** yóujì send by post
   我 想 邮寄 书籍。
   Wǒ xiǎng yóujì shūjí.
   I'd like to post these books.

5. **邮票** yóupiào stamp
   寄 美国 的 明信片 要 贴
   Jì Měiguó de míngxìnpiàn yào tie
   多少 邮票?
   duōshao yóupiào?
   What's the postage on a postcard to the United States?

The sixth stroke looks like the number 3.												7 strokes
丶	冂	冃	由	由	由阝	邮						

jú bureau

The character is a phonetic used as a character. The presence of *dwelling* 尸 suggests that it is some kind of *institution housed in a building*.

Radical: 尸 'dwelling' **Index # 61**

Character components: 尸 + 刁 + 口 **Character configuration:**

Compounds, sentences and meanings

1. **局 jú** game, set, innings
   第一局 谁 赢 了?
   Dìyī jú shéi yíng le?
   Who won the first set?

2. **局部 júbù** part
   局部 地区 下雪。
   Júbù dīqū xiàxuě.
   It snows in some places.

3. **局势 júshì** situation
   最近 国际 局势 不 太 稳定。
   Zuìjìn guójì júshì bú tài wěndìng.
   The international situation has been very unstable lately.

4. **邮局 yóujú** post office
   邮局 里面 有 公用 电话。
   Yóujú lǐmiàn yǒu gōngyòng diànhuà.
   There are public phones inside the post office.

5. **公安局 gōng'ānjú** police station
   公安局 就 是 警察局。
   Gōng'ānjú jiù shì jǐngchájú.
   The Public Security Bureau is the same as the Police.

The fourth stroke is a horizontal-bend-hook. **7 strokes**

㇆	㇆	尸	尸	局	局	局					

Quiz 37 (361–370)

A. Look at the 16-character grid and CIRCLE words or phrases. They can be written horizontally or vertically. (Look at the circled characters in the Key if you are unsure.) Copy the word or phrase next to the grid and write down the pinyin and meaning.

						Word or phrase			Pinyin	Meaning
也	里	商	许	(i)		商	场		shāngchǎng	arcade
银	行	场	对	(ii)						
清	楚	如	太	(iii)						
果	往	回	走	(iv)						

B. Using the characters in the 16-character grid, convert the pinyin sentences into characters and write the English meaning.

(i)	Shāngchǎng lǐ yǒu méiyǒu yínháng?									
(ii)	Wǒ bú tài qīngchu, yěxǔ méiyǒu.									
(iii)	Rúguǒ méiyǒu, nǐ wǎng huí zǒu.									
(iv)	Yóujú duìmiàn yǒu yì jiā yínháng.									

C. Match the Chinese words with their English meaning.

(i)

市场	if
许多	nowadays
不许	clear
也许	not allow
清楚	many
清 lǐ	market
如果	perhaps
如今	tidy up

(ii)

后果	stamp
果 rán	consequence
回 dá	come back
回来	post office
回去	as expected
邮 bāo	reply
邮票	go back
邮局	postal parcel

Full form

 yán color; face

The full form of the character combines *page* 页, which in olden times meant *forehead*, and *handsome* 彦 to suggest the idea of a handsome person's *face*.

Radical: 页 'page'

Index # 140

Character components: 彦 + 页

Character configuration:

Compounds, sentences and meanings

1. **颜 yán** face
   他 犯了大 错误，觉得 无 颜 见 人。
   Tā fànle dà cuòwù, juéde wú yán jiàn rén.
   He made a grave mistake and felt that he couldn't face people.

2. **颜料 yánliào** pigment
   这 是 天然 颜料。
   Zhè shì tiānrán yánliào.
   This is a natural pigment.

3. **颜色 yánsè** color
   你 最 喜欢 什么 颜色?
   Nǐ zuì xǐhuan shénme yánsè?
   What color do you like most?

4. **颜面 yánmiàn** face, prestige
   说话 请 客气点儿，要 顾全
   Shuōhuà qǐng kèqi diǎnr, yào gùquán
   他的 颜面。
   tāde yánmiàn.
   Please speak politely so that he doesn't lose face.

5. **五颜六色 wǔyán-liùsè** of various (or all) colors
   五颜六色 的 云霞 真 好看。
   Wǔyán-liùsè de yúnxiá zhēn hǎokàn.
   The multi-colored clouds are really beautiful.

The three strokes of 彡 taper down from right to left.												15 strokes
丶	二	亠	产	立	产	产	彦	彦	彦	彦	颜	颜
颜	颜											

sè color

The character combines *knife* 刀 and *eyebrow* 巴, which was the simplified form of 眉, to suggest the idea of *complexion*. It later came to mean *color*.

Radical: 刀 'knife'　　　　　　　　　　**Index # 30**

Character components: 勹 + 巴

Character configuration:

Compounds, sentences and meanings

1. **色　sè**　color
   这 道 菜色，香， 味 俱佳。
   Zhè dào cài sè, xiāng, wèi jù jiā.
   This dish looks good, smells good, and tastes good.

2. **色彩　sècǎi**　characteristic quality, flavor
   这 种　 服装 富有 民族 色彩。
   Zhè zhǒng fúzhuāng fùyǒu mínzú sècǎi.
   This costume is rich in ethnic flavor.

3. **色情　sèqíng**　pornographic
   色情 杂志 在　 中国　 是 非法 的。
   Sèqíng zázhì zài Zhōngguó shì fēifǎ de.
   Pornographic magazines are illegal in China.

4. **色泽　sèzé**　color and luster
   我 喜欢 这 幅画儿,它的色泽 鲜明。
   Wǒ xǐhuan zhè fú huàr, tāde sèzé xiānmíng.
   I like this painting for its bright luster.

5. **黄色　huángsè**　yellow, pornographic
   中国　 严禁 黄色 书刊。
   Zhōngguó yánjìn huángsè shūkān.
   China strictly forbids pornographic books and magazines.

The last stroke ends with a hook.									6 strokes
⺈	⺈	夕	名	叾	色				

黑 hēi black

The character represents *soot* accumulated in a chimney. Thus, it came to mean *black*.

Radical: 黑 'black'

Index # 187

Character components: 里 + 灬

Character configuration:

Compounds, sentences and meanings

1. 黑 **hēi** dark, black
   天 黑 了。
   Tiān hēi le.
   It is already dark.

2. 黑暗 **hēi'àn** darkness
   山洞 里一 片 黑暗。
   Shāndòng lǐ yī piàn hēi'àn.
   It's all darkness in the cave.

3. 黑白 **hēibái** black and white
   这 个 电视 是 黑白 的。
   Zhè ge diànshì shì hēibái de.
   This is a black-and-white television.

4. 黑板 **hēibǎn** blackboard
   黑板 上 写着 什么?
   Hēibǎn shàng xiězhe shénme?
   What's written on the blackboard?

5. 黑人 **hēirén** black people
   黑人 在 美国 的 社会 地位 提高了。
   Hēirén zài Měiguó de shèhuì dìwèi tígāo le.
   The social status of blacks in America has improved.

The bottom horizontal stroke is longer.											12 strokes
丶	冂	冂	冂	四	甲	甲	里	里	黑	黑	黑

chèn   set off

The full form of the character combines *clothing* 衤 and *close* 親 to suggest the idea of *clothing worn close to the body* or *underneath*. It also means *provide a background for*.

Radical: 衤 'clothing'

Character components: 衤 + 寸

Index # 113

Character configuration:

Compounds, sentences and meanings

1. 衬 **chèn** place something underneath
   你 说 红色 衬 不 衬 黑色?
   Nǐ shuō hóngsè chèn bu chèn hēisè?
   Do you think red and black go well together?

2. 衬裙 **chènqún** petticoat
   这 种 裙子 要 穿 衬裙。
   Zhè zhǒng qúnzi yào chuān chènqún.
   This type of skirt needs a petticoat.

3. 衬衫 **chènshān** shirt
   这 是 女装 衬衫。
   Zhè shì nǚzhuāng chènshān.
   This is a blouse.

4. 衬托 **chèntuō** set off
   红花 要 有 绿叶 衬托。
   Hónghuā yào yǒu lǜyè chèntuō.
   Red flowers should be set off by green leaves.

5. 衬衣 **chènyī** shirt
   这 是 女装 衬衣。
   Zhè shì nǚzhuāng chènyī
   This is a blouse.

Note the component 衤. It has two dots on the left side.   8 strokes

丶	㇇	衤	衤	衤	衤	衬	衬				

lán blue

The full form of the character represents the color of *indigo* from the indigo plant. It means the color *blue*.

Radical: ⺾ 'grass'

Index # 42

Character components: ⺾ + ⼁ + ⼃ + 皿

Character configuration: ⊟

Compounds, sentences and meanings

1. 蓝　**lán**　blue
   这里的天很蓝。
   Zhèlǐ de tiān hěn lán.
   The sky here is blue.

2. 蓝宝石　**lánbǎoshí**　sapphire
   蓝宝石戒指很贵。
   Lánbǎoshí jièzhǐ hěn guì.
   Sapphire rings are expensive.

3. 蓝鲸　**lánjīng**　blue whale
   蓝鲸是最大的鲸鱼。
   Lánjīng shì zuìdà de jīngyú.
   The blue whale is the largest whale.

4. 蓝领　**lánlǐng**　blue collar
   他是蓝领工人。
   Tā shì lánlǐng gōngrén.
   He is a blue-collar worker.

5. 蓝色　**lánsè**　blue color
   这个湖的水是蓝色的。
   Zhè ge hú de shuǐ shì lánsè de.
   The water in the lake is blue.

The bottom horizontal stroke is longer. | 13 strokes

一 十 艹 艹 艹 艹 芷 芷 萨 蓝 蓝 蓝 蓝

白　**bái**　white

The character originally represented the *white nut* of an acorn. It means *white*.

Radical: 白 'white'　　　　　　　　　　**Index # 125**

Character component: 白　　　　　　　　**Character configuration:** ☐

Compounds, sentences and meanings

1. 白　**bái**　white
   她的皮肤 很 白。
   Tāde pífū hěn bái.
   She has a fair complexion.

2. 白白　**báibái**　in vain, for nothing
   不要 让 时光 白白 过去。
   Bǔyào ràng shíguāng báibái guòqù.
   Don't let time slip by.

3. 白菜　**báicài**　Chinese cabbage
   白菜 做 汤 好喝。
   Báicài zuò tāng hǎohē.
   Chinese cabbage soup is delicious.

4. 白费　**báifèi**　waste
   再 等下去 是 白费 时间。
   Zài děngxiàqù shì báifèi shíjiān.
   It's a waste of time to wait any longer.

5. 白天　**báitiān**　daytime
   白天 我 睡不着。
   Báitiān wǒ shuìbuzháo.
   I can't sleep in the daytime.

There should be equal spacing between the horizontal lines.　　　　5 strokes

′	′	白	白	白					

别

biế other

The character combines *joint in the body* 另 and *sword* 刂 to express the idea of *separating the joint with a sword* and means *part from*.

Radical: 刂 'upright knife'　　　　　　**Index # 15**

Character components: 口 + 力 + 刂　　　**Character configuration:**

Compounds, sentences and meanings

1. **别** biế　don't
   别 忘 了。
   Biế wàng le.
   Don't forget.

2. **别的** biếde　other
   还 要 别的 吗?
   Hái yào biếde ma?
   Would you like something else?

3. **别人** biếren　other people
   认真 考虑 别人 的 意见。
   Rènzhēn kǎolǜ biếren de yǐjiàn.
   Give other people's suggestions serious consideration.

4. **别致** biếzhì　unique
   天坛 的 建筑 结构 非常 别致。
   Tiāntán de jiànzhù jiégòu fēicháng biếzhì.
   The architecture of the Temple of Heaven is unique.

5. **特别** tèbiế　special, peculiar
   他的 口音 很 特别。
   Tāde kǒuyīn hěn tèbiế.
   He has a peculiar accent.

The last stroke is a vertical hook.　　　　　　　　　　　**7 strokes**

丶	冖	口	弓	另	别	别					

tè special

The character combines *cow* 牛 and *monastery* 寺. Originally, it meant *a fine cow*. Later it came to mean *superior, out of the ordinary*.

Radical: 牛 'cattle'　　　　　　　　**Index # 95**

Character components: 牛 + 土 + 寸　　**Character configuration:** ⊞

Compounds, sentences and meanings

1. **特** tè specially
   这 种 药 治 咳嗽 特 灵。
   Zhè zhǒng yào zhì késou tè líng.
   This medicine is specially good for coughs.

2. **特长** tècháng special skill
   他 有 什么 特长?
   Tā yǒu shénme tècháng?
   What is he skilled in?

3. **特点** tèdiǎn special features
   日本菜 有 什么 特点?
   Rìběncài yǒu shénme tèdiǎn?
   What are the distinctive features of Japanese cooking?

4. **特色** tèsè characteristic
   这 是 一个 富有 民族 特色的 歌舞 节目。
   Zhè shì yí ge fùyǒu mínzú tèsè de gēwǔ jiémù.
   This musical performance is very characteristic of the ethnic group.

5. **特有** tèyǒu peculiar
   这 是 广东人 特有 的一 种
   Zhè shì Guǎngdōngrén tèyǒu de yì zhǒng
   说法。
   shuōfǎ.
   This is an expression peculiar to people from Guangdong.

The seventh stroke is longer than the ones above and below it.　　　　**10 strokes**

| ノ | ⸝ | 牛 | 牛 | 牛 | 牜 | 牜 | 牜 | 特 | 特 | | |

yīn reason

The character combines *mattress (enclosure)* 口 and *a man with his arms and legs spread* to suggest the idea of being dependent on others or *based on.*

Radical: 口 '4-sided frame'

Index # 51

Character components: 口 + 大

Character configuration:

Compounds, sentences and meanings

1. 因 **yīn** because of
   这 次 他 是 因 病 请假。
   Zhè cì tā shì yīn bìng qǐngjià.
   On this occasion he asked for sick leave.

2. 因此 **yīncǐ** so, therefore
   她 没有 小孩子, 因此 养了 一只 猫。
   Tā méiyǒu xiǎoháizi, yīncǐ yàngle yì zhī māo.
   She has no children, so she keeps a cat.

3. 因循 **yīnxún** be in a rut
   老人 经常 是 因循 守旧。
   Lǎorén jīngcháng shì yīnxún shǒujiù.
   Old folks often stick to old ways.

4. 因为 **yīnwèi** because
   因为 喝了酒, 所以 不 能 开车。
   Yīnwèi hēle jiǔ, suǒyǐ bù néng kāichē.
   I can't drive because I've been drinking.

5. 原因 **yuányīn** reason
   你 知道 是 什么 原因 吗?
   Nǐ zhīdao shì shénme yuányīn ma?
   Do you know the reason?

The fifth stroke ends firmly.

6 strokes

丨	冂	冂	冈	因	因						

Full form

 wéi/wèi do / on behalf of

The full form of the character combines *claw* ⌐ and 爲 which was the figure of an elephant. It represents the act of training an elephant and means *do*.

Radical: 丶 'dot'   **Index # 1**

Character components: 丶 + 力 + 丶   **Character configuration:** ☐

Compounds, sentences and meanings

1. 为 **wéi** do, act
   事 在 人 为。
   Shì zài rén wéi.
   Human effort is the decisive factor.

2. 为难 **wéinán** make things difficult for
   请 别 故意 为难 我。
   Qǐng bié gùyì wéinán wǒ.
   Please don't deliberately make things difficult for me.

3. 为期 **wéiqī** last for a period
   会议 为期 三 天。
   Huìyì wéiqī sān tiān.
   The meeting is scheduled to last for three days.

4. 为了 **wèile** in order to, for
   我 学 英语 是 为了 以后 出国。
   Wǒ xué Yīngyǔ shì wèile yǐhòu chūguó.
   I'm studying English so that I can study abroad later.

5. 为什么 **wèishénme** why
   你 为什么 不 去 美国 看看?
   Nǐ wèishénme bú qù Měiguó kànkan?
   Why don't you go to the US for a visit?

The first dot is placed on the top left, the second dot goes inside.   **4 strokes**

丶	ソ	为	为								

A. Look at the 16-character grid and CIRCLE words or phrases. They can be written horizontally or vertically. (Look at the circled characters in the Key if you are unsure.) Copy the word or phrase next to the grid and write down the pinyin and meaning.

	Word or phrase		Pinyin	Meaning
(i)	白 色		báisè	white
(ii)				
(iii)				
(iv)				

Grid:

喜	白	蓝	欢
颜	色	黄	觉
黑	衬	特	别
容	易	亮	得

B. Using the characters in the 16-character grid, convert the pinyin sentences into characters and write the English meaning.

(i)	Nǐ xǐhuan shénme yánsè?									
(ii)	Wǒ xǐhuan hēisè.									
(iii)	Hēisè róngyì chèn biéde yánsè.									
(iv)	Wǒ juéde lánsè bú chèn huángsè.									

C. Match the Chinese words with their English meaning.

(i)

颜 miàn — shirt
色 zé — waste
黑 àn — color and luster
衬 shān — face, prestige
衬 tuō — daytime
白 fēi — darkness
白天 — other people
别人 — set off

(ii)

别 zhǐ — special skill
特色 — unique
特长 — in order to
yuán 因 — special features
因 cǐ — why
为了 — because
为什么 — reason
因为 — thus

Full form

 shuāng   pair

The full form of the character combines *two birds* 雔 and *again* 又 to suggest the idea of *a pair of birds*. The simplfied form duplicates 又 to give the same idea.

Radical: 又 'again'

Index # 24

Character components: 又 + 又

Character configuration:

Compounds, sentences and meanings

1. 双 shuāng   pair
   我 今天 买了 一 双 运动鞋。
   Wǒ jīntiān mǎile yì shuāng yùndòngxié.
   I bought a pair of sports shoes today.

2. 双胞胎 shuāngbāotāi   twins
   他们 是 双胞胎。
   Tāmen shì shuāngbāotāi.
   They are twins.

3. 双层 shuāngcéng   double-deck
   卧室 里有 一 张 双层床。
   Wòshì lǐ yǒu yī zhāng shuāngcéngchuáng.
   There's a bunkbed in the room.

4. 双重 shuāngchóng   dual, double
   我 是 双重 国籍 人。
   Wǒ shì shuāngchóng guójí rén.
   I have dual nationality.

5. 双人床 shuāngrénchuáng   double bed
   我 要 双人床。
   Wǒ yào shuāngrénchuáng.
   I would like a double bed.

The first 又 ends firmly like a dot, but the second 又 tapers off.										4 strokes
フ	又	刄	双							

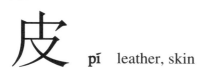

pí leather, skin

The character was composed of three parts: an animal carcass, the hide and the hand that is skinning it. It suggests the idea of peeling the *skin*.

Radical: 皮 'skin'　　　　　　　　　　　　**Index # 131**

Character component: 皮　　　　　　　　**Character configuration:** ☐

Compounds, sentences and meanings

1. **皮　pí**　skin, leather
   当心，别 踩到 香蕉皮。
   Dāngxīn, biě cǎidào xiāngjiāo pí.
   Be careful, don't step on the banana skin.

2. **皮包　píbāo**　briefcase
   我 想 买 一个 皮包。
   Wǒ xiǎng mǎi yī ge píbāo.
   I'd like to buy a briefcase.

3. **皮肤　pífū**　skin
   这 种 冷霜 对皮肤 很 好。
   Zhè zhǒng lěngshuāng duì pífū hěn hǎo.
   This cream is good for the skin.

4. **皮毛　pímáo**　superficial knowledge
   电脑 我 略知 皮毛。
   Diànnǎo wǒ lüè zhī pímáo.
   I have only a superficial knowledge of computers.

5. **皮夹克　pí jiākè**　leather jacket
   我 喜欢 穿 皮夹克。
   Wǒ xǐhuan chuān pí jiākè.
   I like wearing a leather jacket.

The first stroke ends with a hook.　　　　　　　　　　　　　　　5 strokes

一	厂	广	皮	皮							

鞋　**xié**　shoe

The character combines *leather* 革 and the phonetic 圭 to give the idea of *footwear*.

Radical: 革 'leather'　　　　　　　　　　**Index # 179**

Character components: 革 + 土 + 土

Character configuration: ▯▯

Compounds, sentences and meanings

1. **鞋** **xié** shoe
   请 稍 等, 我 把 鞋 穿上。
   Qǐng shāo děng, wǒ bǎ xié chuānshang.
   Please wait while I put my shoes on.

2. **鞋带** **xiédài** shoelace
   请 稍 等, 我 把 鞋带 绑好。
   Qǐng shāo děng, wǒ bǎ xiédài bǎnghǎo.
   Please wait while I tie my shoelaces.

3. **鞋匠** **xiéjiang** cobbler
   附近 有 没有 鞋匠?
   Fùjìn yǒu méiyǒu xiéjiang?
   Is there a cobbler nearby?

4. **鞋油** **xiéyóu** shoe polish
   哪里 能 买到 鞋油?
   Nǎlǐ néng mǎidào xiéyóu?
   Where can I get some shoe polish?

5. **皮鞋** **píxié** leather shoes
   皮鞋 穿起来 没有 布鞋 舒服。
   Píxié chuānqǐlái méiyǒu bùxié shūfu.
   Leather shoes are not as comfortable as shoes made of cloth.

The second and bottom horizontal strokes of 圭 are longer.　　　　　　**15 strokes**

一	十	卅	廿	芈	苦	苩	苣	革	革	革	鞋	鞋
鞋	鞋											

zhēn real

The character combines *straight* 直 and 八 to suggest the idea of something that is *straight-forward* and can be *spread* or *laid before anybody*. Thus, it means *true and real*.

Radical: 十 'ten'　　　　　　　　　　　**Index # 11**

Character components: 直 + 八　　　　**Character configuration:**

Compounds, sentences and meanings

1. **真** zhēn really
   时间 过得 真 快。
   Shíjiān guòde zhēn kuài.
   How time flies.

2. **真话** zhēnhuà truth
   朋友 之间 要 说 真话。
   Péngyou zhījiān yào shuō zhēnhuà.
   Friends should be honest with each other.

3. **真相** zhēnxiàng the real situation
   这 就是 事情 的 真相。
   Zhè jiù shì shìqing de zhēnxiàng.
   This is the actual state of affairs.

4. **真心** zhēnxīn sincere
   我 知道 你 是 真心 对 我 好。
   Wǒ zhīdao nǐ shì zhēnxīn duì wǒ hǎo.
   I know your affections for me are genuine.

5. **真正** zhēnzhèng genuine
   这 是 真正 的吉林 人参。
   Zhè shì zhēnzhèng de Jílín rénshēn.
   This is genuine Jilin ginseng.

There are three horizontal strokes inside.									10 strokes

一	十	广	古	古	肯	肯	直	真	真			

新　**xīn** new

The character combines *ax* 斤 with *standing* 立 and *tree* 木 to give the idea of *cutting or sawing a standing tree* in order to make a *new* building.

Radical: 斤 'ax'　　　　　　　　　　**Index # 101**

Character components: 亲 + 斤　　　**Character configuration:**

Compounds, sentences and meanings

1. 新　**xīn**　new
   这 本 书 是 我 新 买 的。
   Zhè běn shū shì wǒ xīn mǎi de.
   This is the book I've just bought.

2. 新年　**xīnnián**　new year
   新年 好!
   Xīnnián hǎo!
   Happy New Year!

3. 新奇　**xīnqí**　strange, novel
   他 初 到 北京 时, 处处 觉得 新奇。
   Tā chū dào Běijīng shí, chùchù juéde xīnqí.
   Whe he first got to Beijing, everything struck him as new.

4. 新闻　**xīnwén**　news
   现在 是 新闻 简报。
   Xiànzài shì xīnwén jiǎnbào.
   Here are the (news) headlines.

5. 新鲜　**xīnxiān**　fresh
   这 条 鱼 有点 不 新鲜。
   Zhè tiáo yú yǒudiǎn bù xīnxiān.
   This fish is slightly stale.

The bottom horizontal stroke of 亲 is shorter.　　　　　　　13 strokes

丶	亠	一	一	立	立	辛	辛	亲	亲	新	新	新

Full form

 gāng just

The full form of the character combines *knife* 刂 and the phonetic 岡 to suggest the idea of *just now*. In simplification, the stereotype 冈 is used to abbreviate 岡.

Radical: 刂 'upright knife'

Index # 15

Character components: 冈 + 刂

Character configuration: ⬚

Compounds, sentences and meanings

1. **刚 gāng** just
   这 双 鞋 大小 刚 合适。
   Zhè shuāng xié dàxiǎo gāng héshì.
   This pair of shoes is just the right size.

2. **刚才 gāngcái** just now
   他 刚才 还 说 要 去 呢。
   Tā gāngcái hái shuō yào qù ne.
   He was saying only a moment ago that he wanted to go.

3. **刚刚 gānggāng** a moment ago
   他 刚刚 走, 你 去 追 吧。
   Tā gānggāng zǒu, nǐ qù zhuī ba.
   He left just a minute ago. Run and try to catch him.

4. **刚好 gānghǎo** exactly
   你们 来得 刚 好。
   Nímen láide gāng hǎo.
   You came in the nick of time.

5. **刚巧 gāngqiǎo** by chance
   我 刚巧 在 车站 碰见 她。
   Wǒ gāngqiǎo zài chēzhàn pèngjiàn tā.
   I happened to run into her at the station.

冈 does not close at the bottom.

6 strokes

丨	冂	刀	冈	刚	刚						

穿 chuān wear

The character combines *cave* 穴 and 牙 to represent the idea of *going through something*, possibly a cave. By extension, it means *to wear*.

Radical: 穴 '**cave**'

Character components: 穴 + 牙

Index # 110

Character configuration:

Compounds, sentences and meanings

1. 穿 **chuān** wear
   穿得 这么 少, 不 冷 吗?
   Chuānde zhème shǎo, bù lěng ma?
   Aren't you cold with so little on?

2. 穿不住 **chuānbuzhù** cannot go on wearing
   天 热 了, 毛衣 穿不住 了。
   Tiān rè le, máoyī chuānbuzhù le.
   It's too warm to wear woolen sweaters now.

3. 穿过 **chuān'guò** go across or through
   我们 从 操场 穿过 去吧。
   Wǒmen cóng cāochǎng chuān'guò qù ba.
   Let's cut across the sports field.

4. 穿越 **chuānyuè** pass through
   这 条 铁路 穿越 国境。
   Zhè tiáo tiělù chuānyuè guójǐng.
   This railroad goes across the border.

5. 穿着 **chuānzhuó** apparel, dress
   他 不 讲究 穿着。
   Tā bù jiǎngjiu chuānzhuó.
   He is not particular about what he wears.

The last stroke sweeps down from right to left.   **9 strokes**

丶	丷	宀	宀	穴	空	空	穿	穿			

shū   stretch

The character combines *house* 舍 and the phonetic 予 to suggest the idea of relaxing at home. It means to *relax*.

Radical: 人 'people'   **Index # 18**

Character components: ⼈ + 干 + 口 + 予   **Character configuration:**

Compounds, sentences and meanings

1. 舒 **shū** stretch
   舒 筋 活 络。
   Shū jīn huó luò.
   Stretching stimulates blood circulation.

2. 舒畅 **shūchàng** entirely free from worry
   山上 的 空气 使人 感到 舒畅。
   Shānshang de kōngqì shǐ rén gǎndào shūchàng.
   Mountain air is very refreshing.

3. 舒服 **shūfu** comfortable
   这 把 椅子 又 软 又 舒服。
   Zhè bǎ yǐzi yòu ruǎn yòu shūfu.
   This chair is soft and comfortable.

4. 舒散 **shūsàn** stretch and flex
   跑完步 应该 舒散 一下 筋骨。
   Pǎowánbù yīnggāi shūsàn yíxià jīngǔ.
   After a run, you should do some stretching exercises.

5. 舒适 **shūshì** comfortable, cozy
   房间 不大, 但 很 舒适。
   Fángjiān bú dà, dàn hěn shūshì.
   The room is not big, but it is very cozy.

The last stroke ends with a hook.   12 strokes

| 丿 | 𠆢 | 𠂉 | 𠂤 | 𠂤 | 𠆢 | 舍 | 舍 | 舍 | 舍 | 舒 | 舒 | |

fú clothes; service

The character combines *flesh* 月 and 𠬝, which was the figure of the hand pressing firmly down on a kneeling person, and suggests the idea of *serve* or *obey*.

Radical: 月 'moon/flesh'

Index # 103

Character components: 月 + 𠬝

Character configuration:

Compounds, sentences and meanings

1. 服 **fú** be convinced
   你 说得 有 道理, 我 服 了。
   Nǐ shuōde yǒu dàoli, wǒ fú le.
   What you've said makes sense. I'm convinced.

2. 服从 **fúcóng** be subordinated to
   少数 服从 多数。
   Shǎoshù fúcóng duōshù.
   The minority should give way to the majority.

3. 服软 **fúruǎn** yield to persuasion
   他 服软 不 服硬。
   Tā fúruǎn bù fúyìng.
   He yields to persuasion but not to coercion.

4. 服务 **fúwù** give service to
   这 个 饭店 的 服务 非常 好。
   Zhè ge fàndiàn de fúwù fēicháng hǎo.
   The service at the hotel is very good.

5. 服装店 **fúzhuāngdiàn** boutique
   这 家 服装店 的衣服 很 时髦。
   Zhè jiā fúzhuāngdiàn de yīfu hěn shímáo.
   The clothes in this boutique are very fashionable.

The fifth stroke ends with a hook.							8 strokes
丿	刀	月	月	肌	胛	服	服

Full form

旧 jiù old

舊

The full character combines *grass* ⺾, *bird* 隹 and the phonetic 臼 to refer to something *old*. The simplified form uses the association of a *vertical stroke* 丨 and the *sun* 日 to express the same idea.

Radical: 丨 'vertical stroke'　　　　**Index # 3**

Character components: 丨 + 日　　　　**Character configuration:**

Compounds, sentences and meanings

1. **旧 jiù** old, used
   你的 鞋 旧 了,买 一 双 新的 吧。
   Nǐde xié jiù le, mǎi yì shuāng xīnde ba.
   Your shoes are worn. Buy a new pair.

2. **旧货 jiùhuò** secondhand goods
   我 买 的 是 旧货。
   Wǒ mǎi de shì jiùhuò.
   I bought it secondhand.

3. **旧事 jiùshì** a past event
   请 不要 重提 旧事 了。
   Qǐng búyào chóngtí jiùshì le.
   Please don't dwell on the past.

4. **陈旧 chénjiù** outdated
   你 也 应该 改改 你的 陈旧 思想。
   Nǐ yě yīnggāi gǎigai nǐde chénjiù sīxiǎng.
   You should change your outdated thinking.

5. **破旧 pòjiù** old and shabby
   那个 老头儿 穿着 一 身 破旧 的 衣服。
   Nà ge lǎotóur chuānzhe yì shēn pòjiù de yīfu.
   That old man is shabbily dressed.

The vertical stroke takes up one third of the space.				5 strokes
丨	刂	旧	旧	旧

Quiz 39 (381–390)

A. Look at the 16-character grid and CIRCLE words or phrases. They can be written horizontally or vertically. (Look at the circled characters in the Key if you are unsure.) Copy the word or phrase next to the grid and write down the pinyin and meaning.

真	新	皮	刚
运	动	鞋	过
觉	慢	舒	服
穿	起	来	得

	Word or phrase			Pinyin	Meaning
(i)	运	动	鞋	yùndòngxié	sports shoes
(ii)					
(iii)					
(iv)					

B. Using the characters in the 16-character grid, convert the pinyin sentences into characters and write the English meaning.

(i)	Zhè shuāng píxié zhēn hǎokàn.									
(ii)	Shì xīn de, shàng xīngqī gāng mǎi de.									
(iii)	Búguò chuānqǐlái hái bù shūfu.									
(iv)	Nǐ mànmàn jiù juéde shūfu le.									

C. Match the Chinese words with their English meaning.

(i)

双 chóng	superficial knowledge
双 bāotāi	the real situation
皮 bāo	dual, double
皮毛	twins
真话	truth
真心	briefcase
真相	genuine
真正	sincere

(ii)

刚才	exactly
刚好	fresh
新 xiān	just now
穿过	obey
舒 chàng	service
服从	old and shabby
服 wù	go across
pò 旧	free from worry

紧　jǐn　tight

The full form of the character has three components: *official (minister)* 臣, *again* 又 and *silk* 糸. It is not clear how it came to mean *tight*.

Radical: 糸 'silk'

Index # 152

Character components: 刂 + 又 + 幺 + 小

Character configuration:

Compounds, sentences and meanings

1. 紧　**jǐn**　tight
   这 双 鞋 太 紧。
   Zhè shuāng xié tài jǐn.
   These shoes are too tight.

2. 紧凑　**jǐncòu**　compact
   这 个 电影 情节 很 紧凑。
   Zhè ge diànyǐng qíngjié hěn jǐncòu.
   The film has a neat plot.

3. 紧急　**jǐnjí**　urgent
   这 是 紧急 出口, 不能 堵塞。
   Zhè shì jǐnjí chūkǒu, bùnéng dǔsè.
   This is an emergency exit. Keep clear.

4. 紧迫　**jǐnpò**　pressing
   我 今天 有 一件 紧迫 的 事情 要 做。
   Wǒ jīntiān yǒu yí jiàn jǐnpò de shìqing yào zuò.
   Today I have urgent business.

5. 紧张　**jǐnzhāng**　nervous
   慢慢 讲, 别 紧张。
   Mànmàn jiǎng, bié jǐnzhāng.
   Speak slowly, don't be nervous.

The first vertical stroke is shorter.　　　　10 strokes

丨	刂	刂⁷	刂又	刂又	竖	竖	紧	紧	紧			

xiàng resemble

The character combines *person* 亻 and *picture* 象 to suggest the idea that the portrait *resembles* the person. Thus, it means *resemble*.

Radical: 亻 'upright person'　　　　　**Index # 19**

Character components: 亻 + 象　　　　　**Character configuration:** ⊟

Compounds, sentences and meanings

1. **像 xiàng** resemble
   这 孩子 像 他 父亲。
   Zhè háizi xiàng tā fùqin.
   The child takes after his father.

2. **像样 xiàngyàng** up to the mark, presentable
   她 跳舞 还 挺 像样 的。
   Tā tiàowǔ hái tǐng xiàngyàng de.
   Her dancing is pretty good.

3. **不像话 bú xiànghuà** unreasonable
   这 种 行为 真 不像话。
   Zhè zhǒng xíngwéi zhēn búxiànghuà.
   Behavior like that is really shocking.

4. **好像 hǎoxiàng** seem, be like
   这 个 人 我 好像 是 在 哪儿 见过。
   Zhè ge rén wǒ hǎoxiàng shì zài nǎr jiànguo.
   I seem to have met this man before.

5. **录像 lùxiàng** video tape
   这 是 你 跳舞 的 录像。
   Zhè shì nǐ tiàowǔ de lùxiàng.
   This is a video tape of your dancing.

The tenth stroke curves and ends with a hook.　　　　　**13 strokes**

ノ	亻	亻	亻	伫	伫	伯	伊	俤	像	像	像	像

肥

féi   fat/loose-fitting

The character combines *flesh* or *body part* 月 and the phonetic 巴 to suggest the idea of *being fat* or *loose-fitting*.

Radical: 月 'flesh/moon'

Index # 103

Character components: 月 + 巴

Character configuration:

Compounds, sentences and meanings

1. **肥** **féi** loose-fitting
   这 条 裤子 太 肥 了。
   Zhè tiáo kùzi tài féi le.
   These trousers are too baggy.

2. **肥大** **féidà** loose, large
   现在 流行 肥大 的 衣服。
   Xiànzài liúxíng féidà de yīfu.
   Loose clothing is fashionable at the moment.

3. **肥胖** **féipàng** fat, obese
   如今 中国 的 小孩 偏向 肥胖。
   Rújīn Zhōngguó de xiǎohái piānxiàng féipàng.
   Nowadays Chinese children tend to be overweight.

4. **肥瘦** **féishòu** the girth of a garment
   你 看 这 件 外衣 的 肥瘦 怎么样?
   Nǐ kàn zhè jiàn wàiyī de féishòu zěnmeyàng?
   Do you think this coat is a good fit?

5. **肥沃** **féiwò** fertile, rich
   这里 土地 肥沃。
   Zhèlǐ tǔdì féiwò.
   The land here is fertile.

The last stroke ends with a hook.   8 strokes

丿	刀	月	月	月⁻	月⁻	月ᴵ	肥				

bǎ handle/ with regard to

The character combines *hand* or *grasp* 扌 and the phonetic 巴 to suggest the idea of a *sure, tight hold of something.* It is used as an *object marker* and can be translated as *with regard to.*

Radical: 扌 'hand'　　　　　　　　**Index # 48**

Character components: 扌 + 巴　　　　**Character configuration:**

Compounds, sentences and meanings

1. **把　bǎ**　preposition (used to shift the object before the verb)
   我 把 这 件 事 忘 了。
   Wǒ bǎ zhè jiàn shì wàng le.
   I forgot all about it.

2. **一把刀子　yì bǎ dāozi**　a knife (*bǎ* is used as a measure word)
   请 给 我 一 把 刀子。
   Qǐng gěi wǒ yì bǎ dāozi.
   Please give me a knife.

3. **把柄　bǎbìng**　handle
   不要 给 人 留下 把柄。
   Búyào gěi rén liúxià bǎbìng.
   Don't do anything that people can hold against you.

4. **把握　bǎwò**　certainty
   他 有 把握 通过 考试。
   Tā yǒu bǎwò tōngguò kǎoshì.
   He's confident that he will pass the exam.

5. **把戏　bǎxì**　cheap trick, game
   他 玩 的 把戏 我 都 看穿 了。
   Tā wán de bǎxì wǒ dōu kànchuān le.
   I saw through his game.

The last stroke ends with a hook.　　　　　　　　**7 strokes**

一	扌	扌	扣	扣	扣	把				

ná take

The character consisting of *hand* 手 and *join together* 合, represents the idea of *holding something in your hands*. It means *hold*.

Radical: 手 'whole hand'   **Index # 96**

or 人 'people'   **Index # 18**

Character components: 合 + 手   **Character configuration:** ⊟

Compounds, sentences and meanings

1. 拿 **ná** take
   请 把 这些 东西 拿走。
   Qǐng bǎ zhèxiē dōngxi názǒu.
   Please take these things away.

2. 拿主意 **ná zhǔyi** make a decision
   究竟 去不去,你拿 主意 吧。
   Jiùjìng qù buqù, nǐ ná zhǔyi ba.
   Please decide whether to go or not.

3. 拿不起来 **nábuqǐlái** cannot manage
   这样 的 工作 他拿不起来。
   Zhèyàng de gōngzuò tā nábuqǐlái.
   He can't handle this kind of work.

4. 拿定主意 **nádìng zhǔyi** make up one's mind
   她 一直 拿不定 主意。
   Tā yìzhí nábudìng zhǔyi.
   She just can't make up her mind.

5. 拿手 **náshǒu** good at
   他 很 拿手 做饭。
   Tā hěn náshǒu zuòfàn.
   He's a good cook.

The last stroke ends with a hook.   **10 strokes**

ノ	人	𠆢	𠆢	合	合	拿	拿	拿	拿			

 **hé** join

The character represents *the act of collecting objects and keeping them.* By extension, it means *to fit.*

Radical: 人 'people'   **Index # 18**

Character components: 人 + 一 + 口   **Character configuration:** ⊟

Compounds, sentences and meanings

1. **合 hé** close
   把 书 合上。
   Bǎ shū héshàng.
   Close the book.

2. **合不来 hébulái** be incompatible
   她 跟 母亲 合不来。
   Tā gēn mǔqin hébulái.
   She doesn't get along with her mother.

3. **合口 hékǒu** (of a dish) be to one's taste
   你 做 的 菜 很 合口。
   Nǐ zuò de cài hěn hékǒu.
   The food you cook is very much to my taste.

4. **合理 hélǐ** reasonable
   这 家 饭馆儿 收费 合理。
   Zhè jiā fànguǎnr shōufèi hélǐ.
   Prices at this restaurant are reasonable.

5. **合适 héshì** suitable, appropriate
   这 个 词 用 在 这里 不 合适。
   Zhè ge cí yòng zài zhèlǐ bù héshì.
   This isn't the right word to use here.

The line in the middle does not touch the side strokes.   **6 strokes**

丿	人	스	合	合	合						

shì appropriate

The full form of the character combines *movement* 辶 and 商 which originally meant *going straight to one's destination*. Later, it came to mean *to fit*.

Radical: 辶 'movement'

Index # 38

Character components: 舌 + 辶

Character configuration:

Compounds, sentences and meanings

1. 适 **shì** suitable
   这 个 电影 不 适于 儿童 观看。
   Zhè ge diànyǐng bú shì yú értóng guānkàn.
   This movie is not suitable for children.

2. 适当 **shìdàng** appropriate
   到 适当 的 时候 我 会 告诉 你。
   Dào shìdàng de shíhou wǒ huì gàosu nǐ.
   I'll tell you in due course.

3. 适合 **shìhé** suit, fit
   他 适合 做 教师。
   Tā shìhé zuò jiàoshī.
   He's well suited to a teaching career.

4. 适宜 **shìyí** suitable
   游泳 对 老年人 也 是 适宜的。
   Yóuyǒng duì lǎoniánrén yě shì shìyí de.
   Swimming is good for old people too.

5. 适中 **shìzhōng** well situated
   这 家 饭店 地点 适中。
   Zhè jiā fàndiàn dìdiǎn shìzhōng.
   This hotel is well situated.

The top stroke of 舌 sweeps from right to left.								9 strokes
丿	二	千	千	舌	舌	适	话	适

着

Full form

著

zhe/zhǎo/zhuó   verbal particle

The full form combines *grass* ^艹 and *person* 者 to refer to the idea of *to wear*. The simplified form combines *sheep* 羊 and *eye* 目. It is used to indicate a *continuous state of being*.

Radical: 羊 'sheep'

Index # 133

Character components: 羊 + 目

Character configuration:

Compounds, sentences and meanings

1. 着 **zhe** *verbal suffix*
   她 穿着 一 身 新 衣服。
   Tā chuānzhe yì shēn xīn yīfu.
   She is wearing new clothes.

2. 着急 **zháojí** get worried
   冷静 点儿, 别 着急。
   Lěngjìng diǎnr, biě zháojǐ.
   Keep calm, don't panic.

3. 着凉 **zháoliáng** catch a chill
   外面 有点 冷, 当心 着凉。
   Wàimiàn yǒudiǎn lěng, dāngxīn zháoliáng.
   It's chilly outside, be careful not to catch cold.

4. 着想 **zhuóxiǎng** consider (the interest of somebody or something)
   他 是 为 你 着想, 才 劝 你 不要
   去 的。
   Tā shì wèi nǐ zhuóxiǎng, cái quàn nǐ bùyào
   qù de.
   It was for your own good that he advised you not to go.

5. 着重 **zhuózhòng** stress, emphasize
   这里 我 想 着重地 讲 一 个 问题。
   Zhèlǐ wǒ xiǎng zhuózhòngde jiǎng yǐ ge wèntí.
   Here I would like to go into one question in particular.

The second horizontal stroke is shorter.

11 strokes

| 丶 | 丷 | 丷 | 兰 | 兰 | 羊 | 羊 | 羔 | 着 | 着 | 着 | | |

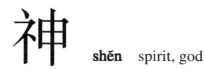

shén spirit, god

The character combines *ritual* 礻 and the phonetic 申 to express the idea of a *deity* or *god*.

Radical: 礻 'ritual'　　　　　　**Index # 78**

Character components: 礻 + 申

Character configuration:

Compounds, sentences and meanings

1. 神 **shén** god
   神 不 知, 鬼 不 觉。
   Shén bù zhī, guǐ bù jué.
   Unknown to god or ghost.

2. 神经 **shénjīng** nerve
   比赛 之前, 我 有点 神经 紧张。
   Bǐsài zhīqián, wǒ yǒudiǎn shénjīng jǐnzhāng.
   I was a bit nervous before the competition.

3. 神情 **shénqíng** expression, look
   跳舞 的 时候, 要 露出 愉快 的 神情。
   Tiàowǔ de shíhou, yào lùchū yúkuài de shénqíng.
   When you dance, you should look happy.

4. 神态 **shéntài** manner, bearing
   看 她的 神态 像 舞蹈 演员。
   Kàn tāde shéntài xiàng wǔdǎo yǎnyuán.
   From the way she carries herself, she must be a dancer.

Note the component 礻 has only one dot on the left.								9 strokes

丶　礻　礻　礻　衤　祁　祁　神　神

Full form

qì   air, gas

The full form of the character combines *steam* 气 and *rice* 米 to represent the steam emitted when rice is cooked. It means *steam* or *gas*. In simplification, the 'rice' component is dropped.

Radical: 气 'air'   **Index # 98**

Character component: 气   **Character configuration:** ☐

Compounds, sentences and meanings

1. 气 **qì** air
   自行车　前带　没气了。
   Zìxíngchē qiándài méi qì le.
   The front tire of the bike is flat.

2. 气候 **qìhòu** climate
   他不 适应　北京 的 气候。
   Tā bú shìyìng Běijīng de qìhòu.
   He's not used to the climate in Beijing.

3. 气味 **qìwèi** smell
   这 是 什么 气味?
   Zhè shì shénme qìwèi?
   What kind of smell is that?

4. 气色 **qìsè** complexion
   她气色不好, 脸上 没 什么 血色。
   Tā qìsè bù hǎo, liǎnshàng méi shénme xuèsè.
   She's very pale, there isn't much color on her face.

5. 气力 **qìlì** strength
   学 外国语 要 用 很大 的 气力 才
   Xué wàiguóyǔ yào yòng hěndà de qìlì cái
   能 学好。
   néng xuéhǎo.
   It takes a lot of effort to learn a foreign language well.

The last stroke ends with a hook.							4 strokes
ノ	ト	仁	气				

A. Look at the 16-character grid and CIRCLE words or phrases. They can be written horizontally or vertically. (Look at the circled characters in the Key if you are unsure.) Copy the word or phrase next to the grid and write down the pinyin and meaning.

	Word or phrase		Pinyin	Meaning

Grid:
紧	身	肥	着
把	合	衣	服
好	适	神	件
拿	像	气	穿

	Word or phrase	Pinyin	Meaning
(i)	紧 身	jǐnshēn	tight fit
(ii)			
(iii)			
(iv)			

B. Using the characters in the 16-character grid, convert the pinyin sentences into characters and write the English meaning.

(i)	Wǒ xǐhuan chuān jǐnshēn yīfu.								
(ii)	Zhè jiàn hǎoxiàng féi le diǎnr.								
(iii)	Qǐng bǎ nà jiàn ná gěi wǒ kànkan.								
(iv)	Zhèng héshì, nǐ chuānzhe zhēn shénqì!								

C. Match the Chinese words with their English meaning.

(i)

紧 zhāng	loose, large
紧 jí	seem, be like
像样	urgent
好像	nervous
肥大	certainty
肥 pàng	presentable
把 wò	be good at
拿手	fat, obese

(ii)

合口	reasonable
合理	nerve
适合	smell
着 liáng	be to one's taste
着 xiǎng	catch a cold
神经	consider
气候	suit, fit
气 wèi	climate

CHARACTER BUILDING 8 (351–400)

A. Memorize the following radicals and their English names. As a review exercise, write the pinyin and meaning of each example:

1. [丶] 'dot'
   为 (_____) _____ ; 半 (_____) _____ .

2. [丨] 'vertical stroke'
   旧 (_____) _____ ; 中 (_____) _____ .

3. [丿] 'downward-left stroke'
   向 (_____) _____ ; 千 (_____) _____ .

4. [讠] 'word'
   许 (_____) _____ ; 计 (_____) _____ .

5. [十] 'ten'
   真 (_____) _____ ; 直 (_____) _____ .

6. [刂] 'upright knife'
   刚 (_____) _____ ; 别 (_____) _____ .

7. [人] 'person'
   合 (_____) _____ ; 舒 (_____) _____ .

8. [亻] 'upright person'
   像 (_____) _____ ; 但 (_____) _____ ;

9. [又] 'again'
   双 (_____) _____ ; 难 (_____) _____ .

10. [氵] '3 drops of water'
    清 (_____) _____ ; 湾 (_____) _____ .

11. [辶] 'movement'
    适 (_____) _____ ; 过 (_____) _____ .

12. [艹] 'grass'
    蓝 (_____) _____ ; 黄 (_____) _____ .

13. [扌] 'hand'
    把 (_____) _____ ; 拐 (_____) _____ .

14. [囗] '4-sided frame'
    因 (_____) _____ ; 回 (_____) _____ .

15. [女] 'female'
    如 (_____) _____ ; 好 (_____) _____ .

16. [纟] 'silk'
    红 (_____) _____ ; 绿 (_____) _____ .

17. [木] 'tree'
    果 (_____) _____ ; 相 (_____) _____ .

18. [斤] 'catty'
    所 (_____) _____ ; 新 (_____) _____ .

19. ［月］ 'flesh/moon'
肥（＿＿＿＿＿）＿＿＿＿＿＿ ; 服（＿＿＿＿＿）＿＿＿＿＿＿ .

20. ［穴］ 'cave'
穿（＿＿＿＿＿）＿＿＿＿＿＿ ; 容（＿＿＿＿＿）＿＿＿＿＿＿ .

21. ［白］ 'white'
白（＿＿＿＿＿）＿＿＿＿＿＿ ; 百（＿＿＿＿＿）＿＿＿＿＿＿ .

22. ［页］ 'page'
颜（＿＿＿＿＿）＿＿＿＿＿＿ ; 题（＿＿＿＿＿）＿＿＿＿＿＿ .

B. Write the pinyin and meaning against the characters classified under the following radicals.

1. ［厂］ 'building' 厕 （＿＿＿＿＿）＿＿＿＿＿＿

2. ［阝］ 'left ear-lobe' 附 （＿＿＿＿＿）＿＿＿＿＿＿

3. ［刀］ 'knife' 色 （＿＿＿＿＿）＿＿＿＿＿＿

4. ［尸］ 'dwelling' 局 （＿＿＿＿＿）＿＿＿＿＿＿

5. ［弓］ 'bow' 弯 （＿＿＿＿＿）＿＿＿＿＿＿

6. ［火］ 'fire' 灯 （＿＿＿＿＿）＿＿＿＿＿＿

7. ［礻］ 'ritual' 神 （＿＿＿＿＿）＿＿＿＿＿＿

8. ［牛］ 'cattle' 特 （＿＿＿＿＿）＿＿＿＿＿＿

9. ［衤］ 'clothing' 衬 （＿＿＿＿＿）＿＿＿＿＿＿

10. ［疋］ 'roll of cloth' 楚 （＿＿＿＿＿）＿＿＿＿＿＿

11. ［羊］ 'sheep' 着 （＿＿＿＿＿）＿＿＿＿＿＿

12. ［系］ 'upright silk' 紧 （＿＿＿＿＿）＿＿＿＿＿＿

13. ［革］ 'leather' 鞋 （＿＿＿＿＿）＿＿＿＿＿＿

C. Write the pinyin and meaning against the characters which share the following components. (Note that these components are not necessarily used as radicals.)

1. ［艮］ 银（＿＿＿＿＿）＿＿＿＿＿＿ ; 跟（＿＿＿＿＿）＿＿＿＿＿＿ .

2. ［巴］ 肥（＿＿＿＿＿）＿＿＿＿＿＿ ; 把（＿＿＿＿＿）＿＿＿＿＿＿ .

3. ［舌］ 适（＿＿＿＿＿）＿＿＿＿＿＿ ; 话（＿＿＿＿＿）＿＿＿＿＿＿ .

4. ［斤］ 新（＿＿＿＿＿）＿＿＿＿＿＿ ; 听（＿＿＿＿＿）＿＿＿＿＿＿ .

5. ［另］ 拐（＿＿＿＿＿）＿＿＿＿＿＿ ; 别（＿＿＿＿＿）＿＿＿＿＿＿ .

REVIEW 8 (351–400)

The following are words and phrases classified under parts of speech. Write their pinyin and meaning.

Nouns 附近 (_____) _____ ; 女厕 (_____) _____ ;

厕所 (_____) _____ ; 红绿灯 (_____) _____ ;

绿灯 (_____) _____ ; 向导 (_____) _____ ;

弯路 (_____) _____ ; 弯子 (_____) _____ ;

米饭 (_____) _____ ; 商场 (_____) _____ ;

银行 (_____) _____ ; 银色 (_____) _____ ;

邮票 (_____) _____ ; 邮局 (_____) _____ ;

颜面 (_____) _____ ; 颜色 (_____) _____ ;

黑人 (_____) _____ ; 衬衣 (_____) _____ ;

蓝色 (_____) _____ ; 别的 (_____) _____ ;

别人 (_____) _____ ; 特长 (_____) _____ ;

特点 (_____) _____ ; 特色 (_____) _____ ;

双人床 (_____) _____ ; 皮毛 (_____) _____ ;

皮鞋 (_____) _____ ; 真话 (_____) _____ ;

真相 (_____) _____ ; 新年 (_____) _____ ;

穿着 (_____) _____ ; 服务 (_____) _____ ;

神经 (_____) _____ ; 神气 (_____) _____ ;

气候 (_____) _____ ; 气色 (_____) _____ .

Interrogative 为什么 (_____) _____ .
Pronouns

Measure 双 (_____) _____ .
Word

Verbs 附上 (_____) _____ ; 向往 (_____) _____ ;

拐弯 (_____) _____ ; 清理 (_____) _____ ;

回来 (_____) _____ ; 回去 (_____) _____ ;

为难 (_____) _____ ; 为期 (_____) _____ ;

穿过 (_____) _____ ; 服从 (_____) _____ ;

合不来 (_____) _____ ; 适合 (_____) _____ ;

着想 (_____) _____ .

Adjectives 所有 (_____) _____ ; 弯弯 (_____) _____ ;

178

弯曲 (_____) _____ ；　清楚 (_____) _____ ；

许多 (_____) _____ ；　黄色 (_____) _____ ；

黑白 (_____) _____ ；　特别 (_____) _____ ；

特有 (_____) _____ ；　真心 (_____) _____ ；

真正 (_____) _____ ；　舒服 (_____) _____ ；

舒适 (_____) _____ ；　肥大 (_____) _____ ；

拿手 (_____) _____ ；　合口 (_____) _____ ；

合理 (_____) _____ ；　合适 (_____) _____ ；

适宜 (_____) _____ ；　适中 (_____) _____ .

Adverbs　　向来 (_____) _____ ；　许久 (_____) _____ ；

不许 (_____) _____ ；　也许 (_____) _____ ；

如今 (_____) _____ ；　白天 (_____) _____ ；

刚才 (_____) _____ ；　刚刚 (_____) _____ ；

刚好 (_____) _____ .

Conjunctions　因为 (_____) _____ ；　所以 (_____) _____ ；

如果 (_____) _____ .

Prepositions　为了 (_____) _____ ；　把 (_____) _____ .

WORD/SENTENCE PUZZLE 8

Find and circle words, phrases and sentences hidden in the puzzle. They can be found horizontally from left to right or vertically . The lines across and down are indicated by numbers. Write their meaning next to the pinyin. The first one is done for you.

ACROSS

1. Zhè shuāng xié chuānqilái hěn shūfu.　　*This pair of shoes is very comfortable.*

4. Qǐng bié wéinán wǒ.　　_____

6. (i) Gāng lái Běijīng bùjiǔ　　_____

    (ii) shēngyīn　　_____

8. Tā shuōhuà de shénqì tèbié xiàng tā bà.　　_____

13. Nǐ wèishénme bù jiǎng qīngchu?　　_____

16. Xué wàiguóyǔ yào huā hěnduō shíjiān.　　_____

DOWN

1. Zhè shuāng xié dàxiǎo gāng héshì.　　_____

3. Tā xué Yīngyǔ shì wèile chūguó.　　_____

179

5.　Zhè zhǒng xíngwéi zhēn bùxiànghuà.　　_____

7.　jiǎnglǐ.　　_____

9.　Tāde kǒuyīn hěn tèbié.　　_____

11.　Zhè ge rén wǒ hǎoxiàng zài nǎr jiànguo.　　_____

13.　Tā gēn tā bàba hébulái.　　_____

	1	2	3	4	5	6	7	8	9	10	11	12	13
1	这	价	音	建	这	双	鞋	穿	起	来	很	舒	服
2	双	正	改	界	种	难	绿	应	调	流	山	谈	验
3	鞋	附	教	世	行	容	拐	议	她	才	这	俗	容
4	大	厕	请	别	为	难	我	首	的	黑	个	找	趣
5	小	帮	所	表	真	的	红	唱	口	曲	人	建	他
6	刚	来	北	京	不	久	弯	声	音	听	我	又	跟
7	合	价	蓝	建	像	快	紧	河	很	容	好	衬	他
8	适	首	他	说	话	的	神	气	特	别	像	他	爸
9	识	银	学	空	张	比	做	来	别	看	在	心	爸
10	子	知	英	体	电	场	会	着	台	肥	哪	吧	合
11	样	昨	语	分	请	问	邮	局	在	那	儿	如	不
12	向	把	是	回	许	口	城	年	灯	游	见	会	来
13	星	你	为	什	么	不	讲	清	楚	果	过	出	哥
14	颜	决	了	请	她	去	理	怎	就	还	狗	白	给
15	语	色	出	新	期	明	心	旧	拿	的	米	题	公
16	学	外	国	语	要	花	很	多	时	间	黄	因	友

yù beforehand

The full form of the character combines *head* 页 and the phonetic 予 which means *I, me* to suggest that by applying my head, I am *ahead of time.*

Radical: 页 'page'

Index # 140

Character components: 予 + 页

Character configuration:

Compounds, sentences and meanings

1. **预 yù** beforehand
   预 祝 你 取得 成功。
   Yù zhù nǐ qǔdé chénggōng.
   I wish you success.

2. **预报 yùbào** forecast
   天气 预报 说 明天 会下雨。
   Tiānqì yùbào shuō míngtiān huì xiàyǔ.
   The weather forecast says it will rain tomorrow.

3. **预备 yùbèi** get ready
   你们 预备好 了 吗?
   Nǐmen yùbèihǎo le ma?
   Are you ready?

4. **预订 yùdìng** place an order
   我 预订 火车票 了。
   Wǒ yùdìng huǒchēpiào le.
   I've booked the train ticket.

5. **预约 yùyuē** make an appointment
   你 跟 医生 预约 了 吗?
   Nǐ gēn yīshēng yùyuē le ma?
   Have you made an appointment with the doctor?

Finish the last stroke firmly.

10 strokes

フ	マ	ヱ	予	予	予	预	预	预	预			

Full form

报 **bāo** report

報

The full form of the character combines *luck* 幸 and the character component 及 to give the idea of *returning with a piece of information* or *to report*.

Radical: 扌 'hand'

Index # 48

Character components: 扌 + 及

Character configuration:

Compounds, sentences and meanings

1. 报 **bāo** report
   请假 要 报 上级 批准。
   Qǐngjià yào bāo shàngjí pīzhǔn.
   You need your boss's approval to take leave.

2. 报酬 **bāochou** remuneration
   这 个 工作 很 累, 报酬 不多。
   Zhè ge gōngzuò hěn lèi, bāochou bùduō.
   This job is hard, and it pays very little.

3. 报告 **bāogào** report
   现在 报告 新闻。
   Xiànzài bāogào xīnwén.
   Here is the news.

4. 报关 **bāoguān** declare something at customs
   你 有 什么 东西 要 报关 吗?
   Nǐ yǒu shénme dōngxi yào bāoguān ma?
   Have you got anything to declare?

5. 报名 **bāomíng** sign up
   我 报名 参加了 百 米 赛跑。
   Wǒ bāomíng cānjiāle bǎi mǐ sàipǎo.
   I've signed up for the 100 meter dash.

The fourth stroke is a horizontal-bend-hook.   7 strokes

一	十	扌	扩	护	报	报					

晴

qíng   fine, sunny

The character combines *sun* 日 and *blue* 青 to refer to *blue sky* or *fine day*.

Radical: 日 'sun'

Character components: 日 + 青

Index # 90

Character configuration: ⊞

Compounds, sentences and meanings

1. **晴** qíng   fine day
   天 晴 了。
   Tiān qíng le.
   It's clearing up.

2. **晴朗** qínglǎng   fine, sunny
   今天 天气 晴朗。
   Jīntiān tiānqì qínglǎng.
   Today is sunny.

3. **晴天** qíngtiān   sunny day
   昨天 是 晴天。
   Zuótiān shì qíngtiān.
   Yesterday was a fine day.

4. **晴间多云** qíng jiān duōyún   fine with occasional clouds
   预报 说 明天 晴 间 多云。
   Yùbào shuō míngtiān qíng jiān duōyún.
   The weather forecast says tomorrow will be fine with occasional clouds.

5. **晴转阴** qíng zhuǎn yīn   fine changing to overcast
   下午 晴 转 阴。
   Xiàwǔ qíng zhuǎn yīn.
   It will cloud over in the afternoon.

The third horizontal stroke of 青 is the longest.   12 strokes

丿	刀	月	日	日⁻	日⁼	日‡	晴	晴	晴	晴	晴

lì strength

The hieroglyphic character is that of *a hand attempting to hold an object in a raised position.* It expresses the meaning of *force* or *power.*

Radical: 力 'strength'　　　　　　　　**Index # 31**

Character component: 力　　　　　　　**Character configuration:** ⬚

Compounds, sentences and meanings

1. **力　lì**　power, strength
   我 想 帮 你,可是 恐怕 力 不 从 心。
   Wǒ xiǎng bāng nǐ, kěshì kǒngpà lì bù cóng xīn.
   I wanted to help but I'm afraid I don't have the ability.

2. **力量　lìliang**　strength
   我 一定 尽 我的 力量 帮忙。
   Wǒ yídìng jǐn wǒde lìliang bāngmáng.
   I'll certainly do everything in my power to help.

3. **力气　lìqi**　physical strength
   他的力气不 小。
   Tāde lìqi bù xiǎo.
   He's very strong.

4. **力求　lìqiú**　make every effort to
   我们 力求 取得 一致 意见。
   Wǒmen lìqiú qǔdé yízhì yìjiàn.
   We'll do our best to reach a consensus.

5. **力争　lìzhēng**　work hard for
   力争　上游。
   Lìzhēng shàngyóu.
   Try hard to come first.

The first stroke ends with a hook.　　　　　　　　**2 strokes**

フ	力								

jí grade

The character combines *silk* 纟 and the phonetic 及 to suggest *different grades of silk*. Thus, it means *grade*.

Radical: 纟 'silk' **Index # 68**

Character components: 纟 + 及

Character configuration: ▯▯

Compounds, sentences and meanings

1. 级 **jí** grade
   长城 饭店 是 五星级 宾馆。
   Chángchéng Fàndiàn shì wǔxīngjí bīnguǎn.
   The Great Wall Hotel is a five-star hotel.

2. 级别 **jíbié** rank
   她的 级别 比我 高。
   Tāde jíbié bǐ wǒ gāo.
   She is my senior.

3. 超级 **chāojí** super grade
   这家 超级 市场 东西 很 全。
   Zhè jiā chāojí shìchǎng dōngxi hěn quán.
   This supermarket has a wide range of goods.

4. 初级 **chūjí** novice level
   这 是 汉语 初级 读本。
   Zhè shì Hànyǔ chūjí dúběn.
   This is an elementary Chinese reader.

5. 高级 **gāojí** advanced level
   这 个 旅馆 真 高级。
   Zhè ge lǚguǎn zhēn gāojí.
   This hotel is really first class.

The second stroke of 及 has two bends.						6 strokes
乚	纟	纟	纠	级	级	

温 wēn warm

The full form of the character combines *water* 氵 and the phonetic 昷 to give the idea of *temperature*.

Radical: 氵 '3 drops of water'   **Index # 32**

Character components: 氵 + 日 + 皿   **Character configuration:**

Compounds, sentences and meanings

1. 温 **wēn** warm
   请 把 牛奶 温 一下。
   Qǐng bǎ niúnǎi wēn yíxià.
   Please heat the milk.

2. 温差 **wēnchā** difference in temperature
   这里 白天 和 夜晚 的 温差 很 大。
   Zhèlǐ báitiān hé yèwǎn de wēnchā hěn dà.
   The temperature here varies greatly between day and night.

3. 温度 **wēndù** temperature
   晚上 室外 温度 比较 冷。
   Wǎnshang shìwài wēndù bǐjiào lěng.
   At night the temperature outside is pretty cold.

4. 温和 **wēnhé** gentle
   她的 性情 温和。
   Tāde xìngqíng wēnhé.
   She has a gentle disposition.

5. 温暖 **wēnnuǎn** warm
   今天 天气 温暖。
   Jīntiān tiānqì wēnnuǎn.
   Today's weather is warm.

The bottom line extends beyond both sides of the rectangle.											12 strokes
丶	冫	氵	沪	沪	沪	沪	沪	渇	温	温	温

dù degree

The character is a phonetic used as a character. It means *degree*.

Radical: 广 'broad'　　　　　　　　　　**Index # 36**

Character components: 广 + 廿 + 又　　　　**Character configuration:**

Compounds, sentences and meanings

1. **度　dù**　degree
   这里 夏天 最热 是 摄氏三十五度。
   Zhèlǐ xiàtiān zuìrè shì shèshì 35 dù.
   It gets to 35°C in summer here.

2. **度过　dùguò**　pass, spend time in
   他 在 农村 度过 童年。
   Tā zài nóngcūn dùguò tóngnián.
   He spent his childhood in the countryside.

3. **度假　dùjià**　take a holiday
   下 个 月 我 到 海边 去 度假。
   Xià ge yuè wǒ dào hǎibiān qù dùjià.
   I'll be spending my holidays at the beach next month.

4. **风度　fēngdù**　demeanor, bearing
   她的 风度 很 大方。
   Tāde fēngdù hěn dàfāng.
   She has an easy manner.

5. **湿度　shīdù**　humidity
   广州 夏天 湿度 很 高。
   Guǎngzhōu xiàtiān shīdù hěn gāo.
   The humidity in Guangzhou is very high in summer.

The last stroke tapers off.									9 strokes		
丶	亠	广	广	庐	庐	庐	庐	度			

 **yè** night

The character combines *person* 亻, *roof* 宀, and *evening* 夕 to give the idea of *a person under a roof at night*. It came to mean *night*.

Radical: 宀 'top of 六'   **Index # 6**

Character components: 宀 + 亻 + 夕 + 乀   **Character configuration:**

Compounds, sentences and meanings

1. 夜 **yè** night
   三 天 三 夜 讲不完。
   Sān tiān sān yè jiǎngbuwán.
   It's a long story. (Literally, three days and three nights wouldn't be enough time to finish it.)

2. 夜间 **yèjiān** night time
   上海 很多 工地 都 进行
   Shànghǎi hěnduō gōngdì dōu jìngxíng
   夜间 施工。
   yèjiān shīgōng.
   In Shanghai, work on lots of building sites goes on all night.

3. 夜景 **yèjǐng** night scene
   香港 的 夜景 很 有名。
   Xiānggǎng de yèjǐng hěn yǒumíng.
   Hong Kong's night scene is very famous.

4. 夜生活 **yèshēnghuó** night life
   这里 的 夜生活 很 丰富。
   Zhèlǐ de yèshēnghuó hěn fēngfù.
   The night life here is vibrant.

5. 夜总会 **yèzǒnghuì** night club
   我们 常常 去 夜总会 跳舞。
   Wǒmen chángcháng qù yèzǒnghuì tiàowǔ.
   We often go to night clubs to dance.

The bottom component is tucked under the horizontal stroke.   8 strokes

丶	亠	广	疒	疒	夜	夜	夜			

 dī low

The character combines *person* 亻 and the phonetic 氐 to suggest the idea of *low*.

Radical: 亻 'upright person'　　　　**Index # 19**

Character components: 亻 + 氏 + 丶　　　　**Character configuration:**

Compounds, sentences and meanings

1. **低** **dī** low
   飞机 飞得 很 低。
   Fēijī fēide hěn dī.
   The plane flew very low.

2. **低沉** **dīchén** (of voice) low and deep
   他的 声音 很 低沉。
   Tāde shēngyīn hěn dīchén.
   He's got a low voice.

3. **低估** **dīgū** underrate
   我 低估了 她的 英语 水平。
   Wǒ dīgūle tāde Yīngyǔ shuǐpíng.
   I underestimated the standard of her English.

4. **低头** **dītóu** yield, submit
   我 决不 向 困难 低头。
   Wǒ juébù xiàng kùnnan dītóu.
   I will never give in to difficulties.

5. **降低** **jiàngdī** drop, lower
   今天 气温 降低 了。
   Jīntiān qìwēn jiàngdī le.
   The temperature has dropped today.

Don't forget the dot at the bottom.　　　　**7 strokes**

ノ	亻	亻	仟	仟	低	低					

Full form

 yīn dark, cloudy

The full form of the character combines *place* 阝 , *this* 今 and *clouds* 云 to suggest the idea that when a place is covered with clouds, it is *overcast*.

Radical: 阝 'left ear-lobe'   **Index # 27**

Character component: 阝 + 月   **Character configuration:** ⊟

Compounds, sentences and meanings

1. 阴 **yīn** overcast
   天 阴 了。
   Tiān yīn le.
   The sky is overcast.

2. 阴暗 **yīn'àn** dark, gloomy
   这 个 房间 又 阴暗 又 潮湿。
   Zhè ge fángjiān yòu yīn'àn yòu cháoshī.
   This room is dark and damp.

3. 阴沉 **yīnchén** cloudy, gloomy
   天色 阴沉。
   Tiānsè yīnchén.
   The sky is cloudy.

4. 阴黑 **yīnhēi** gloomy, somber
   他的 脸色 阴黑。
   Tāde liǎnsè yīnhēi.
   His face looks glum.

5. 阴凉 **yīnliáng** shady and cool
   找 个 阴凉 的 地方 休息。
   Zhǎo ge yīnliáng de dìfang xiūxi.
   Let's find a cool, shady spot and rest.

The fourth stroke ends with a hook.   **6 strokes**

了	阝	阝月	阴	阴	阴						

Quiz 41 (401–410)

A. Look at the 16-character grid and CIRCLE words or phrases. They can be written horizontally or vertically. (Look at the circled characters in the Key if you are unsure.) Copy the word or phrase next to the grid and write down the pinyin and meaning.

	Word or phrase		**Pinyin**	**Meaning**
(i)	预 报		yùbào	forecast
(ii)				
(iii)				
(iv)				

Grid:

风	预	力	阴
南	报	夜	间
最	高	快	级
向	晴	气	温

B. Using the characters in the 16-character grid, convert the pinyin sentences into characters and write the English meaning.

(i)	Tiānqì yùbào shuō jīntiān qíngtiān.							
(ii)	Fēngxiàng nán fēng, fēnglì èrjí.							
(iii)	Zuìgāo qìwēn 18 dù.							
(iv)	Yèjiān zuìdī qìwēn 9 dù.							

C. Match the Chinese words with their English meaning.

(i)

预 bèi   sign up
预 yuē   rank
报告   make an appointment
报名   make every effort to
力气   get ready
力求   report
级别   physical strength
高级   advanced level

(ii)

温度   spend holiday
温和   night view
度过   temperature
度假   shady and cool
夜景   underrate
低 gū   drop, lower
jiàng 低   gentle
阴凉   pass, spend

chūn spring

The character combines *sun* 日 and *budding plant* 夫 to refer to *spring*.

Radical: 日 'sun'　　　　　　　　　**Index # 90**

Character components: 夫 + 日　　　**Character configuration:**

Compounds, sentences and meanings

1. **春 chūn** spring
   这里的气候四季如春。
   Zhèlǐ de qìhòu sìjì rú chūn.
   The climate here is like spring all year round.

2. **春天 chūntiān** spring
   北京 春天 还 很 冷。
   Běijīng chūntiān hái hěn lěng.
   Spring is still quite cold in Beijing.

3. **春节 Chūnjié** Chinese New Year or Spring Festival
   在 中国 过 春节 很 热闹。
   Zài Zhōngguó guò Chūnjié hěn rè'nào.
   Chinese New Year in China is very lively.

4. **春风 chūnfēng** spring breeze
   他 今天 春风 满面 的, 不 知
   Tā jīntiān chūnfēng mǎnmiàn de, bù zhī
   是 为什么。
   shì wèishénme.
   His face is beaming with satisfaction. I wonder what happened.

5. **春药 chūnyào** aphrodisiac
   有 人 说 吃 春药 对 身体 有害。
   Yǒu rén shuō chī chūnyào duì shēntǐ yǒuhài.
   People say that taking aphrodisiacs is harmful to health.

The third horizontal stroke is longer than those above it.									9 strokes
一	二	三	声	夫	未	春	春	春	

tǎo discuss

The character is formed by the combination of *word* 讠 and *inch* 寸. It is not clear how the association came to mean *beg*.

Radical: 讠 'word'

Index # 9

Character components: 讠 + 寸

Character configuration:

Compounds, sentences and meanings

1. 讨 tǎo incur, invite
   大熊猫　温和　驯良，讨人喜欢。
   Dàxióngmāo wēnhé xúnliáng, tǎo rén xǐhuan.
   The gentleness and good nature of the giant panda make them especially likeable.

2. 讨价还价 tǎojià-huánjià haggle over price
   在　中国　买东西　得　讨价还价。
   Zài Zhōngguó mǎi dōngxi děi tǎojià-huánjià.
   You need to bargain when you shop in China.

3. 讨论 tǎolùn discuss
   这件事 我们 得 讨论 讨论。
   Zhè jiàn shì wǒmen děi tǎolùn tǎolùn.
   We must talk it over.

4. 讨厌 tǎoyàn disagreeable, annoying
   每天　刮风，真　讨厌!
   Měitiān guāfēng, zhēn tǎoyàn!
   It's been windy every day. What a nuisance!

5. 不讨好 bùtǎohǎo not have one's labor rewarded
   这 个　工作　怎么　干 也费力 不讨好。
   Zhè ge gōngzuò zěnme gàn yě fèilì bùtǎohǎo.
   No matter how hard you work on this job, it's a thankless task.

The fourth stroke ends with a hook.　　　　5 strokes

丶	讠	计	讨	讨							

Full form

厌　**yàn**　detest

厭

The full form of the character has four components: *building* 厂, *sun* 日, *moon* 月 and *dog* 犬. The second and third components are missing in the simplified form.

Radical: 厂 'building'

Index # 12

Character components: 厂 + 犬

Character configuration:

Compounds, sentences and meanings

1. 厌　**yàn**　be fed up with
   这 个 广告 我 看厌 了。
   Zhè ge guǎnggào wǒ kànyàn le.
   I've seen more than enough of this ad.

2. 厌烦　**yànfán**　be fed up with
   这 首 歌 我 听 多少 次 也 不 觉得 厌烦。
   Zhè shǒu gē wǒ tīng duōshao cì yě bù juéde yànfán.
   I never tire of listening to this song.

3. 厌倦　**yànjuàn**　be tired of
   整天 坐 办公室, 我 早 就 厌倦 了。
   Zhěngtiān zuò bàn'gōngshì, wǒ zǎo jiù yànjuàn le.
   Long ago, I grew tired of sitting in an office all day.

4. 厌食症　**yànshízhèng**　(esp. in young women) anorexia
   她 什么 都 不吃, 恐怕 是 得了 厌食症。
   Tā shénme dōu bù chī, kǒngpà shì déle yànshízhèng.
   She's not eating anything. I'm worried that she has become anorexic.

5. 厌恶　**yànwù**　detest
   大家 都 厌恶 他。
   Dàjiā dōu yànwù tā.
   Everyone is disgusted with him.

Note the difference between 厌 and 庆.　6 strokes

一	厂	厍	厈	厌	厌						

刮

gūa (of the wind) blow

颳

The full form of the character combines *wind* 風 and *tongue* 舌 to suggest the idea of the wind *blowing*. Note that only the full form is restricted to this meaning. 刮 by itself means *scrape*.

Radical: 刂 'upright knife'

Index # 15

Character components: 舌 + 刂

Character configuration:

Compounds, sentences and meanings

1. **刮 gūa** blow (of the wind)
   刮 大 风 了。
   Gūa dà fēng le.
   There's a gale blowing.

2. **刮破 guāpò** scratched
   就 刮破 一点 皮。
   Jiù guāpò yìdiǎn pí.
   It's only a scratch.

3. **刮脸 guāliǎn** shave
   我 天天 早上 刮脸。
   Wǒ tiāntiān zǎoshang guāliǎn.
   I shave every morning.

4. **刮脸刀 guāliǎndāo** razor
   我 要 买 刮脸刀。
   Wǒ yào mǎi guāliǎndāo.
   I need to buy some razor blades.

5. **刮目相看 gūa mù xiāng kàn** look at someone with new eyes
   她 从 美国 回来 以后, 大家 都
   Tā cóng Měiguó huílai yǐhòu, dàjiā dōu
   刮 目 相 看。
   gūa mù xiāng kàn.
   Everyone treats her with increased respect since her return from the United States.

The first stroke sweeps from right to left.									8 strokes
丿	二	千	千	舌	舌	刮	刮		

shā sand

The character combines *water* 氵 and *few* 少 to suggest the idea of *sand*.

Radical: 氵 '3 drops of water'　　　　　　**Index # 32**

Character components: 氵 + 少　　　　　**Character configuration:**

Compounds, sentences and meanings

1. **沙 shā** hoarse, husky (of voice)
   我的 嗓子 沙 了。
   Wǒde sǎngzi shā le.
   My voice has become husky.

2. **沙尘 shāchén** dust and sand in the air
   卡车 驶过，扬起 一 片 沙尘。
   Kǎchē shǐguò, yángqǐ yī piàn shāchén.
   The truck raised a cloud of dust as it drove by.

3. **沙发 shāfā** sofa
   客厅 里 摆着 一 套 沙发。
   Kètīng lǐ bǎizhe yī tào shāfā.
   There is a sofa in the lounge.

4. **沙拉 shālā** salad
   我 喜欢 吃 沙拉。
   Wǒ xǐhuan chī shālā.
   I love salad.

5. **沙子 shāzi** sand
   这 海滩 的 沙子 又 细 又 白。
   Zhè hǎitān de shāzi yòu xì yòu bái.
   The sand on this beach is fine and white.

The last stroke sweeps from right to left.						7 strokes

丶	氵	氵	氵丿	氵小	氵少	沙					

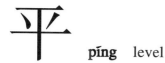

píng level

This character is a pictograph of *a scale with two objects balancing* on it. It means *flat* or *calm*.

Radical: 一 'horizontal-stroke'　　　　　**Index # 2**

Character components: 干 + ⺀

Character configuration: ☐

Compounds, sentences and meanings

1. 平 **píng** level
   桌面 不 平。
   Zhuōmiàn bù píng.
   The table is not level.

2. 平安 **píng'ān** safe
   平安 到达 目的地。
   Píng'ān dàodá mùdìdì.
   Get there safe and sound.

3. 平常 **píngcháng** ordinary
   平常 我 很少 进城。
   Píngcháng wǒ hěnshǎo jìnchéng.
   As a rule, I seldom go to town.

4. 平等 **píngděng** equality
   我们 家里 男 女 平等。
   Wǒmen jiāli nán nǚ píngděng.
   In our family, there is equality between the sexes.

5. 平静 **píngjìng** calm down
   他 很 激动，心情 久久 不能 平静。
   Tā hěn jīdòng, xīnqíng jiǔjiǔ bùnéng píngjìng.
   He was very excited, and it was a long time before he calmed down.

The two dots come towards each other at an angle.　　　　　5 strokes

一	丷	亓	平	平							

s— **suī** although

The full form of the character combines *mouth* 口, *insect* 虫 and *bird* 隹 to suggest the notion of *although*. In the simplified form, only the left component is retained.

Radical: 口 'mouth'   **Index # 50**

or   虫 'insect'   **Index # 142**

Character components: 口 + 虫   **Character configuration:**

Compounds, sentences and meanings

1. **虽 suī** although
   问题 虽 小, 但 很 典型。
   Wèntí suī xiǎo, dàn hěn diǎnxíng.
   The problem is trivial, but common.

2. **虽然 suīrán** although
   路上 虽然 很 辛苦, 但是 他 觉得
   Lùshàng suīrán hěn xīnkǔ, dànshì tā juéde
   很 高兴。
   hěn gāoxìng.
   Although the journey was tiring, he felt very happy.

3. **虽说 suīshuō** although
   虽说 我 已 认识 他 很 久 了, 但 我
   Suīshuō wǒ yǐ rènshi tā hěn jiǔ le, dàn wǒ
   并 不 了解 他。
   bìng bù liǎojiě tā.
   Though I've known him for a long time, I don't understand him at all.

The top rectangle is slightly narrower.										9 strokes
丶	冂	口	尸	吕	吕	串	虽	虫		

rán   right, correct

The character combines *flesh* 月, *dog* 犬 and *fire* 灬 to suggest *cooking the flesh of a dog over the fire*. It came to mean *burn*. Later it acquired the meaning of *right* or *correct*.

Radical: 灬 '4 dots of fire'

Index # 71

Character components: 月 + 犬 + 灬

Character configuration:

Compounds, sentences and meanings

1. 然 **rán**   right, correct
   他 不 以 为 然。
   Tā bù yǐ wéi rán.
   He doesn't think so.

2. 然而 **rán'ér**   but, however
   这 篇 文章 写得 不错，然而
   Zhè piān wénzhāng xiěde bùcuò, rán'ér
   还 可以 改进。
   hái kěyǐ gǎijìn.
   The essay is all right, but there is room for improvement.

3. 然后 **ránhòu**   then, afterwards
   我们 看了 一 场 电影，然后 就 回家了。
   Wǒmen kànle yì chǎng diànyǐng, ránhòu jiù huíjiā le.
   We saw a movie, and after that we went home.

4. 忽然 **hūrán**   suddenly
   我 正 要 出去，忽然 下起 大雨 来了。
   Wǒ zhèng yào chūqu, hūrán xiàqǐ dàyǔ lái le.
   I was about to go out when suddenly it started to rain heavily.

5. 果然 **guǒrán**   sure enough
   他 说 要 下雪，果然 就 下了。
   Tā shuō yào xiàxuě, guǒrán jiù xià le.
   He said it would snow, and sure enough it did.

The top left component slants slightly to the left.											12 strokes
丿	勺	夕	夕	夕-	夗	狁	狀	然	然	然	然

wū house, room

The character combines *dwelling* 尸 and *reach* 至 to suggest *a place a man reaches and stays*. It came to mean *room*.

Radical: 尸 'dwelling'

Index # 61

Character components: 尸 + 至

Character configuration:

Compounds, sentences and meanings

1. **屋 wū** house
   山上 有 一 座 小 屋。
   Shānshàng yǒu yí zuò xiǎo wū.
   There's a small house on the hill.

2. **屋顶 wūdǐng** roof
   我们 家 的 屋顶 要 修理。
   Wǒmen jiā de wūdǐng yào xiūlǐ.
   The roof of our house needs to be repaired.

3. **屋里 wūlǐ** inside the room
   请 到 屋里 坐。
   Qǐng dào wūlǐ zuò.
   Please come in and sit down.

4. **屋子 wūzi** room
   这 套 单元 有 三 间 屋子。
   Zhè tào dānyuán yǒu sān jiān wūzi.
   This apartment has three rooms.

5. **房屋 fángwū** housing
   这里 高 质量 的 房屋 短缺。
   Zhèlǐ gāo zhìliàng de fángwū duǎnquē.
   There's a shortage of quality housing here.

The middle horizontal stroke is the shortest.　　　**9 strokes**

㇕	㇕	尸	尸	尼	层	屋	屋	屋			

420

暖　**nuǎn**　warm

The character combines *sun* 日 and the phonetic 爰 to suggest the idea of *warmth*.

Radical: 日 'sun'

Character components: 日 + 爰

Index # 90

Character configuration: ⊟

Compounds, sentences and meanings

1. **暖　nuǎn**　warm
   天 暖 了。
   Tiān nuǎn le.
   It's getting warm.

2. **暖呼呼　nuǎnhūhū**　warm
   听了 这 番 话，我们 大家 心里
   Tīngle zhè fān huà, wǒmen dàjiā xīnlǐ
   暖呼呼 的。
   nuǎnhūhū de.
   The words warmed our hearts.

3. **暖和　nuǎnhuo**　nice and warm
   炉子 一 着，屋子 就 暖和 了。
   Lúzi yì zháo, wūzi jiù nuǎnhuo le.
   The room became warm when the fire got going.

4. **暖气　nuǎnqì**　central heating
   北京 不 冷，室内 有 暖气。
   Běijīng bù lěng, shìnèi yǒu nuǎnqì.
   It's not cold in Beijing, there's central heating.

5. **温暖　wēnnuǎn**　warm
   我 喜欢 温暖 的 天气。
   Wǒ xǐhuan wēnnuǎn de tiānqì.
   I like the warm weather.

There's a horizontal stroke above 友.　13 strokes

丨	冂	冂	日	日′	日″	日″	日″	日″	睅	睅	暖	暖

A. Look at the 16-character grid and CIRCLE words or phrases. They can be written horizontally or vertically. (Look at the circled characters in the Key if you are unsure.) Copy the word or phrase next to the grid and write down the pinyin and meaning.

					Word or phrase			Pinyin	Meaning
最	刮	风	沙	(i)	刮	风	沙	guā fēngshā	dust storm
虽	气	冷	内	(ii)					
然	讨	厌	暖	(iii)					
平	常	屋	温	(iv)					

B. Using the characters in the 16-character grid, convert the pinyin sentences into characters and write the English meaning.

(i)	Běijīng chūntiān hái bǐjiào lěng.								
(ii)	Zuì tǎoyàn shì guā fēngshā.								
(iii)	Qìwēn píngcháng 10 dù zuǒyòu.								
(iv)	Suīrán lěng, dàn wūlǐ yǒu nuǎnqì.								

C. Match the Chinese words with their English meaning.

(i)

春天	discuss
春 jié	safe and sound
讨 lùn	ordinary
沙发	spring
平 ān	Chinese New Year
平常	calm down
平 děng	sofa
平 jìng	equality

(ii)

然后	room
然 ér	housing
hū 然	then, afterwards
果然	central heating
屋子	suddenly
房屋	sure enough
暖气	but, however
温暖	warm

421

 qiū autumn

The character combines *grain* 禾 and *fire* 火 to refer to drying the grain stalks after the *autumn* harvest.

Radical: 禾 'grain'　　　　　　　　　**Index # 124**

Character components: 禾 + 火

Character configuration: ⊞

Compounds, sentences and meanings

1. **秋 qiū** autumn
   二零零一年 秋，美国 遭到 恐怖
   Èrlínglíngyīnián qiū, Měiguó zāodào kǒngbù
   份子 攻击。
   fènzi gōngjī.
   In the autumn of 2001, the United States was attacked by terrorists.

2. **秋季 qiūjì** autumn
   广州 每年 秋季有 一个 交易会。
   Guǎngzhōu měinián qiūjì yǒu yí ge jiāoyìhuì.
   There is a Trade Fair in Guangzhou every autumn.

3. **秋色 qiūsè** autumn scenery
   这里 秋色 宜人。
   Zhèlǐ qiūsè yírén.
   The autumn scenery here is delightful.

4. **秋收 qiūshōu** autumn harvest
   农民 都 忙着 秋收。
   Nóngmín dōu mángzhe qiūshōu.
   The farmers are all busy with the autumn harvest.

5. **秋天 qiūtiān** autumn
   秋天 是 北京 最好 的 季节。
   Qiūtiān shì Běijīng zuìhǎo de jìjié.
   Autumn is the loveliest season in Beijing.

The last stroke tapers off.　　　　　　　　　　　　**9 strokes**

ノ	二	千	禾	禾	禾	禾	秒	秋			

liáng cool

The character combines *ice* 冫 and *capital* 京 to suggest *cool weather*.

Radical: 冫 'ice'　　　　　　**Index # 7**

Character components: 冫 + 亠 + 口 + 小　　　**Character configuration:**

Compounds, sentences and meanings

1. **凉　liáng**　cool, cold
   天气　忽然　凉　了。
   Tiānqì hūrán liáng le.
   The weather has suddenly turned cold.

2. **凉拌　liángbàn**　(of food) cold and dressed
   with sauce
   我　喜欢　吃　凉拌面。
   Wǒ xǐhuan chī liángbànmiàn.
   I like cold noodles in sauce.

3. **凉爽　liángshuǎng**　nice and cool
   我　喜欢　凉爽　的　秋天。
   Wǒ xǐhuan liángshuǎng de qiūtiān.
   I like the brisk autumn days.

4. **凉快　liángkuài**　pleasantly cool
   这里　凉快，　坐下来　歇会儿。
   Zhèlǐ liángkuài, zuòxiàlai xiē huìr.
   *It's nice and cool here, let's sit down and
   have a rest.*

5. **凉鞋　liángxié**　sandals
   这　双　凉鞋　很　好看。
   Zhè shuāng liángxié hěn hǎokàn.
   This pair of sandals is very attractive.

The second stroke of 冫 is a rounded dot that lifts.　　　　**10 strokes**

丶	冫	冫	广	亠	冹	洁	涫	凉	凉		

jì   season

The character combines *grain* 禾 and the phonetic 子 to suggest that grains are grown according to seasons. Thus it means *season*.

Radical: 禾 'grain'   **Index # 124**

Character components: 禾 + 子   **Character configuration:**

Compounds, sentences and meanings

1. **季** jì   season
   昆明 的 气候 四季 如 春。
   Kūnmíng de qìhòu sìjì rú chūn.
   In Kunming it's like spring all year round.

2. **季节** jìjié   season
   秋天 是 北京 最 好 的 季节。
   Qiūtiān shì Běijīng zuì hǎo de jìjié.
   Autumn is the loveliest season in Beijing.

3. **季节性** jìjiéxìng   seasonal
   这 是 季节性 工作。
   Zhè shì jìjiéxìng gōngzuò.
   This is seasonal work.

4. **季候风** jìhòufēng   monsoon
   这里 的 天气 受 季候风 影响。
   Zhèlǐ de tiānqì shòu jìhòufēng yǐngxiǎng.
   The monsoon has an influence on the climate here.

5. **冬季** dōngjì   winter
   滑雪 是 冬季 体育 运动。
   Huáxuě shì dōngjì tǐyù yùndòng.
   Skiing is a winter sport.

The top stroke sweeps from right to left.							8 strokes
一	二	千	禾	禾	秂	季	季

424 **Full form**

节 jié festival 節

The full form of the character combines *bamboo* 竹 and *cut off* 即 to represent *a bamboo joint*. The simplified form uses *grass* ⺾ and *half a gem* 卩. It means *festival*.

Radical: ⺾ 'grass'   **Index # 42**

Character components: ⺾ + 卩   **Character configuration:**

Compounds, sentences and meanings

1. 节 **jié** session (measure word)
   我 每 个 星期 有 三 节 中文 课。
   Wǒ měi ge xīngqī yǒu sān jié Zhōngwén kè.
   I have three Chinese lessons a week.

2. 节假日 **jiéjiàrì** festivals and holidays
   每逢 节假日 黄山 有 很多 游人。
   Měiféng jiéjiàrì Huángshān yǒu hěnduō yóurén.
   During festivals and holidays, the Yellow Mountain has lots of tourists.

3. 节目 **jiémù** program
   你 想 看 什么 电视 节目?
   Nǐ xiǎng kàn shénme diànshì jiémù?
   Which TV program would you like to watch?

4. 节食 **jiéshí** on a diet
   要 保持 身材 苗条 就 得 节食。
   Yào bǎochí shēncái miáotiáo jiù děi jiéshí.
   You have to diet if you want to stay slim.

5. 中秋节 **Zhōngqiūjié** the Mid-Autumn Festival
   我 喜欢 中秋节 的 天气。
   Wǒ xǐhuan Zhōngqiūjié de tiānqì.
   I like the weather around the time of the Mid-Autumn Festival.

The fourth stroke ends with a hook.   5 strokes

一 十 艹 节 节

206

jiāo   countryside

The character combines *city* 阝 and the phonetic 交 which means *joining and crossing* to express the idea of a place where city and countryside cross each other. It means *outskirts*.

Radical: 阝 'right ear-lobe'   **Index # 28**

Character components: 交 + 阝   **Character configuration:**

Compounds, sentences and meanings

1. 郊   **jiāo**   suburb
   他 住 在 北京 西郊。
   Tā zhù zài Běijīng xījiāo.
   He lives in the western suburbs of Beijing.

2. 郊区   **jiāoqū**   suburb
   中关村 是 北京 的 一 个 郊区。
   Zhōngguāncūn shì Běijīng de yí ge jiāoqū.
   Zhongguancun is a suburb of Beijing.

3. 郊外   **jiāowài**   outskirts
   周末 我门 经常 去 郊外 玩儿。
   Zhōumò wǒmen jīngcháng qù jiāowài wánr.
   We often go to the countryside on the weekend.

4. 郊游   **jiāoyóu**   outing
   周末 我们 去 郊游, 你 感 兴趣 吗?
   Zhōumò wǒmen qù jiāoyóu, nǐ gǎn xìngqù ma?
   We're going out on the weekend. Would you like to come?

5. 城郊   **chéngjiāo**   outskirts of town
   城郊 的 房子 便宜。
   Chéngjiāo de fángzi piányi.
   Houses in the outer suburbs are inexpensive.

The seventh stroke is written like the figure 3.								8 strokes
丶	二	亠	六	产	交	交阝	郊	

Full form

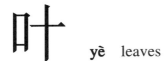
yè leaves

The full form of the character combines *grass* ⺿, *world* 世 and *tree* 木 to suggest the idea of *foliage*. The simplified form uses *mouth* 口 and *ten* 十 to represent the same idea.

Radical: 口 'mouth'   **Index # 50**

Character components: 口 + 十   **Character configuration:** ⊟

Compounds, sentences and meanings

1. **叶** yè leaves
   红 花 绿 叶 真 好看。
   Hóng huā lǜ yè zhēn hǎokàn.
   Red flowers set off by green leaves are really pretty.

2. **叶子** yèzi leaves
   秋天 了，树上 的叶子 都 红 了。
   Qiūtiān le, shùshang de yèzi dōu hóng le.
   It's autumn, the leaves have turned red.

3. **末叶** mòyè closing historical period
   清朝 末叶 政府 腐败。
   Qīngcháo mòyè, zhèngfǔ fǔbài.
   In the final days of the Manchu Dynasty, the government was corrupt.

4. **中叶** zhōngyè middle historical period
   二十世纪 中叶， 中国 发生了
   Èrshíshìjì zhōngyè, Zhōngguó fāshēngle
   巨大的 变化。
   jùdà de biànhuà.
   Tremendous changes took place in China in the middle of the twentieth century.

5. **树叶** shùyè leaves
   树叶 在 水上 漂着。
   Shùyè zài shuǐshang piāozhe.
   Leaves were floating on the water.

The horizontal stroke is shorter than the vertical stroke.								5 strokes
丨	丨丨	口	口一	叶				

427

 漂 **piāo/piǎo/piào** adrift/bleach/beautiful

The character combines *water* 氵 and the phonetic 票 to refer to the idea of *floating about*.
It also means *to bleach* or *to rinse*. A third meaning is *handsome*.

Radical: 氵 '3 drops of water'　　　　**Index # 32**

Character components: 氵 + 西 + 示　　　**Character configuration:**

Compounds, sentences and meanings

1. 漂 **piāo** float
   树叶 在 水上 漂着。
   Shùyè zài shuǐshang piāozhe.
   Leaves were floating on the water.

2. 漂游 **piāoyóu** lead a wandering life
   他 喜欢 四处 漂游。
   Tā xǐhuan sìchù piāoyóu.
   He likes to wander from place to place.

3. 漂白粉 **piǎobáifěn** bleaching powder
   有 没有 漂白粉？
   Yǒu méiyǒu piǎobáifěn?
   Do you have bleaching powder?

4. 漂亮 **piàoliang** pretty
   女孩子 都 喜欢 穿 漂亮 的衣服。
   Nǚháizi dōu xǐhuan chuān piàoliang de yīfu.
   Girls like to wear pretty dresses.

5. 漂亮话 **piàolianghuà** fancy talk
   说 漂亮话 没 用，干出来
   Shuō piàolianghuà méi yòng, gànchūlái
   才 算。
   cái suàn.
   Actions speak louder than words.

The eighth stroke is a short vertical without a bend.　　　**14 strokes**

丶	冫	氵	氵	汀	沪	沪	沪	湮	漂	漂	漂
漂											

209

Full form

极　jí　extreme

極

The full form of the character combines *tree* 木 and 亟 which represents *a pole stretching from floor to ceiling to support a roof*. Thus it means *extreme*.

Radical: 木 'tree'

Index # 81

Character components: 木 + 及

Character configuration:

Compounds, sentences and meanings

1. 极 **jí** extremely
   我 最近 忙极了。
   Wǒ zuìjìn mángjíle.
   I've been extremely busy lately.

2. 极大 **jídà** enormous
   人类 给自然 带来极大的 损害。
   Rénlèi gěi zìrán dàilái jídà de sǔnhài.
   Humans have caused great environmental harm.

3. 极端 **jíduān** extreme
   他 是 个 极端 个人主义者。
   Tā shì ge jíduān gèrénzhǔyìzhě.
   He is an out-and-out egoist.

4. 极力 **jílì** do everything possible
   我们 将 极力避免 发生 事故。
   Wǒmen jiāng jílì bìmiǎn fāshēng shìgù.
   We'll do our utmost to avoid accidents.

5. 南极 **Nánjí** the South Pole
   中国 也派 探险队 去过 南极。
   Zhōngguó yě pài tànxiǎnduì qùguo Nánjí.
   China also sent an expedition to the South Pole.

The sixth stroke has two bends.　　　　7 strokes

一	十	扌	木	朸	朹	极			

shù   tree

The full form of the character combines *tree* 木 and the non-character component 尌 to suggest the idea of something upright or a *tree*. The simplified form combines 木 with 对.

Radical: 木 'tree'

Index # 81

Character components: 木 + 又 + 寸

Character configuration:

Compounds, sentences and meanings

1. 树　shù　tree
   这 是 什么 树?
   Zhè shì shénme shù?
   What kind of tree is this?

2. 树立　shùlì　set up
   当 老师 要 树立 好 榜样。
   Dāng lǎoshī yào shùlì hǎo bǎngyàng.
   A teacher has to set a good example.

3. 树林　shùlín　forest
   前面 是 树林, 走不过去。
   Qiánmiàn shì shùlín, zǒubuguòqu.
   There's a forest ahead, we can't get through.

4. 树阴　shùyīn　the shade of a tree
   树阴 下面 凉快, 坐下来 歇 会儿。
   Shùyīn xiàmiàn liángkuài, zuòxiàlai xiē huǐr.
   It's nice and cool under the tree, let's sit down and have a rest.

5. 树枝　shùzhī　branch
   这 树枝 可以 用 来 做 拐杖。
   Zhè shùzhī kěyǐ yòng lái zuò guǎizhàng.
   This branch can be used as a walking stick.

The eighth stroke ends with a hook.								9 strokes
一	十	才	木	朾	权	枚	树	树

lín forest

The character combines two of the characters for *tree* 木, suggesting *trees* or *bamboo growing together in a woods*.

Radical: 木 'tree'   **Index # 81**

Character components: 木 + 木

Character configuration:

Compounds, sentences and meanings

1. **林 lín** forest
   前面　有　一个 竹林。
   Qiánmiàn yǒu yí ge zhúlín.
   There is a bamboo grove ahead.

2. **松林 sōnglín** pine forest
   黄山　有　很多　松林。
   Huángshān yǒu hěnduō sōnglín.
   There are many pine forests in the Yellow Mountain.

3. **林业 línyè** forestry
   很多 林业　工人　现在　面临　失业。
   Hěnduō línyè gōngrén xiànzài miànlín shīyè.
   Many forestry workers are now facing unemployment.

4. **山林 shānlín** wooded and hilly lands
   中国　政府　现在 保护 山林
   Zhōngguó zhèngfǔ xiànzài bǎohù shānlín
   地区。
   dìqū.
   The Chinese government is now protecting wooded and hilly lands.

5. **森林 sēnlín** forest
   森林 火灾　损失　很 大。
   Sēnlín huǒzāi sǔnshī hěn dà.
   Forest fires cause a great deal of damage.

The two horizontal strokes do not join.							8 strokes

一	十	才	木	木	杵	材	林				

A. Look at the 16-character grid and CIRCLE words or phrases. They can be written horizontally or vertically. (Look at the circled characters in the Key if you are unsure.) Copy the word or phrase next to the grid and write down the pinyin and meaning.

						Word or phrase			Pinyin	Meaning
叶	凉	快	游		(i)	凉	快		liángkuài	cool
树	看	漂	红		(ii)					
季	节	亮	郊		(iii)					
极	林	旅	外		(iv)					

B. Using the characters in the 16-character grid, convert the pinyin sentences into characters and write the English meaning.

(i)	Běijīng de qiūtiān hěn liángkuài.								
(ii)	Shì lǚyóu de hǎo jìjié.								
(iii)	Rénmen dào jiāowài qù kàn qiūyè.								
(iv)	Huángde, hóngde piàoliangjíle!								

C. Match the Chinese words with their English meaning.

(i)

凉 shuǎng	on a diet
凉鞋	rhythm
秋季	outing
节 shí	program (TV etc.)
节 zòu	nice and cool
节 mù	sandals
郊 qū	autumn
郊游	suburb

(ii)

漂亮话	extreme
极大	establish
极 duān	high-sounding words
极力	forest
树叶	enormous
树 lì	shade of a tree
树阴	do one's utmost
sēn 林	leaves

病 bìng sick, ill

The character combines *sickness* 疒 and the phonetic 丙 to refer to things connected with *sickness*.

Radical: 疒 'sickness'

Index # 112

Character components: 疒 + 丙

Character configuration:

Compounds, sentences and meanings

1. 病 **bìng** sick
   他 有 病。
   Tā yǒu bìng.
   He is ill.

2. 病假 **bìngjià** sick leave
   医生 给 我 三 天 病假。
   Yīshēng gěi wǒ sān tiān bìngjià.
   The doctor gave me three days' sick leave.

3. 病历 **bìnglì** medical history
   请 填上 病历。
   Qǐng tiánshàng bìnglì.
   Please fill in your medical history.

4. 病情 **bìngqíng** patient's condition
   孩子 的 病情 有 好转。
   Háizi de bìngqíng yǒu hǎozhuǎn.
   The child's condition took a turn for the better.

5. 病人 **bìngrén** patient
   这 家 医院 医生 不够, 病人 太 多。
   Zhè jiā yīyuàn yīshēng búgòu, bìngrén tài duō.
   This hospital does not have enough doctors; there are too many patients.

The sixth stroke is shorter than the one above it.										10 strokes
丶	亠	广	疒	疒	疒	疒	病	病	病	

tóu   head

The full form of the character combines *head* 页 and the phonetic 豆 to give the idea of *head*. In simplification, 头 is used.

Radical: 、 'dot'   **Index # 1**

Character components: 、 + 、 + 大   **Character configuration:** ☐

Compounds, sentences and meanings

1. **头** **tóu**   head
   走路 要 抬高 头。
   Zǒulù yào táigāo tóu.
   One should lift one's head when walking.

2. **头等** **tóuděng**   first class
   他 买 的 是 头等舱。
   Tā mǎi de shì tóuděngcāng.
   He bought tickets for a first-class cabin.

3. **头发** **tóufa**   hair
   她 把 头发 染成 金色。
   Tā bǎ tóufa rǎnchéng jīnsè.
   She dyed her hair blonde.

4. **头脑** **tóunǎo**   brains, mind
   她 很 有 头脑。
   Tā hěn yǒu tóunǎo.
   She has plenty of brains.

5. **头痛** **tóutòng**   (have a) headache
   我 头痛得 很 厉害。
   Wǒ tóutòngde hěn lìhai.
   I have a very bad headache.

End the last stroke firmly.   **5 strokes**

、	丷	三	头	头							

痛

tòng sore, hurt

The character combines *sickness* 疒 and the phonetic 甬 to suggest the sensation of *pain*.

Radical: 疒 'sickness'

Index # 112

Character components: 疒 + 甬

Character configuration:

Compounds, sentences and meanings

1. 痛 **tòng** pain
   这里 痛 不 痛?
   Zhèlǐ tòng bu tòng?
   Does it hurt here?

2. 痛哭 **tòngkū** weep bitterly
   她 为 这 件 事 痛哭了 一 场。
   Tā wèi zhè jiàn shì tòngkūle yì chǎng.
   She had a good cry about it.

3. 痛苦 **tòngkǔ** suffering
   我 得 离开 老家, 感到 很 痛苦。
   Wǒ děi líkāi lǎojiā, gǎndào hěn tòngkǔ.
   It pains me to have to leave my home.

4. 痛快 **tòngkuài** delighted
   今天 遇到了 一 件 不 痛快 的 事。
   Jīntiān yùdàole yī jiàn bú tòngkuài de shì.
   I had an unpleasant experience today.

5. 痛心 **tòngxīn** distressed
   这样 浪费 食物 令 人 痛心。
   Zhèyàng làngfèi shíwù lìng rén tòngxīn.
   It is distressing to see food being wasted like this.

The sixth stroke is a horizontal-bend. | **12 strokes**

| 、 | 亠 | 广 | 疒 | 疒 | 疒 | 疒 | 疒 | 病 | 病 | 痛 | 痛 | |

shāo burn

The full form of the character combines *fire* 火 and the phonetic 堯 to suggest the idea of something *burning*. The simplified form replaces the component 垚 with 戈.

Radical: 火 'fire'

Index # 75

Character components: 火 + 尧

Character configuration:

Compounds, sentences and meanings

1. **烧 shāo** burn
   干柴 好 烧。
   Gānchái hǎo shāo.
   Dry wood burns well.

2. **烧乳猪 shāo rǔzhū** roast suckling pig
   这 个 烧 乳猪 的 皮 很 脆。
   Zhè ge shāo rǔzhū de pí hěn cuì.
   The skin of this roast suckling pig is very crisp.

3. **烧饼 shāobǐng** sesame seed cake
   这 家 饭馆 的 烧饼 不错。
   Zhè jiā fànguǎn de shāobǐng búcuò.
   This restaurant makes nice sesame seed cakes.

4. **烧烤 shāokǎo** barbecue
   我 喜欢 吃 烧烤。
   Wǒ xǐhuan chī shāokǎo.
   I love barbecues.

5. **发烧 fāshāo** run a temperature
   你 有点 发烧, 应该 去 看 医生。
   Nǐ yǒudiǎn fāshāo, yīnggāi qù kàn yīshēng.
   You're running a temperature, you should see a doctor.

The top part of the phonetic component is made up of 3 strokes.										10 strokes		
丶	丷	少	火	灯	灶	烤	烤	烤	烧			

liáng/liàng   *measure/quantity*

The character combines *sun* 日, *one* 一 and the *Chinese measure of distance* 里 to suggest the idea of *using the sun to measure the passage of time*. By extension, it means *measure*.

Radical: 日 'sun'

Index # 90

Character components: 日 + 一 + 里

Character configuration:

Compounds, sentences and meanings

1. **量 liáng** measure
   我 给 你 量量 体温 吧。
   Wǒ gěi nǐ liángliang tǐwēn ba.
   Let me take your temperature.

2. **量词 liàngcí** measure word, quantifier
   中文 量词 很多。
   Zhōngwén liàngcí hěnduō.
   There are many measure words in Chinese.

3. **量力 liànglì** estimate strength or ability
   我们 应该 量力 而 行。
   Wǒmen yīnggāi liànglì ér xíng.
   We should do what we are capable of.

4. **气量 qìliàng** tolerance, forbearance
   气量 大 的 人 对 这点 小事 是
   Qìliàng dà de rén duì zhè diǎn xiǎoshì shì
   不会 介意 的。
   búhuì jièyì de.
   Broad-minded people don't bother about such trifles.

5. **力量 lìliang** power, force
   我 一定 尽 我的 力量 帮忙。
   Wǒ yídìng jìn wǒde lìliang bāngmáng.
   I'll certainly do everything in my power to help.

The second last horizontal stroke of 里 is shorter than the last one.											12 strokes
丶	冂	日	日	旦	昃	昻	昌	昌	畕	量	量

张 zhāng measure word

The full form of the character combines *bow* 弓 and the phonetic 長 to suggest the idea of *pulling a bow* or *open*.

Radical: 弓 'bow'

Index # 63

Character components: 弓 + 长

Character configuration:

Compounds, sentences and meanings

1. **张** zhāng measure word
   这 间 房 有 两 张 床。
   Zhè jiān fáng yǒu liǎng zhāng chuáng.
   There are two beds in this room.

2. **张开** zhāngkāi open
   张开 嘴。
   Zhāngkāi zuǐ.
   Open your mouth.

3. **紧张** jǐnzhāng nervous
   慢慢 讲，别 紧张。
   Mànmàn jiǎng, bié jǐnzhāng.
   Speak slowly, don't be nervous.

4. **张罗** zhāngluó get busy
   要 带 的 东西 早点儿 收拾 好，不要
   Yào dài de dōngxi zǎodiǎnr shōushí hǎo, búyào
   临时 张罗。
   línshí zhāngluó.
   Get your things ready in advance so as to avoid a last-minute rush.

5. **张扬** zhāngyáng make widely known
   这 事 还 没 定下来，先 别
   Zhè shì hái méi dìngxiàlai, xiān bié
   张扬出去。
   zhāngyángchūqu.
   The final decision hasn't been made yet, so don't spread this around.

Both downward strokes to left and the right on 长 are diagonals.

7 strokes

フ	ヲ	弓	弓ʼ	弘	张	张				

嘴

zuǐ mouth

The character combines *mouth* 口, *this* 此 and *corner* 角 to suggest the idea of *mouth*.

Radical: 口 'mouth'　　　　　　　　**Index # 50**

Character components: 口 + 此 + 角

Character configuration:

Compounds, sentences and meanings

1. **嘴** zuǐ　mouth
   闭上 嘴。
   Bìshàng zuǐ.
   Shut your mouth.

2. **嘴馋** zuǐchán　fond of good food
   他一见 有 好吃 的 东西 就 嘴馋。
   Tā yī jiàn yǒu hǎochī de dōngxi jiù zuǐchán.
   He starts drooling at the sight of good food.

3. **嘴尖** zuǐjiān　be choosy about what one eats
   别 嘴尖 了,给 你 什么 你 吃 什么。
   Biě zuǐjiān le, gěi nǐ shénme nǐ chī shénme.
   Don't be so choosy. Take what you're given.

4. **嘴快** zuǐkuài　have a loose tongue
   她 嘴快, 跟 谁 都 会 说。
   Tā zuǐkuài, gēn shéi dōu huì shuō.
   She's a gossip, she'll tell everyone.

5. **张嘴** zhāngzuǐ　open one's mouth (to say something)
   他 正要 张嘴, 一个 同学
   Tā zhèngyào zhāngzuǐ, yī ge tóngxué
   抢先 说 了。
   qiǎngxiān shuō le.
   He was on the verge of saying something when a classmate started to speak.

口 is stretched lengthwise to balance the components on the right.												16 strokes
丶	口	口	口丿	口卜	口卟	叱	叱丿	口此	口此	嘴	嘴	嘴
嘴	嘴	嘴										

mào give off

The character combines *speech* 曰 and *eye* 目 to suggest the idea of liquid or steam *coming out* or *overflowing*.

Radical: 曰 'speech'

Index # 91

Character components: 曰 + 目

Character configuration:

Compounds, sentences and meanings

1. 冒 **mào** give off
   水壶 正 冒着 气。
   Shuǐhū zhèng màozhe qì.
   The kettle is boiling.

2. 冒充 **màochōng** pretend to be (somebody or something else)
   他 冒充 记者 走进来。
   Tā màochōng jìzhě zǒujìnlai.
   He came in passing himself off as a journalist.

3. 冒牌 **màopái** fake
   这 是 冒牌 货。
   Zhè shì màopái huò.
   This is a fake.

4. 冒险 **màoxiǎn** take risk
   骑 自行车 得 戴 安全帽, 别 冒险。
   Qí zìxíngchē děi dài ānquánmào, bié màoxiǎn.
   Wear a helmet when riding a bicycle. Don't take the risk.

5. 感冒 **gǎnmào** common cold, flu
   医生 说 我 得了 感冒。
   Yīshēng shuō wǒ déle gǎnmào.
   The doctor said that I've got the flu.

The bottom component has two horizontal strokes inside.   9 strokes

丶	冂	冂	曰	冃	冐	冐	冒	冒			

Full form

药　**yào**　medicine

The full form of the character combines *grass* ⺿ and *happy* 樂 to suggest the idea that *certain plants* if taken will *restore health* and *make people happy*. It came to mean *medicine*.

Radical: ⺿ 'grass'

Index # 42

Character components: ⺿ + 纟 + 勹

Character configuration:

Compounds, sentences and meanings

1. **药　yào**　medicine
   你 吃过 药 了吗?
   Nǐ chīguo yào le ma?
   Have you taken your medicine?

2. **药材　yàocái**　medicinal materials
   人参 是 一 种 补身 药材。
   Rénshēn shì yì zhǒng bǔshēn yàocái.
   Ginseng is a tonic.

3. **药方　yàofāng**　prescription
   这 是 治 感冒 的 药方。
   Zhè shì zhì gǎnmào de yàofāng.
   This is the prescription for the flu.

4. **药店　yàodiàn**　pharmacy, chemist
   这 种 药 在 大 药店 才 有。
   Zhè zhǒng yào zài dà yàodiàn cái yǒu.
   This medicine is only available at large pharmacies.

5. **药水　yàoshuǐ**　liquid medicine, mixture
   这 药水 吃下去 就 见效。
   Zhè yàoshuǐ chīxiàqu jiù jiànxiào.
   This medicine works immediately.

The eighth stroke ends with a hook.　　　　　9 strokes

| 一 | 十 | 艹 | 艿 | 药 | 药 | 茐 | 药 | 药 | | |

情

qíng emotion

The character combines *upright heart* 忄 and the phonetic 青 which means *blue* or *pure* to represent a *pure and beautiful heart* or *tender and considerate feelings*. It means *emotions*.

Radical: 忄 **'upright heart'**　　　　**Index # 33**

Character components: 忄 + 青

Character configuration:

Compounds, sentences and meanings

1. **情** **qíng** emotion, affection
   她 情 不自禁 地 笑起来。
   Tā qíng bù zì jīn de xiàoqǐlai.
   She can't help laughing.

2. **情节** **qíngjié** plot
   这 个 剧本 情节 很 复杂。
   Zhè ge jùběn qíngjié hěn fùzá.
   The play has a very complicated plot.

3. **情况** **qíngkuāng** situation
   现在 情况 不同 了。
   Xiànzài qíngkuāng bùtóng le.
   Now things are different.

4. **情趣** **qíngqù** temperament and interest
   他们 两 人 情趣 相投。
   Tāmen liǎng rén qíngqù xiāngtóu.
   The two of them are compatible.

5. **情人** **qíngrén** lover
   情人 眼里 出 西施。
   Qíngrén yǎnlǐ chū Xīshī.
   The beloved is always beautiful. (Literally, Xishi, a famous beauty).

The fifth stroke is shorter than the one above it.　　　　11 strokes

| 丶 | 丷 | 忄 | 忄一 | 忄二 | 忄丰 | 忄丰 | 情 | 情 | 情 | 情 | | |

Quiz 44 (431–440)

A. Look at the 16-character grid and CIRCLE words or phrases. They can be written horizontally or vertically. (Look at the circled characters in the Key if you are unsure.) Copy the word or phrase next to the grid and write down the pinyin and meaning.

					Word or phrase				Pinyin	Meaning
药	紧	医	感	(i)	感	冒			gǎnmào	have the flu
嘴	体	温	冒	(ii)						
发	量	张	痛	(iii)						
烧	头	开	病	(iv)						

B. Using the characters in the 16-character grid, convert the pinyin sentences into characters and write the English meaning.

(i)	Wǒ bìngle. Tóutòng, fāshāo.									
(ii)	Liángliang tǐwēn ba, qǐng zhāngkāi zuǐ.									
(iii)	38 dù, bú yàojǐn, gǎnmào le.									
(iv)	Chī diǎn yào, guò jǐ tiān jiù hǎo le.									

C. Match the Chinese words with their English meaning.

(i)

病人	delighted
头发	tolerance
头脑	strength
痛 kǔ	hair
痛快	patient
痛心	brains, mind
气量	suffering
力量	distressed

(ii)

张 yáng	prescription
嘴快	fake
冒 pái	make widely known
冒 xiǎn	plot
药方	temperament and interest
情节	have a loose tongue
情 kuàng	take risk
情趣	situation

lǐ politeness/gift

The full form of the character has three components: *ritual* 礻, *song* 曲 and *beans* 豆. It is not clear how it came to mean *polite* or *manners*.

Radical: 礻 'ritual'   **Index # 78**

Character components: 礻 + 乚   **Character configuration:** ▯▯

Compounds, sentences and meanings

1. 礼 lǐ gift
   这 份 礼 很 重。
   Zhè fèn lǐ hěn zhòng.
   This is a generous gift.

2. 礼拜 lǐbài week
   今天 礼拜几?
   Jīntiān lǐbài jǐ?
   What day is it today?

3. 礼拜三 lǐbàisān Wednesday
   今天 礼拜三。
   Jīntiān Lǐbàisān.
   Today is Wednesday.

4. 礼节 lǐjié etiquette
   中国 有 很多 礼节跟 外国
   Zhōngguó yǒu hěnduō lǐjié gēn wàiguó
   不同。
   bùtóng.
   In China a lot of the rules of etiquette are different.

5. 礼貌 lǐmào courteous
   我 觉得 这么 早 就 走 不大 礼貌。
   Wǒ juéde zhème zǎo jiù zǒu búdà lǐmào.
   I don't think it'd be polite for us to leave so soon.

Note the difference between 礻 and 衤.   5 strokes

丶	㇇	㇒	礻	礼						

物

wù   thing

The character combines *cattle* 牛 and the phonetic 勿 to suggest the idea of an item or *thing*.

Radical: 牛 'cattle'

Index # 95

Character components: 牛 + 勿

Character configuration:

Compounds, sentences and meanings

1. **物** **wù** thing
   物 以 稀 为 贵。
   Wù yǐ xī wéi guì.
   Scarcity increases value.

2. **物价** **wùjià** commodity prices
   这 两 年 的 物价 稳定。
   Zhè liǎng nián de wùjià wěndìng.
   Prices in the last two years have remained stable.

3. **物品** **wùpǐn** goods
   不要 忘记 你 随身 携带 的 物品。
   Búyào wàngjì nǐ suíshēn xiédài de wùpǐn.
   Don't forget your personal belongings.

4. **食物** **shíwù** food
   他 住院 是 因为 食物 中毒。
   Tā zhùyuàn shì yīnwèi shíwù zhòngdú.
   He was hospitalized because of food poisoning.

5. **礼物** **lǐwù** gift
   他 送了 一 份 很 重 的 礼物。
   Tā sòngle yí fèn hěn zhòng de lǐwù.
   His present was very generous.

The sixth stroke is a horizontal-bend-hook.   8 strokes

ノ	⺧	牛	牛	牜	牊	物	物				

kè guest

The character combines *roof* 宀 and *stop for a while* 各 to suggest the idea of a person *visiting and stopping for a while*, that is, *guest* or *customer*.

Radical: 宀 'roof'

Index # 34

Character components: 宀 + 夂 + 口

Character configuration:

Compounds, sentences and meanings

1. **客 kè** guest
   家里 来 客 了。
   Jiālǐ lái kè le.
   We have a guest.

2. **客观 kèguān** objective
   她 看 问题 比较 客观。
   Tā kàn wèntí bǐjiào kèguān.
   She looks at problems objectively.

3. **客气 kèqi** polite
   他 对 人 很 客气。
   Tā duì rén hěn kèqi.
   He is very polite.

4. **客套话 kètàohuà** polite expressions
   "劳驾" 是 客套话。
   "Láojià" shì kètàohuà.
   The phrase "Excuse me" is a polite expression.

5. **顾客 gùkè** customer
   顾客 至上。
   Gùkè zhìshàng.
   The customer is always right.

Note the difference between 客 and 容.   9 strokes

丶	丷	宀	宁	夕	宏	宎	客	客			

 **yì** idea

The character combines *sound* 音 and *heart* 心 to represent the *oral expression of the thought*. It means *will* or *intention*.

Radical: 心 'heart'　　　　　　　　　　**Index # 76**

Character components: 音 + 心　　　　**Character configuration:**

Compounds, sentences and meanings

1. **意　yì**　trace, hint
   今天 的 天气 颇 有 秋 意。
   Jīntiān de tiānqì pō yǒu qiū yì.
   Today's weather has a hint of autumn.

2. **意见　yìjiàn**　idea, opinion
   我们的 意见 一致。
   Wǒmende yìjiàn yízhì.
   We have identical views.

3. **意思　yìsi**　meaning
   我 不 明白 你的 意思。
   Wǒ bù míngbai nǐde yìsi.
   I don't understand what you mean.

4. **没意思　méi yìsi**　boring, uninteresting
   这 本 书 没意思。
   Zhè běn shū méi yìsi.
   This book is boring.

5. **拿主意　ná zhǔyi**　make a decision
   究竟 去 不去, 你拿 主意 吧。
   Jiūjìng qù buqù, nǐ ná zhǔyi ba.
   Please decide whether to go or not.

The second horizontal stroke is longer.　　　　　　　**13 strokes**

| 丶 | 亠 | 亠 | 产 | 立 | 产 | 产 | 音 | 音 | 音 | 意 | 意 | 意 |

思 sī think

The character combines *brain* 田 and *mind* 心 to suggest *the thinking process*. Thus, it means *think*. When it comes after 意思 (yìsi), the character takes on the neutral tone.

Radical: 心 'heart'　　　　　　　　　**Index # 76**

Character components: 田 + 心　　　　**Character configuration:**

Compounds, sentences and meanings

1. 思　sī　think
   我 思, 故 我 在。
   Wǒ sī, gù wǒ zài.
   I think, therefore I am.

2. 思考　sīkǎo　think deeply
   大学 主要 培养 独立 思考。
   Dàxué zhǔyào péiyǎng dúlì sīkǎo.
   The main aim of a university education is to develop independent thinking.

3. 思路　sīlù　train of thought
   你的思路 很 清楚。
   Nǐde sīlù hěn qīngchu.
   You think very clearly.

4. 思索　sīsuǒ　think deeply
   我 一 夜 没　睡着，反复 思索 这 个
   Wǒ yí yè méi shuìzháo, fǎnfù sīsuǒ zhè ge
   问题。
   wèntí.
   I lay awake all night, turning the problem over and over in my mind.

5. 思想　sīxiǎng　thought
   美国　有　思想 自由。
   Měiguó yǒu sīxiǎng zìyóu.
   There is freedom of thought in the United States.

The vertical stroke does not cross the enclosing box.　　　　　　　9 strokes

丶	冂	曰	甲	田	甩	思	思	思			

chéng become

The character combines *spear* 戈 and the character component 勹 to give the meaning of *accomplished*.

Radical: 戈 'spear' **Index # 85**

Character components: 勹 + 戈 **Character configuration:**

Compounds, sentences and meanings

1. 成 **chéng** become
   他们 两 个 人 成了 好 朋友。
   Tāmen liǎng ge rén chéngle hǎo péngyou.
   The two of them became good friends.

2. 成绩 **chéngjī** result (of work or study)
   他的 学习 成绩 不太 好。
   Tāde xuéxí chéngjī bútài hǎo.
   He's not doing very well in his studies.

3. 成就 **chéngjiù** achievement
   她 是 个 很 有 成就 的 科学家。
   Tā shì ge hěn yǒu chéngjiù de kēxuéjiā.
   She is an accomplished scientist.

4. 成问题 **chéng wèntí** be a problem
   雨 再 不 停, 明天 的比赛 就 要
   Yǔ zài bù tíng, míngtiān de bǐsài jiù yào
   成 问题 了。
   chéng wèntí le.
   If the rain doesn't stop, I doubt we can have the competition tomorrow.

5. 完成 **wánchéng** finish
   她的 论文 完成 了。
   Tāde lùnwén wánchéng le.
   She has finished her thesis.

The third stroke is a horizontal-bend-hook. **6 strokes**

一	厂	厉	成	成	成								

敬 jìng respect

The character combines *careless* 苟 and *stick* 攵. It is not clear how this came to be associated with the idea of *respect*.

Radical: 攵 'tap'

Index # 99

Character components: 苟 + 攵

Character configuration:

Compounds, sentences and meanings

1. 敬 jìng respect
   敬 你 一 杯!
   Jìng nǐ yì bēi!
   To your health! (Literally, respectfully offer you a cup)

2. 敬佩 jìngpèi esteem, admire
   我 对 她的 文材 非常 敬佩。
   Wǒ duì tāde wéncái fēicháng jìngpèi.
   I have the highest regard for her literary ability.

3. 敬请 jìngqǐng kindly give
   敬请 指教。
   Jìngqǐng zhǐjiào.
   Kindly give me your advice.

4. 敬意 jìngyì respect
   一点 小 礼物, 不 成 敬意。
   Yìdiǎn xiǎo lǐwù, bù chéng jìngyì.
   Here's a small gift as a token of my regard.

5. 尊敬 zūnjìng respect, honor
   我们 都 非常 尊敬 他。
   Wǒmen dōu fēicháng zūnjìng tā.
   We have the greatest respect for him.

The second stroke of 攵 is a horizontal.

12 strokes

| 一 | 十 | 艹 | 艹 | 芍 | 芍 | 苟 | 苟 | 苟 | 苟 | 敬 | 敬 | |

zhù   express good wishes

The character combines *ritual* 礻 and *older brother* 兄 to express the idea of *showing respect when congratulating someone*. It means *congratulations*.

Radical: 礻 'ritual'   **Index # 78**

Character components: 礻 + 兄

Character configuration:

Compounds, sentences and meanings

1. 祝 **zhù**   congratulate
   祝 你 生日 快乐!
   Zhù nǐ shēngrì kuàilè!
   Happy birthday!

2. 祝福 **zhùfú**   blessing
   为 你 祝福。
   Wèi nǐ zhùfú.
   Blessings on you.

3. 祝贺 **zhùhè**   congratulate
   祝贺 你 生了 一 个 女儿。
   Zhùhè nǐ shēngle yī ge nǚ'ér.
   Congratulations! You have a daughter.

4. 祝愿 **zhùyuàn**   wish
   致 以 良好 的 祝愿。
   Zhì yǐ liánghǎo de zhùyuàn.
   With best wishes.

5. 庆祝 **qìngzhù**   celebrate
   我们 去 饭馆儿 庆祝 父亲的 生日。
   Wǒmen qù fànguǎnr qìngzhù fùqin de shēngrì.
   We're going to a restaurant to celebrate dad's birthday.

Note the difference between 礻 and 衤.   **9 strokes**

丶	亍	礻	礻	礻	祀	祀	祀	祝			

Full form

 lè/yuè music/joy

The full form of the character depicts a rough sketch of a *hand-drum on a wooden stand*. It came to mean *music* (pronounced **lè**). It also means *happy* (pronounced **yuè**).

Radical: 丿 **'downward-left stroke'**

Index # 4

Character components: 丿 + 乚 + 小

Character configuration: ☐

Compounds, sentences and meanings

1. **乐　lè**　laugh, be amused
   他 说 的 笑话 把 大家 都 逗 乐了。
   Tā shuō de xiàohuà bǎ dàjiā dōu dòu lè le.
   His joke made everyone laugh.

2. **快乐　kuàilè**　happy
   我的 童年 过得 很 快乐。
   Wǒde tóngnián guòde hěn kuàilè.
   I had a happy childhood.

3. **乐观　lèguān**　optimistic
   我 对 中国 的 将来 很 乐观。
   Wǒ duì Zhōngguó de jiānglái hěn lèguān.
   I'm optimistic about China's future.

4. **乐器　yuèqì**　musical instrument
   这 是 什么 乐器?
   Zhè shì shénme yuèqì?
   What sort of musical instrument is this?

5. **音乐　yīnyuè**　music
   我 喜欢 听 古典 音乐。
   Wǒ xǐhuan tīng gǔdiǎn yīnyuè.
   I like classical music.

The second stroke is a slanting-bend-horizontal.											5 strokes
一	匚	乐	乐	乐							

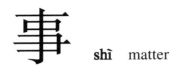

450

事　*shì*　matter

The character combines *scribe* 吏 and *hand* 手 to give the idea that when a scribe put something down in writing, he was recording a *matter*. It also means a *thing*.

Radical: 一 'horizontal stroke'　　**Index # 2**

Character components: 一 + 口 + ヨ + 亅

Character configuration: ☐

Compounds, sentences and meanings

1. 事　**shì**　matter
   我把这件事忘了。
   Wǒ bǎ zhè jiàn shì wàng le.
   I've forgotten all about it.

2. 事情　**shìqing**　matter
   我把这件事情忘了。
   Wǒ bǎ zhè jiàn shìqing wàng le.
   I've forgotten all about it

3. 事故　**shìgù**　accident
   路滑慢驶，防止发生事故。
   Lù huá màn shǐ, fángzhǐ fāshēng shìgù.
   The road is slippery, try to avoid accidents.

4. 事后　**shìhòu**　after the event
   不要老是作事后的批评。
   Búyào lǎoshì zuò shìhòu de pīpíng.
   Don't get into the habit of criticizing after the event.

5. 事先　**shìxiān**　in advance, beforehand
   应该事先作好准备。
   Yīnggāi shìxiān zuòhǎo zhǔnbèi.
   We should get everything ready beforehand.

The vertical stroke ends with a hook.							8 strokes
一	丆	丆	写	写	写	写	事

A. Look at the 16-character grid and CIRCLE words or phrases. They can be written horizontally or vertically. (Look at the circled characters in the Key if you are unsure.) Copy the word or phrase next to the grid and write down the pinyin and meaning.

					Word or phrase				Pinyin	Meaning
礼	物	事	万	(i)	礼	物			lǐwù	gift
日	客	快	乐	(ii)						
祝	气	神	意	(iii)						
成	给	敬	思	(iv)						

B. Using the characters in the 16-character grid, convert the pinyin sentences into characters and write the English meaning.

(i)	Zhè shì gěi nǐ de shēngrì lǐwù.								
(ii)	Nín tài kèqi le!								
(iii)	Yīdiǎn xiǎo yìsi, bù chéng jìngyì.								
(iv)	Zhù shēngrì kuàilè, wànshì-rúyì!								

C. Match the Chinese words with their English meaning.

(i)

礼节　　　　　think deeply
礼 mào　　　　commodity prices
物价　　　　　opinion
gù 客　　　　　etiquette
意见　　　　　courtesy
没意思　　　　thought
思 kǎo　　　　customer
思想　　　　　boring

(ii)

成就　　　　　finish
wán 成　　　　music
zūn 敬　　　　matter
qìng 祝　　　　achievement
乐 guān　　　　celebrate
音乐　　　　　optimistic
事情　　　　　respect
事 gù　　　　　accident

CHARACTER BUILDING 9 (401–450)

A. Memorize the following radicals and their English names. As a review exercise, write the pinyin and meaning of each example:

1. 　[、] 　'dot'
　　　头 (＿＿＿＿) ＿＿＿＿＿＿ ; 为 (＿＿＿＿) ＿＿＿＿＿＿ .

2. 　[一] 　'horizontal stroke'
　　　平 (＿＿＿＿) ＿＿＿＿＿＿ ; 事 (＿＿＿＿) ＿＿＿＿＿＿ .

3. 　[丿] 　'downward-left stroke'
　　　乐 (＿＿＿＿) ＿＿＿＿＿＿ ; 向 (＿＿＿＿) ＿＿＿＿＿＿ .

4. 　[亠] 　'top of 六 '
　　　夜 (＿＿＿＿) ＿＿＿＿＿＿ ; 交 (＿＿＿＿) ＿＿＿＿＿＿ .

5. 　[冫] 　'ice'
　　　凉 (＿＿＿＿) ＿＿＿＿＿＿ ; 冷 (＿＿＿＿) ＿＿＿＿＿＿ .

6. 　[讠] 　'word'
　　　讨 (＿＿＿＿) ＿＿＿＿＿＿ ; 许 (＿＿＿＿) ＿＿＿＿＿＿ .

7. 　[厂] 　'dwelling'
　　　厌 (＿＿＿＿) ＿＿＿＿＿＿ ; 厕 (＿＿＿＿) ＿＿＿＿＿＿ .

8. 　[刂] 　'upright knife'
　　　刮 (＿＿＿＿) ＿＿＿＿＿＿ ; 刚 (＿＿＿＿) ＿＿＿＿＿＿ ;

9. 　[亻] 　'upright person'
　　　低 (＿＿＿＿) ＿＿＿＿＿＿ ; 但 (＿＿＿＿) ＿＿＿＿＿＿ .

10. [阝] 　'left ear-lobe'
　　　阴 (＿＿＿＿) ＿＿＿＿＿＿ ; 附 (＿＿＿＿) ＿＿＿＿＿＿ .

11. [阝] 　'right ear-lobe'
　　　郊 (＿＿＿＿) ＿＿＿＿＿＿ ; 邮 (＿＿＿＿) ＿＿＿＿＿＿ .

12. [力] 　'strength'
　　　力 (＿＿＿＿) ＿＿＿＿＿＿ ; 办 (＿＿＿＿) ＿＿＿＿＿＿ .

13. [氵] 　'3 drops of water'
　　　沙 (＿＿＿＿) ＿＿＿＿＿＿ ; 温 (＿＿＿＿) ＿＿＿＿＿＿ .
　　　漂 (＿＿＿＿) ＿＿＿＿＿＿ ; 清 (＿＿＿＿) ＿＿＿＿＿＿ .

14. [忄] 　'upright heart'
　　　情 (＿＿＿＿) ＿＿＿＿＿＿ ; 忙 (＿＿＿＿) ＿＿＿＿＿＿ .

15. [宀] 'roof'

客 (_____) _____ ； 定 (_____) _____ .

16. [广] 'broad'

度 (_____) _____ ； 应 (_____) _____ .

17. [艹] 'grass'

节 (_____) _____ ； 药 (_____) _____ .

18. [扌] 'hand'

报 (_____) _____ ； 把 (_____) _____ .

19. [口] 'mouth'

叶 (_____) _____ ； 虽 (_____) _____ ；

嘴 (_____) _____ .

20. [尸] 'dwelling'

屋 (_____) _____ ； 局 (_____) _____ .

21. [纟] 'silk'

级 (_____) _____ ； 红 (_____) _____ .

22. [灬] '4 dots of fire'

然 (_____) _____ ； 热 (_____) _____ .

23. [火] 'fire'

烧 (_____) _____ ； 灯 (_____) _____ .

24. [心] 'heart'

意 (_____) _____ ； 思 (_____) _____ .

25. [礻] 'ritual'

礼 (_____) _____ ； 祝 (_____) _____ .

26. [木] 'tree'

林 (_____) _____ ； 极 (_____) _____ ；

树 (_____) _____ ； 果 (_____) _____ .

27. [戈] 'spear'

成 (_____) _____ ； 我 (_____) _____ .

28. [日] 'sun'

春 (_____) _____ ； 晴 (_____) _____ ；

量 (_____) _____ ； 暖 (_____) _____ .

29. [曰] 'speech'

冒 (_____) _____ ； 最 (_____) _____ .

30. ［牛］ 'cattle'

物 (＿＿＿＿) ＿＿＿＿＿＿＿ ； 特 (＿＿＿＿) ＿＿＿＿＿＿＿ .

31. ［攵］ 'tap'

敬 (＿＿＿＿) ＿＿＿＿＿＿＿ ； 改 (＿＿＿＿) ＿＿＿＿＿＿＿ .

32. ［疒］ 'sickness'

病 (＿＿＿＿) ＿＿＿＿＿＿＿ ； 痛 (＿＿＿＿) ＿＿＿＿＿＿＿ .

33. ［禾］ 'grain'

秋 (＿＿＿＿) ＿＿＿＿＿＿＿ ； 季 (＿＿＿＿) ＿＿＿＿＿＿＿ .

34. ［页］ 'page'

预 (＿＿＿＿) ＿＿＿＿＿＿＿ ； 题 (＿＿＿＿) ＿＿＿＿＿＿＿ .

B. Write the pinyin and meaning against the characters which share the following components. (Note that these components are not necessarily used as radicals.)

1. ［及］ 服 (＿＿＿＿) ＿＿＿＿＿＿ ； 报 (＿＿＿＿) ＿＿＿＿＿＿ .

2. ［月］ 阴 (＿＿＿＿) ＿＿＿＿＿＿ ； 肥 (＿＿＿＿) ＿＿＿＿＿＿ .

3. ［舌］ 刮 (＿＿＿＿) ＿＿＿＿＿＿ ； 适 (＿＿＿＿) ＿＿＿＿＿＿ .

4. ［至］ 屋 (＿＿＿＿) ＿＿＿＿＿＿ ； 到 (＿＿＿＿) ＿＿＿＿＿＿ .

5. ［寸］ 讨 (＿＿＿＿) ＿＿＿＿＿＿ ； 对 (＿＿＿＿) ＿＿＿＿＿＿ .

6. ［京］ 凉 (＿＿＿＿) ＿＿＿＿＿＿ ； 就 (＿＿＿＿) ＿＿＿＿＿＿ .

REVIEW 9 (401–450)

The following are words and phrases classified under parts of speech. Write their pinyin and meaning.

Nouns

预报 (＿＿＿＿) ＿＿＿＿＿ ； 力量 (＿＿＿＿) ＿＿＿＿＿ ；

力气 (＿＿＿＿) ＿＿＿＿＿ ； 级别 (＿＿＿＿) ＿＿＿＿＿ ；

温度 (＿＿＿＿) ＿＿＿＿＿ ； 风度 (＿＿＿＿) ＿＿＿＿＿ ；

夜间 (＿＿＿＿) ＿＿＿＿＿ ； 夜生活 (＿＿＿＿) ＿＿＿＿＿ ；

夜景 (＿＿＿＿) ＿＿＿＿＿ ； 春天 (＿＿＿＿) ＿＿＿＿＿ ；

春节 (＿＿＿＿) ＿＿＿＿＿ ； 春风 (＿＿＿＿) ＿＿＿＿＿ ；

沙发 (＿＿＿＿) ＿＿＿＿＿ ； 沙子 (＿＿＿＿) ＿＿＿＿＿ ；

屋子 (＿＿＿＿) ＿＿＿＿＿ ； 房屋 (＿＿＿＿) ＿＿＿＿＿ ；

暖气 (＿＿＿＿) ＿＿＿＿＿ ； 秋季 (＿＿＿＿) ＿＿＿＿＿ ；

秋色 (＿＿＿＿) ＿＿＿＿＿ ； 秋天 (＿＿＿＿) ＿＿＿＿＿ ；

凉鞋 (＿＿＿＿) ＿＿＿＿＿ ; 季节 (＿＿＿＿) ＿＿＿＿＿ ;

季候风 (＿＿＿) ＿＿＿＿＿ ; 冬季 (＿＿＿＿) ＿＿＿＿＿ ;

节假日 (＿＿＿＿) ＿＿＿＿＿ ; 郊外 (＿＿＿＿) ＿＿＿＿＿ ;

城郊 (＿＿＿＿) ＿＿＿＿＿ ; 叶子 (＿＿＿＿) ＿＿＿＿＿ ;

树叶 (＿＿＿＿) ＿＿＿＿＿ ; 树林 (＿＿＿＿) ＿＿＿＿＿ ;

树阴 (＿＿＿＿) ＿＿＿＿＿ ; 山林 (＿＿＿＿) ＿＿＿＿＿ ;

漂亮话 (＿＿＿) ＿＿＿＿＿ ; 南极 (＿＿＿＿) ＿＿＿＿＿ ;

病假 (＿＿＿＿) ＿＿＿＿＿ ; 病情 (＿＿＿＿) ＿＿＿＿＿ ;

病人 (＿＿＿＿) ＿＿＿＿＿ ; 头发 (＿＿＿＿) ＿＿＿＿＿ ;

头脑 (＿＿＿＿) ＿＿＿＿＿ ; 量词 (＿＿＿＿) ＿＿＿＿＿ ;

气量 (＿＿＿＿) ＿＿＿＿＿ ; 感冒 (＿＿＿＿) ＿＿＿＿＿ ;

药方 (＿＿＿＿) ＿＿＿＿＿ ; 药水 (＿＿＿＿) ＿＿＿＿＿ ;

情节 (＿＿＿＿) ＿＿＿＿＿ ; 情趣 (＿＿＿＿) ＿＿＿＿＿ ;

情人 (＿＿＿＿) ＿＿＿＿＿ ; 事情 (＿＿＿＿) ＿＿＿＿＿ ;

物价 (＿＿＿＿) ＿＿＿＿＿ ; 礼物 (＿＿＿＿) ＿＿＿＿＿ ;

礼节 (＿＿＿＿) ＿＿＿＿＿ ; 动物园 (＿＿＿) ＿＿＿＿＿ ;

意见 (＿＿＿＿) ＿＿＿＿＿ ; 意思 (＿＿＿＿) ＿＿＿＿＿ ;

主意 (＿＿＿＿) ＿＿＿＿＿ ; 思路 (＿＿＿＿) ＿＿＿＿＿ ;

思想 (＿＿＿＿) ＿＿＿＿＿ ; 敬意 (＿＿＿＿) ＿＿＿＿＿ ;

成就 (＿＿＿＿) ＿＿＿＿＿ ; 音乐 (＿＿＿＿) ＿＿＿＿＿ ;

Measure Word 节 (＿＿＿＿＿) ＿＿＿＿＿ .

Verbs 报告 (＿＿＿＿) ＿＿＿＿＿ ; 报名 (＿＿＿＿) ＿＿＿＿＿ ;

力求 (＿＿＿＿) ＿＿＿＿＿ ; 度过 (＿＿＿＿) ＿＿＿＿＿ ;

度假 (＿＿＿＿) ＿＿＿＿＿ ; 漂游 (＿＿＿＿) ＿＿＿＿＿ ;

头痛 (＿＿＿＿) ＿＿＿＿＿ ; 发烧 (＿＿＿＿) ＿＿＿＿＿ ;

量力 (＿＿＿＿) ＿＿＿＿＿ ; 张开 (＿＿＿＿) ＿＿＿＿＿ ;

张嘴 (＿＿＿＿) ＿＿＿＿＿ .

Adjectives 中级 (＿＿＿＿) ＿＿＿＿＿ ; 高级 (＿＿＿＿) ＿＿＿＿＿ ;

温暖 (＿＿＿＿) ＿＿＿＿＿ ; 阴黑 (＿＿＿＿) ＿＿＿＿＿ ;

阴凉 (＿＿＿＿) ＿＿＿＿＿ ; 讨厌 (＿＿＿＿) ＿＿＿＿＿ ;

不讨好 (＿＿＿) ＿＿＿＿＿ ; 暖和 (＿＿＿＿) ＿＿＿＿＿ ;

凉快 (_____) _____ ; 漂亮 (_____) _____ ;

极大 (_____) _____ ; 痛快 (_____) _____ ;

痛心 (_____) _____ ; 紧张 (_____) _____ ;

嘴快 (_____) _____ ; 客气 (_____) _____ ;

没意思 (_____) _____ ; 快乐 (_____) _____ .

Adverbs 平常 (_____) _____ ; 然后 (_____) _____ ;

果然 (_____) _____ ; 极力 (_____) _____ ;

事先 (_____) _____ ; 事后 (_____) _____ ;

Conjunctions 虽然 (_____) _____ ; 虽说 (_____) _____ .

WORD/SENTENCE PUZZLE 9

Find and circle words, phrases and sentences hidden in the puzzle. They can be found horizontally from left to right or vertically . The lines across and down are indicated by numbers. Write their meaning next to the pinyin. The first one is done for you.

ACROSS

1. Měitiān guāfēng, zhēn tǎoyàn.   *It's been windy every day. It's annoying!*

4. Wǒ kànle yì chǎng diànyǐng, ránhòu jiù huíjiā le.   _____

7. Zhōngguó de lǐjié gēn wàiguó bù yíyàng.   _____

9. Wǒ bù míngbai nǐde yìsi.   _____

12. (i) ná zhǔyi   _____
    (ii) qīnglǐ   _____

14. Wàimiàn lěng, róngyì zháoliáng.   _____

DOWN

1. Wǒ xǐhuan Zhōngqiūjié.   _____

3. Tiān qíng le.   _____

4. Yìdiǎn xiǎo lǐwù, bù chéng jìngyì.   _____

6. (i) diànhuà   _____
    (ii) Báitiān wǒ shuìbuzháo.   _____

7. jiāowài   _____

8. Guówài de qìchē hěn guì.   _____

9. hòuguǒ _____

10. Sīlù hěn qīngchu. _____

11. Nǐ jǐ diǎn huíjiā? _____

13. Qiūtiān dàole, shùshàng de yèzi dōu hóng le. _____

	1	2	3	4	5	6	7	8	9	10	11	12	13
1	鞋	附	教	世	行	容	拐	议	度	夜	你	俗	秋
2	预	每	天	刮	风	真	讨	厌	阴	黑	几	找	天
3	树	帮	晴	表	真	力	极	温	低	曲	点	建	到
4	我	看	了	一	场	电	影	然	后	就	回	家	了
5	喜	价	蓝	点	像	话	紧	河	果	容	家	衬	树
6	欢	病	漂	小	报	事	郊	气	特	别	像	春	上
7	中	国	的	礼	节	跟	外	国	不	一	样	平	的
8	秋	乐	英	物	季	场	暖	外	台	肥	然	虽	叶
9	节	昨	我	不	明	白	你	的	意	思	痛	如	子
10	向	把	林	成	许	天	城	汽	灯	路	烧	会	都
11	量	头	为	敬	客	我	讲	车	楚	很	张	出	红
12	颜	拿	主	意	她	睡	理	很	祝	清	理	白	了
13	语	色	出	新	成	不	心	贵	拿	楚	米	题	公
14	外	面	冷	容	易	着	凉	嘴	冒	药	黄	因	情

喝

hē   drink

The character combines *mouth* 口 and the phonetic 曷 to suggest *drinking*.

Radical: 口 'mouth'

Index # 50

Character components: 口 + 日 + 勹

Character configuration:

Compounds, sentences and meanings

1. **喝** hē drink
   你 喝 什么 饮料?
   Nǐ hē shénme yǐnliào?
   What would you like to drink?

2. **喝墨水** hē mòshuǐ drink ink (meaning: go to school)
   他 没 喝过 几 年 墨水。
   Tā méi hēguo jǐ nián mòshuǐ.
   He's had only a few years of school.

3. **喝茶** hēchá drink tea
   中国人 有 喝茶 的 习惯。
   Zhōngguórén yǒu hēchá de xíguàn.
   Chinese people drink a lot of tea.

4. **喝醉** hēzuì drunk
   昨晚 他 喝醉了。
   Zuówǎn tā hēzuì le.
   He was drunk last night.

5. **好喝** hǎohē tasty (drink)
   你 觉得 中国 的 啤酒 好喝 吗?
   Nǐ juéde Zhōngguó de píjiǔ hǎohē ma?
   Do you like Chinese beer?

The ninth stroke ends with a hook.   **12 strokes**

| 丶 | 口 | 口 | 口丶 | 口冂 | 口日 | 口日 | 口甲 | 喝 | 喝 | 喝 | 喝 | |

yǐn drink

The full form of the character combines *food* 食 and *owe* 欠 to suggest the idea of *drinking*.

Radical: 饣 'food'

Index # 59

Character components: 饣 + 欠

Character configuration:

Compounds, sentences and meanings

1. **饮** yǐn drink
   饮 水 不忘 掘井人。
   Yǐn shuǐ búwàng juéjǐngrén.
   When you drink the water, think of those who dug the well.

2. **饮料** yǐnliào drinks
   你 喝 什么 饮料?
   Nǐ hē shénme yǐnliào?
   What would you like to drink?

3. **饮食** yǐnshí food and drink
   要 注意 饮食 卫生。
   Yào zhùyì yǐnshí wèishēng.
   We have to pay attention to culinary hygiene.

4. **饮用水** yǐnyòngshuǐ drinking water
   这 不是 饮用水。
   Zhè búshì yǐnyòngshuǐ.
   This is not drinking water.

5. **冷饮** lěngyǐn cold drink
   天气 这么 热,要 点 冷饮 吗?
   Tiānqì zhème rè, yào diǎn lěngyǐn ma?
   It's so hot today, what about some cold drinks?

The second stroke of 饣 is a horizontal-hook.　　　　**7 strokes**

ノ	⺈	饣	饮	饮	饮	饮				

料 **liào** material

The character combines *rice* 米 and *ladle for measuring* 斗 to suggest the idea of sorting *material*.

Radical: 米 'rice'

Character components: 米 + 斗

Index # 134

Character configuration:

Compounds, sentences and meanings

1. 料 **liào** material
   我 不是 唱歌 的 料。
   Wǒ búshì chànggē de liào.
   I haven't got the makings of a singer.

2. 料到 **liàodào** foresee, expect
   没 料到 他 会 来。
   Méi liàodào tā huì lái.
   We didn't expect him to come.

3. 料理 **liàolǐ** take care of
   孩子们 已经 能 自己 料理 生活。
   Háizimen yǐjīng néng zìjǐ liàolǐ shēnghuó.
   The children can take care of themselves now.

4. 料想 **liàoxiǎng** expect
   这 真 是 料想不到 的 事情。
   Zhè zhēn shì liàoxiǎngbudào de shìqing.
   Who would have thought that would happen?

5. 材料 **cáiliào** material
   做 个 书架 需要 些 什么 材料?
   Zuò ge shūjià xūyào xiē shénme cáiliào?
   What materials do you need to make a bookcase?

The last stroke tapers.   10 strokes

丶	丷	丷	斗	米	米	米	米	料	料			

奶 nǎi milk

The character combines *female* 女 and the phonetic 乃 to suggest the female breasts from which *milk* is derived.

Radical: 女 'female'

Index # 65

Character components: 女 + 乃

Character configuration:

Compounds, sentences and meanings

1. **奶** **nǎi** milk
   我的 孩子 都 是 奶 大 的。
   Wǒde háizi dōu shì nǎi dà de.
   All my children were breast-fed.

2. **奶茶** **nǎichá** tea with milk
   我 习惯 喝 奶茶。
   Wǒ xíguàn hē nǎichá.
   I'm used to milk in my tea.

3. **奶粉** **nǎifěn** powdered milk
   冲 一 杯 奶粉。
   Chōng yī bēi nǎifěn.
   Mix a cup of powdered milk.

4. **奶油** **nǎiyóu** cream
   草莓 放 点儿 奶油 很 好吃。
   Cǎoméi fàng diǎnr nǎiyóu hěn hǎochī.
   Strawberries taste better with cream.

5. **牛奶** **niúnǎi** milk
   牛奶 是 很 有 营养 的 食品。
   Niúnǎi shì hěn yǒu yíngyǎng de shípǐn.
   Milk is a very nutritious food.

The fourth stroke is a horizontal-bend-bend-hook. 5 strokes

㇗	女	女	奶	奶							

茶 chá tea

The character combines *grass* 艹, *people* 人 and *tree* 木 to suggest the idea that people pick the tips of the leaves of certain trees and make them into *tea*.

Radical: 艹 'grass' **Index # 42**

Character components: 艹 + 人 + 木 **Character configuration:**

Compounds, sentences and meanings

1. 茶 **chá** tea
   我们 喝 点儿 茶 吧。
   Wǒmen hē diǎnr chá ba.
   Let's have some tea.

2. 茶褐色 **cháhèsè** dark brown
   我 觉得 茶褐色 那 件 也 不错。
   Wǒ juéde cháhèsè nà jiàn yě búcuò.
   I think the dark brown one looks quite nice.

3. 茶壶 **cháhú** teapot
   我 喜欢 这 个 小 茶壶。
   Wǒ xǐhuan zhè ge xiǎo cháhú.
   I like this little teapot.

4. 茶碗 **cháwǎn** tea-bowl (without handles)
   这 是 茶碗，那 是 茶杯。
   Zhè shì cháwǎn, nà shì chábēi.
   This is a tea-bowl, that is a teacup.

5. 茶叶 **cháyè** tea leaves, tea
   龙井 是 名贵 的 茶叶。
   Lóngjǐng shì míngguì de cháyè.
   Longjing tea is famous and precious.

The last two strokes do not meet in the center. **9 strokes**

| 一 | 十 | 艹 | 艹 | 犬 | 苶 | 茶 | 茶 | 茶 | | | |

糖

táng sugar

The character combines *rice* 米 and the phonetic 唐. It is not clear how it came to mean *sugar*.

Radical: 米 'rice'

Character components: 米 + 唐

Index # 134

Character configuration: ⬚

Compounds, sentences and meanings

1. **糖** táng sugar
   你喝茶搁糖吗?
   Nǐ hē chá gē táng ma?
   Do you take sugar in your tea?

2. **糖醋** tángcù sweet and sour
   我 喜欢 吃 糖醋 排骨。
   Wǒ xǐhuan chī tángcù páigǔ.
   I like sweet and sour spare ribs.

3. **糖果** tángguǒ sweets, candy
   你吃 糖果 吗?
   Nǐ chī tángguǒ ma?
   Do you eat candy?

4. **糖尿病** tángniàobìng diabetes
   很多 老人 都 有 糖尿病。
   Hěnduō lǎorén dōu yǒu tángniàobìng.
   Many elderly people have diabetes.

5. **白糖** báitáng refined sugar
   我们 只有 白糖, 没有 黄糖。
   Wǒmen zhǐyǒu báitáng, méiyǒu huángtáng.
   We have only white sugar, no brown sugar.

The middle horizontal stroke of 唐 is longer.   16 strokes

、	丷	䒑	半	米	米	米	米	米	米	米	米	糖
糖	糖	糖										

甜

tián sweet

The character combines *tongue* 舌 and *sweet* 甘 to give the idea of *sweetness*.

Radical: 舌 'tongue'

Character components: 舌 + 甘

Index # 144

Character configuration:

Compounds, sentences and meanings

1. **甜** **tián** sweet
   这 西瓜 真 甜!
   Zhè xīguā zhēn tián!
   This watermelon is really sweet!

2. **甜蜜** **tiánmì** sweet, happy
   孩子们 笑得 多么 甜蜜!
   Háizimen xiàode duōme tiánmì!
   The children laughed happily.

3. **甜食** **tiánshí** sweets, sweet food
   她爱吃 甜食。
   Tā ài chī tiánshí.
   She has a sweet tooth.

4. **甜丝丝** **tiánsīsī** pleasantly sweet
   收到 男朋友 的信,她心里 感到
   Shōudào nánpéngyou de xīn, tā xīnli gǎndào
   甜丝丝 的。
   tiánsīsī de.
   She was really happy to get a letter from her boyfriend.

5. **甜头** **tiántóu** incentive
   要 给他点儿 甜头 他才会 干下去。
   Yào gěi tā diǎnr tiántóu tā cái huì gànxiàqù.
   You'll have to offer him an incentive to keep working.

The top horizontal stroke of 甘 is longer.　　　　　　　　**11 strokes**

ノ	二	千	千	舌	舌	舌	甜	甜	甜	甜		

chǎng   taste

The full form of the character combines *value* ⸯⁿ, *mouth* 口 and *good taste* 旨 to suggest the idea of *evaluating taste*.

Radical: 小 'small'   **Index # 49**

Character components: 小 + 宀 + 云   **Character configuration:**

Compounds, sentences and meanings

1. 尝 **chǎng** taste
   你 尝尝 味道。
   Nǐ chángchang wèidao.
   Try it and see if it tastes all right.

2. 尝试 **chángshì** try
   最后 一次 尝试 成功 了。
   Zuìhòu yí cì chángshì chénggōng le.
   The last attempt was successful.

3. 尝味 **chángwèi** try the flavor
   我 想 尝味 一下。
   Wǒ xiǎng chángwèi yíxià.
   I'd like to try the flavor.

4. 何尝 **hécháng** ever so
   我 何尝 不想 去, 只是 没 工夫
   Wǒ hécháng bùxiǎng qù, zhǐ shì méi gōngfu
   罢 了。
   ba le.
   It's not that I don't want to go; I just haven't got the time.

5. 未尝 **wèicháng** might not be
   这 未尝 不是 好 主意。
   Zhè wèicháng búshì hǎo zhǔyi.
   This might not be a bad idea.

The middle vertical stroke is written first and is taller than the side dots.   9 strokes

丨	丬	丷	丷	屮	屵	尙	尝	尝			

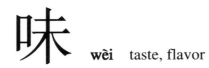 **wèi** taste, flavor

The character combines *mouth* 口 and the phonetic 未 to suggest the idea of *flavor*.

Radical: 口 'mouth'　　　　　　　　　**Index # 50**

Character components: 口 + 未

Character configuration:

Compounds, sentences and meanings

1. **味　wèi**　flavor
   这 糖 有 巧克力 的 味儿。
   Zhè táng yǒu qiǎokèlì de wèir.
   The candy has a chocolate flavor.

2. **味道　wèidao**　taste, flavor
   这 个 菜 味道 很 好。
   Zhè ge cài wèidao hěn hǎo.
   This dish is delicious.

3. **味精　wèijīng**　gourmet powder (MSG)
   常 吃 味精 对 身体 不 好。
   Cháng chī wèijīng duì shēntǐ bù hǎo.
   It's bad for you to eat MSG too often.

4. **美味　měiwèi**　delicious
   北京 有 很多 美味 小吃。
   Běijīng yǒu hěnduō měiwèi xiǎochī.
   Beijing has a lot of delicious snacks.

5. **气味　qìwèi**　smell, odor
   有些 花儿 气味 浓郁。
   Yǒuxiē huār qìwèi nóngyù.
   The scent of some flowers is strong.

The second horizontal stroke of 未 is longer.　　　　　　　**8 strokes**

⺀	口	口	口⁻	口⁼	叶	呋	味				

 shì try

The full form of the character combines *word* 言 and the phonetic 式 to suggest the idea of *trying something out*. It means *try*.

Radical: 讠 'word'

Index # 9

Character components: 讠 + 式

Character configuration:

Compounds, sentences and meanings

1. **试** **shì** try
   让 我 试一试。
   Ràng wǒ shìyishì.
   Let me try.

2. **试探** **shìtàn** sound out
   试探 一下他 对 这 个 问题 的 看法。
   Shìtàn yíxià tā duì zhè ge wèntí de kànfǎ.
   Sound him out about it.

3. **试行** **shìxíng** try out
   先 试行，后 推广。
   Xiān shìxíng, hòu tuīguǎng.
   Test it before general use.

4. **试用** **shìyòng** try out (a product)
   我 想 试用 一下。
   Wǒ xiǎng shìyòng yíxià.
   I'd like to try it out.

5. **考试** **kǎoshì** exam
   他 这 次 考试 的 成绩 很 好。
   Tā zhè cì kǎoshì de chéngjī hěn hǎo.
   He got excellent grades in this exam.

Note the difference between 弋 and 戈.   8 strokes

`	讠	讠	讠	讠	讠	试	试				

A. Look at the 16-character grid and CIRCLE words or phrases. They can be written horizontally or vertically. (Look at the circled characters in the Key if you are unsure.) Copy the word or phrase next to the grid and write the pinyin and meaning.

				Word or phrase				Pinyin	Meaning
错	甜	点	心	(i)	甜	点	心	tián diǎnxīn	pastry
奶	尝	饮	糖	(ii)					
茶	得	料	喝	(iii)					
里	味	道	吧	(iv)					

B. Using the characters in the 16-character grid, convert the pinyin sentences into characters and write the English meaning.

(i)	Nǐ hē shénme yǐnliào?								
(ii)	Nǎichá ba, búyào táng.								
(iii)	Zhèlǐ de tián diǎnxīn búcuò.								
(iv)	Shì ma? Nà wǒ děi chángchang wèidao.								

C. Match the Chinese words with their English meaning.

(i)

喝 zuǐ	expect, foresee
喝 mò 水	go to school
饮用水	drunk
冷饮	material
料到	drinking water
cǎi 料	cold drink
料理	milk
牛奶	take care of

(ii)

茶 hè 色	sweet, happy
茶 yè	try
甜 mì	smell, odor
甜头	dark brown
尝试	exam
美味	benefit
气味	tea
考试	delicious

 **xiū** rest

The character is an ideogram which combines *person* 亻 and *tree* 木 to represent the idea that when a person is standing next to or under a tree, he is *resting*. It means *rest*.

Radical: 亻 'upright person'　　　　**Index # 19**

Character components: 亻 + 木　　　　**Character configuration:**

Compounds, sentences and meanings

1. **休** **xiū** stop
   他们 两 个 争论 不休。
   Tāmen liǎng ge zhēnglùn bùxiū.
   The two of them cannot stop arguing.

2. **休假** **xiūjià** take a holiday
   今年 国庆节 休假 一 周。
   Jīnnián Guóqìngjié xiūjià yì zhōu.
   This year we have a week off for National Day.

3. **休息** **xiūxi** rest
   百货 公司 元旦 不 休息。
   Bǎihuò gōngsī Yuándàn bù xiūxi.
   Department stores are open as usual on New Year's Day.

4. **休养** **xiūyǎng** recuperate
   他 到 北戴河 休养 去了。
   Tā dào Běidàihé xiūyǎng qù le.
   He has gone to Beidaihe to convalesce.

5. **休业** **xiūyè** suspend business
   今天 休业 一 天。
   Jīntiān xiūyè yì tiān.
   Closed today.

The last stroke tapers off.　　　　　　　　　　　　　　6 strokes

ノ	亻	仁	什	休	休						

息　**xī**　stop

The character has two parts: *oneself* 自 and *heart* 心. It is not clear how this came to be associated with the idea of *rest* or *stop*.

Radical: 自 'self'　　　　　　　**Index # 147**
or　　　心 'heart'　　　　　　**Index # 76**
Character components: 自 + 心　　　**Character configuration:**

Compounds, sentences and meanings

1. 息　**xī**　stop
   生命　不息，战斗　不止。
   Shēngmìng bù xī, zhàndòu bù zhǐ.
   Life does not stop as struggles continue.

2. 信息　**xìnxī**　news
   我　很 久 没　收到　她的信息。
   Wǒ hěn jiǔ méi shōudào tāde xìnxī.
   I haven't received news from her for a long time.

3. 利息　**lìxī**　interest (on an investment)
   这 家　银行　给 的利息很 高。
   Zhè jiā yínháng gěi de lìxī hěn gāo.
   This bank gives high interest.

4. 作息　**zuòxī**　work and rest
   我们　应该　按时 作息。
   Wǒmen yīnggāi ànshí zuòxī.
   We should work and rest according to schedule.

5. 歇息　**xiēxi**　put up for the night
   今晚　就 在 我 这里 歇息 吧。
   Jīnwǎn jiù zài wǒ zhèlǐ xiēxi ba.
   Stay here tonight.

The second stroke of 心 is a level curve ending in a hook.　　　　**10 strokes**

| ´ | ⺁ | 白 | 白 | 自 | 自 | 自 | 息 | 息 | 息 | | |

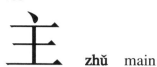

zhǔ   main

The character is the hieroglyphic figure of a candlestick with a flame. It means *center* since the light is usually placed in the center of the house. It came to mean *main*.

Radical: 丶 'dot'   **Index # 1**

or   王 'king'   **Index # 79**

Character components: 丶 + 王   **Character configuration:**

Compounds, sentences and meanings

1. **主** **zhǔ**   hold a definite view about something
   我 一 时 心里 没 主。
   Wǒ yì shí xīnli méi zhǔ.
   For a moment I just didn't know what to do.

2. **主见** **zhǔjiàn**   ideas or thoughts of one's own
   她 这 个 人 很 有 主见。
   Tā zhè ge rén hěn yǒu zhǔjiàn.
   She knows her own mind.

3. **主演** **zhǔyǎn**   act the leading role (in a play or movie)
   巩 俐 主演过 许多 电影。
   Gǒng Lì zhǔyǎnguo xǔduō diànyǐng.
   Gong Li has starred in lots of movies.

4. **主要** **zhǔyào**   main
   会议 主要 讨论了 两 个 问题。
   Huìyì zhǔyào tǎolùnle liǎng ge wèntí.
   The conference dealt mainly with two questions.

5. **主意** **zhǔyi**   idea, plan
   这 是 个 好 主意!
   Zhè shì ge hǎo zhǔyi!
   What a good idea!

The first stroke is a separate dot. It doesn't meet the vertical stroke.	5 strokes

丶	二	三	丯	主							

累 lèi/lěi/léi tired

The character combines *field* 田 and *silk* 糸 to suggest the idea that *working* in the fields was *tiring*.

Radical: 田 'field'　　　　　　　　　　**Index # 119**
or 糸 'raw silk'　　　　　　　　**Index # 152**
Character components: 田 + 幺 + 小　　　**Character configuration:**

Compounds, sentences and meanings

1. 累 **lèi** tired
   我 累了, 想 去 睡觉。
   Wǒ lèi le, xiǎng qù shuìjiào.
   I'm tired and I want to sleep.

2. 累赘 **léizhui** burden, nuisance
   行李 带得 太 多 了, 是 个 累赘。
   Xíngli dàide tài duō le, shì ge léizhui.
   Too much luggage is a nuisance.

3. 积累 **jīlěi** accumulate
   他 在 工作 上 积累了很多 经验。
   Tā zài gōngzuò shàng jīlěile hěnduō jīngyàn.
   He has built up a lot of experience in his work.

4. 日积月累 **rìjī-yuèlěi** accumulate (literally, over days and months)
   日积月累地 练习 就 能 学好。
   Rìjī-yuèlěide liànxí jiù néng xuéhǎo.
   Practice makes perfect.

5. 连累 **liánlěi** get someone into trouble
   这 件 事 连累了你, 真 不 好 意思。
   Zhè jiàn shì liánlěile nǐ, zhēn bù hǎo yìsi.
   I'm sorry to have involved you in this matter.

The last stroke of 幺 is a dot.　　　　　　　　　　**11 strokes**

| 丶 | 冂 | 冋 | 由 | 田 | 甲 | 罗 | 罘 | 累 | 累 | 累 | | |

死 sǐ die, extremely

The character combines *vicious* 歹 and *dagger* 匕 to suggest the idea of *someone stabbed to death*. It means *die* or *dead*.

Radical: 歹 'evil'　　　　　　　　　　**Index # 83**

Character components: 歹 + 匕

Character configuration:

Compounds, sentences and meanings

1. **死** sǐ die
   这 次 车祸 死了 三 个 人。
   Zhè cì chēhuò sǐle sān ge rén.
   The accident took three lives.

2. **死板** sǐbǎn rigid, stiff
   她的 表情 死板。
   Tāde biǎoqíng sǐbǎn.
   She's got an expressionless face.

3. **死记** sǐjì memorize mechanically
   学习 要 思考，不能 死记硬背。
   Xuéxí yào sīkǎo, bùnéng sǐjì-yìngbèi.
   You have to think about what you're learning, not just memorize it.

4. **死心** sǐxīn drop the idea forever
   你 还是 死了 这 条 心 吧。
   Nǐ háishì sǐle zhè tiáo xīn ba.
   You'd better give up the idea altogether.

5. **…死了** … sǐle extremely
   走了 三个 钟头， 把 我 累死了。
   Zǒule sān ge zhōngtóu, bǎ wǒ lèisǐle.
   After walking for three hours, I'm completely exhausted.

The horizontal stroke extends to accommodate the second component.　　　6 strokes

一	厂	歹	歹	歹	死						

cān meal

The character combines *food* 食, the non-character component 歺 and *again* 又 to suggest the idea of a *meal*.

Radical: 食 'eat'　　　　　　　　　　**Index # 181**

Character components: 歺 + 又 + 食　　**Character configuration:**

Compounds, sentences and meanings

1. 餐　**cān**　meal
   我 一日三 餐 都 吃 米饭。
   Wǒ yí rì sān cān dōu chī mǐfàn.
   I eat rice three meals a day.

2. 餐车　**cānchē**　dining car (on a train)
   列车 上 有 餐车。
   Lièchē shàng yǒu cānchē.
   There is a dining car on the train.

3. 餐巾纸　**cānjīnzhǐ**　paper serviette
   请 多给我 一 张 餐巾纸。
   Qǐng duō gěi wǒ yì zhāng cānjīnzhǐ.
   Please give me another serviette.

4. 餐厅　**cāntīng**　restaurant, dining room
   宾馆 里有 西式 餐厅。
   Bīnguǎn lǐ yǒu Xīshì cāntīng.
   There's a Western restaurant in the hotel.

5. 中餐　**Zhōngcān**　Chinese food
   我 吃腻了 中餐， 今天 想 吃 西餐。
   Wǒ chīnǐle Zhōngcān, jīntiān xiǎng chī Xīcān.
   I'm tired of eating Chinese food. Today I'll try some Western food.

The top components drape over the first two strokes of 食.												16 strokes
丶	丄	广	歹	歺	歺	歺	歺	炏	炏	努	努	努
餐	餐	餐										

huán surround

The full form of the character combines *jade* 王 (written without the dot), and the phonetic 睘 to suggest the idea of a *jade bracelet*. It means *encircle*.

Radical: 王 'king'

Index # 79

Character components: 王 + 不

Character configuration:

Compounds, sentences and meanings

1. 环 **huán** link
   这 是 最 薄弱 的 一 环。
   Zhè shì zuì bǎoruò de yì huán.
   This is the weakest link.

2. 环境 **huánjìng** environment
   环境 污染 是 一个 严重 问题。
   Huánjìng wūrǎn shì yí ge yánzhòng wèntí.
   Environmental pollution is a serious problem.

3. 环保 **huánbǎo** environmental protection
   环保 就 是 环境 保护。
   Huánbǎo jiù shì huánjìng bǎohù.
   "Huánbǎo" is the acronym for environmental protection.

4. 环城 **huánchéng** around the city
   这 是 环城 公路, 自行车
   Zhè shì huánchéng gōnglù, zìxíngchē
   不许 驶入。
   bùxǔ shǐrù.
   This is a ring road. Bicycles are not allowed.

5. 环节 **huánjié** link, sector
   减少 环节, 提高 效率。
   Jiǎnshǎo huánjié, tígāo xiàolǜ.
   Streamlining increases efficiency.

The last stroke of 王 lifts when written as a radical.   8 strokes

一	二	干	王	王'	玎	玚	环		

jìng territory

The character combines *earth* 土 and the phonetic 竟 to suggest the idea of *territory*.

Radical: 土 'earth'

Index # 40

Character components: 土 + 竟

Character configuration:

Compounds, sentences and meanings

1. 境 **jìng** territory
   少林寺 在 河南省 境 内。
   Shàolínsì zài Hénánshěng jìng nèi.
   Shaolin Temple is in Henan Province.

2. 境地 **jìngdì** circumstances
   他 把 自己 陷入 完全 孤立 的 境地。
   Tā bǎ zìjǐ xiànrù wánquán gūlì de jìngdì.
   He has completely isolated himself.

3. 境况 **jìngkuàng** (financial) condition
   我 最近 的 境况 不错。
   Wǒ zuìjìn de jìngkuàng búcuò.
   My financial situation is not bad right now.

4. 境遇 **jìngyù** one's lot
   我 很 同情 她 悲惨 的 境遇。
   Wǒ hěn tóngqíng tā bēicǎn de jìngyù.
   I'm truly sympathetic to her difficult circumstances.

5. 困境 **kùnjìng** difficult position
   你 要 想 办法 摆脱 困境。
   Nǐ yào xiǎng bànfǎ bǎituō kùnjìng.
   You must think of a way out of this predicament.

The last stroke is a vertical-bend-hook.

14 strokes

一	十	土	土	圹	圹	圹	垆	垃	培	培	培	境
境												

Full form

 优 **yōu**   excellent

The full form of the character combines *person* 亻 and the phonetic 憂 to suggest the idea of *excellence*. The simplified form uses a different phonetic 尤.

Radical: 亻 'upright person'

Index # 19

Character components: 亻 + 尤

Character configuration:

Compounds, sentences and meanings

1. **优** **yōu**   excellence
   优 胜 劣 败。
   Yōu shèng liè bài.
   Survival of the fittest. (Literally, the superior wins and the inferior loses)

2. **优待** **yōudài**   preferential treatment
   我们 受到了 特别 的 优待。
   Wǒmen shòudàole tèbié de yōudài.
   We were given preferential treatment.

3. **优点** **yōudiǎn**   merit, strong point
   每 个 人 都 有自己的 优点。
   Měi ge rén dōu yǒu zìjǐ de yōudiǎn.
   Each person has their own strong points.

4. **优美** **yōuměi**   graceful, beautiful
   这里 一带 风景 优美。
   Zhèlǐ yídài fēngjǐng yōuměi.
   The scenery around here is beautiful.

5. **优先** **yōuxiān**   have priority
   这 是 必须 优先 考虑 的 问题。
   Zhè shì bìxū yōuxiān kǎolǜ de wèntí.
   This is a question which takes precedence over all others.

The fifth stroke is a vertical-bend-hook.

6 strokes

ノ	亻	仁	忧	优	优							

Full form

馆 guǎn dwelling

The full form combines *accommodation* 舍 and the phonetic 官, which means an official, to suggest a *dwelling fit for honored guests*. The simplified form uses *food* 饣 to replace 舍 in the combination.

Radical: 饣 'food'　　　　　　　　　　**Index # 59**

Character components: 饣 + 官　　　　**Character configuration:**

Compounds, sentences and meanings

1. **馆 guǎn** accommodation for guests
   宾馆 是 高级 的 旅馆。
   Bīnguǎn shì gāojí de lǚguǎn.
   A guest house is a high-class hotel.

2. **博物馆 bówùguǎn** museum
   这 个 博物馆 值得 一 去。
   Zhè ge bówùguǎn zhíde yī qù.
   This museum is well worth visiting.

3. **大使馆 dàshǐguǎn** embassy
   请问, 美国 大使馆 在哪儿?
   Qǐngwèn, Měiguó Dàshǐguǎn zài nǎr?
   Excuse me, can you tell me where the American Embassy is?

4. **领事馆 lǐngshìguǎn** consulate
   我 要 去 领事馆 办 签证。
   Wǒ yào qù lǐngshìguǎn bàn qiānzhèng.
   I need to go to the Consulate to get my visa.

5. **图书馆 túshūguǎn** library
   北京 图书馆 的 藏书 很多。
   Běijīng Túshūguǎn de cángshū hěnduō.
   Beijing Library has a large collection of books.

Note the difference between 官 and 宫.　　　　　　　　　　**11 strokes**

| ノ | ⺈ | 饣 | 饣 | 饣 | 铲 | 馆 | 馆 | 馆 | 馆 | 馆 | |

Quiz 47 (461–470)

A. Look at the 16-character grid and CIRCLE words or phrases. They can be written horizontally or vertically. (Look at the circled characters in the Key if you are unsure.) Copy the word or phrase next to the grid and write the pinyin and meaning.

				Word or phrase			Pinyin	Meaning
饿	休	般	馆	(i)	休	息	xiūxi	rest
优	息	主	意	(ii)				
美	餐	店	又	(iii)				
快	环	境	累	(iv)				

B. Using the characters in the 16-character grid, convert the pinyin sentences into characters and write the English meaning.

(i)	Nǐ xiǎng xiūxi yíxià ma?									
(ii)	Hǎo zhǔyi! Lèisǐ wǒ le!									
(iii)	Zhè ge kuàicāndiàn huánjìng yōuměi.									
(iv)	Jiù zài zhèlǐ xiūxi yíxià ba.									

C. Match the Chinese words with their English meaning.

(i)

休假 — news, information
xìn 息 — accumulate
作息 — memorize mechanically
主见 — drop the idea forever
主要 — take a holiday
jī 累 — work and rest
死 jì — idea of one's own
死心 — main

(ii)

餐 tīng — have priority
环节 — link, sector
境 kuàng — strong point
优点 — museum
优先 — consulate
大 shǐ 馆 — restaurant
lǐng 事馆 — (financial) condition
bó 物馆 — embassy

菜 cài   vegetables

The character combines *grass* ⧾ and the phonetic 采 to suggest the idea of *vegetables*.

Radical: ⧾ '**grass**'   **Index # 42**

Character components: ⧾ + ⼍ + 木   **Character configuration:**

Compounds, sentences and meanings

1. 菜 **cài**   vegetables
    妈妈　上街　买 菜 去了。
    Māma shàngjiē mǎi cài qù le.
    Mother has gone to the market to buy food.
    (Literally, vegetables)

2. 菜单 **càidān**   menu
    请　给 我 菜单。
    Qǐng gěi wǒ càidān.
    Please give me the menu.

3. 蔬菜 **shūcài**   vegetables
    多 吃 蔬菜 对 身体 有 好处。
    Duō chī shūcài duì shēntǐ yǒu hǎochù.
    Eat more vegetables, they're good for you.

4. 菜市场 **càishìchǎng**   food market
    菜市场　里面 卖 蔬菜、肉、 水果、
    Càishìchǎng lǐmiàn mài shūcài, ròu, shuǐguǒ,
    什么的。
    shénmede.
    The food market sells vegetables, meat, fruits,
    and so on.

5. 做菜 **zuòcài**   cook
    我 妈妈 很 会 做菜。
    Wǒ māma hěn huì zuòcài.
    My mother is a good cook.

The middle vertical stroke does not join the dot above it   **11 strokes**

| 一 | 十 | 艹 | 艹 | 芝 | 芝 | 芝 | 苙 | 苹 | 苹 | 菜 | | |

dān single

The full form of the character consists of three parts: *double mouth* 口口, *speech* 曰 and *ten* 十. It is not clear how this combination constitutes the idea of *single*.

Radical: `丷` 'inverted eight'　　　　　**Index # 17**

Character components: `丷` + 曰 + 十　　　**Character configuration:**

Compounds, sentences and meanings

1. 单 **dān**　only, alone
   不要 单 凭 热情 去 工作。
   Búyào dān píng rèqíng qù gōngzuò.
   In work, enthusiasm alone is not enough.

2. 单程 **dānchéng**　one way
   我 只 买了 单程 票。
   Wǒ zhǐ mǎile dānchéng piào.
   I only bought a one-way ticket.

3. 单单 **dāndān**　only
   别人 都 来了, 单单 他 没 来。
   Biéren dōu lái le, dāndān tā méi lái.
   Everyone else is here. He's the only one missing.

4. 单独 **dāndú**　alone
   我 要 和 他 单独 谈一谈。
   Wǒ yào hé tā dāndú tányitán.
   I want to talk privately with him.

5. 单身 **dānshēn**　single (not married)
   她 今年 虽然 三十八, 但 还 是
   Tā jīnnián suīrán sānshíbā, dàn hái shì
   单身。
   dānshēn.
   Although she's 38, she's still single.

The bottom horizontal stroke is longer.　　　　　8 strokes

丶	丷	丷	兯	兯	白	单	单				

酒 **jiǔ** alcohol

The character combines *water* 氵 and the phonetic 酉 to suggest the idea of an *alcoholic drink*.

Radical: 氵 **'3 drops of water'**　　　**Index # 32**

Character components: 氵 + 酉　　　　**Character configuration:**

Compounds, sentences and meanings

1. 酒　**jiǔ**　alcoholic drink
   酒 不 醉 人 人 自 醉。
   Jiǔ bú zuì rén rén zì zuì.
   Alcohol doesn't make you drunk, you make yourself drunk.

2. 酒后　**jiǔhòu**　under the influence of liquor
   酒后 开车 是 犯法 的。
   Jiǔhòu kāichē shì fànfǎ de.
   Driving under the influence of drinks is a crime.

3. 酒量　**jiǔliàng**　capacity for liquor
   他 酒量 很 大。
   Tā jiǔliàng hěn dà.
   He can hold his liquor.

4. 酒肉朋友　**jiǔròu péngyou**　fair-weather friend (Literally, wine-and-meat friend)
   他 只 是 酒肉 朋友，不会 帮助
   Tā zhǐ shì jiǔròu péngyou, búhuì bāngzhù
   你 的。
   nǐ de.
   He's only a fair-weather friend, he won't help you.

5. 啤酒　**píjiǔ**　beer
   夏天 我 喜欢 喝啤酒。
   Xiàtiān wǒ xǐhuan hē píjiǔ.
   I like to drink beer in summer.

The eighth stroke has a bend on the right.　　　**10 strokes**

丶	冫	氵	汀	沂	沔	沔	洒	洒	酒		

474

bēi   glass, cup

Full form

The full form combines *container* 皿 and *not* 不 to suggest the idea that *Chinese cups are too small to be used as containers*. The simplified form uses the combination of *wood* 木 and *not* 不 to give the idea that *cups and glasses* are not made of wood.

Radical: 木 'tree'

Character components: 木 + 不

Index # 81

Character configuration:

Compounds, sentences and meanings

1. 杯 **bēi**   measure word
   我 喝了 两 杯 茶。
   Wǒ hēle liǎng bēi chá.
   I drank two cups of tea.

2. 杯子 **bēizi**   cup, glass
   这 杯子还 没 洗干净 呢。
   Zhè bēizi hái méi xǐgānjìng ne.
   This glass hasn't been washed properly.

3. 茶杯 **chábēi**   teacup
   茶杯、酒杯 中文 都 叫 杯子。
   Chábēi, jiǔbēi Zhōngwén dōu jiào bēizi.
   Teacups and glasses are called "bēizi" in Chinese.

4. 干杯 **gānbēi**   drink a toast (Literally, dry the cup)
   为 我们 的 友谊 干杯!
   Wèi wǒmen de yǒuyī gānbēi!
   Let's drink to our friendship.

5. 世界杯 **Shìjièbēi**   World Cup
   中国 进入 2002 年 世界杯
   Zhōngguó jìnrù Èrlínglíngèrnián Shìjièbēi
   足球 决赛。
   Zúqiú Juésài.
   China got into the finals of the 2002 World Cup Soccer.

End the last stroke firmly.   8 strokes

一	十	才	木	木	杁	杔	杯				

267

jú orange

The character combines *plant* 木 and the character component 矞 to suggest the idea of *tangerine* or *orange*. 桔 is an unofficial simplified form commonly associated with this character.

Radical: 木 'tree'　　　　　　　　**Index # 81**

Character components: 木 + 矛 + 冂 + 冖 + 口　　**Character configuration:**

Compounds, sentences and meanings

1. 橘　jú　orange
   中国 的橘子 没有　美国　的 好吃。
   Zhōngguó de júzi méiyǒu Měiguó de hǎochī.
   Chinese oranges don't taste as good as American oranges.

2. 橘子汁　júzizhī　orange juice
   来 一 杯 橘子汁。
   Lái yì bēi júzizhī.
   I'd like to order a glass of orange juice.

3. 橘黄　júhuáng　orange color
   中国　橘子的皮 一般 不是 橘黄色 的。
   Zhōngguó júzi de pí yìbān búshì júhuángsè de.
   The skin of Chinese oranges is generally not orange in color.

4. 柑橘　gānjú　mandarin orange
   中国　南方　出产 柑橘。
   Zhōngguó nánfāng chūchǎn gānjú.
   Mandarins are produced in the south of China.

5. 蜜橘　mìjú　honey mandarin orange
   柑橘 又 叫 蜜橘。
   Gānjú yòu jiào mìjú.
   Another name for mandarin orange is mìjú.

The last stroke of 矛 sweeps from right to left.　　　　　16 strokes

一	十	才	木	杧	柈	柈	杼	栝	桥	橋	橘	橘
橘	橘	橘										

chǎo   stir-fry

The character combines *fire* 火 and the phonetic 少 to suggest the idea of *stir-fry*.

Radical: 火 'fire'

Index # 75

Character components: 火 + 少

Character configuration:

Compounds, sentences and meanings

1. **炒** **chǎo** stir-fried
   来 一 个 雪菜 炒 肉丝。
   Lái yī ge xuěcài chǎo ròusī.
   I'd like to order stir-fried shredded pork with preserved vegetables.

2. **炒菜** **chǎocài** a stir-fried dish
   我 要了 两 个 炒菜 和 一 个 汤。
   Wǒ yàole liǎng ge chǎocài hé yī ge tāng.
   I ordered two dishes and a soup.

3. **炒鸡蛋** **chǎo jīdàn** scrambled eggs
   来 一 个 西红柿 炒 鸡蛋
   Lái yī ge xīhóngshì chǎo jīdàn.
   I'd like to order scrambled eggs with tomatoes.

4. **炒股票** **chǎo gǔpiào** speculate in shares
   上海 有 很多 人 炒 股票。
   Shànghǎi yǒu hěnduō rén chǎo gǔpiào.
   Many people in Shanghai speculate in shares.

5. **炒鱿鱼** **chǎo yóuyú** give somebody the sack (Literally, fry squid!)
   不要 这样 懒惰， 当心 被 炒
   Búyào zhèyàng lǎnduò, dāngxīn bèi chǎo
   鱿鱼 了。
   yóuyú le.
   Don't be so lazy. Be careful or you'll get the sack.

The last stroke sweeps to the left.   **8 strokes**

丶	丷	少	火	炒	炒	炒	炒				

鸡　jī　chicken

The full form combines *bird* 隹 and the phonetic 奚 to refer to *chicken*. The simplified form reconceptualizes it as a combination of *again* 又 and *bird* 鸟.

Radical:　又 'again'	**Index # 24**
or　　　　鸟 'bird'	**Index # 127**
Character components:　又 + 鸟	**Character configuration:**

Compounds, sentences and meanings

1. 鸡　jī　chicken
   我 爱 吃鸡, 不爱 吃鸭子。
   Wǒ ài chī jī, bú ài chī yāzi.
   I like chicken, but not duck.

2. 鸡毛蒜皮　**jīmáo-suànpí**　trifles (Literally, chicken feathers and garlic skin)
   你何苦 为 这 点 鸡毛蒜皮 的 事 跟
   Nǐ hékǔ wèi zhè diǎn jīmáo-suànpí de shì gēn
   他 吵 呢?
   tā chǎo ne?
   Why argue with him over such trifles?

3. 鸡犬不宁　**jī-quǎn bù níng**　general turmoil (Literally, chickens and dogs in upheaval)
   他们　经常　吵架, 闹得 家里
   Tāmen jīngcháng chǎojià, nàode jiāli
   鸡犬 不 宁。
   jī-quǎn bù níng.
   They fight all the time, turning the whole family upside down.

4. 公鸡　**gōngjī**　rooster
   他 连 公鸡 和 母鸡 都　分不清。
   Tā lián gōngjī hé mǔjī dōu fēnbuqīng.
   He can't even tell the difference between a rooster and a hen.

Note the difference between 鸟 and 乌.	7 strokes

フ	又	又′	又勺	又勺	鸡	鸡					

蛋 dàn egg

The character consists of two parts: *roll of silk* 疋 and *insect* 虫. It's not clear how this gives the idea of *egg*.

Radical: 虫 'insect'   **Index # 142**
or   疋 'roll of silk'   **Index # 130**
Character components: 疋 + 虫   **Character configuration:**

Compounds, sentences and meanings

1. **蛋** **dàn** egg
这 是 什么 蛋? 鸭蛋 吗?
Zhè shì shénme dàn? Yādàn ma?
What kind of egg is this? Is it a duck's egg?

2. **蛋白** **dànbái** egg white
蛋白 的 胆固醇 低。
Dànbái de dǎngùchún dī.
Egg white is low in cholesterol.

3. **蛋黄** **dànhuáng** yolk
蛋黄 的 胆固醇 高。
Dànhuáng de dǎngùchún gāo.
Egg yolk is high in cholesterol.

4. **蛋糕** **dàn'gāo** sponge cake
我 喜欢 吃 西式 蛋糕。
Wǒ xǐhuan chī Xīshì dàn'gāo.
I like Western-style sponge cake.

5. **鸡蛋** **jīdàn** chicken egg
鸡蛋 里 挑 骨头。
Jīdàn lǐ tiāo gǔtou.
Find fault. (Literally, look for a bone in an egg)

The bottom line of 虫 slants upwards.   11 strokes

一 丆 乛 疋 疋 疋 呇 呇 蚤 蛋 蛋

niú cattle

The character was derived from a pictograph of a cow's *head and horns*, viewed from the front.

Radical: 牛 'cattle'　　　　　　　**Index # 95**

Character component: 牛　　　　　　**Character configuration:** ⊡

Compounds, sentences and meanings

1. **牛　niú**　cattle
   我 是 1973年 出生 的, 我 属 牛。
   Wǒ shì Yījiǔqīsānnián chūshēng de, wǒ shǔ niú.
   I was born in 1973, in the year of the Ox.

2. **牛劲　niújìn**　great strength
   我 费了 牛劲 才 把 门 打开。
   Wǒ fèile niújìn cái bǎ mén dǎkāi.
   I had to exert all my strength to open the door.

3. **牛油　niúyóu**　butter
   面包 上 放 点 牛油 才 好吃。
   Miànbāo shàng fàng diǎn niúyóu cái hǎochī.
   Bread doesn't taste good without butter.

4. **牛脾气　niúpíqi**　stubbornness
   他 有 股 牛脾气, 干 什么 事 一定 要
   Tā yǒu gǔ niúpíqi, gàn shénme shì yídìng yào
   干 到底。
   gàn dào dǐ.
   He's very stubborn, once he starts something he must finish it.

5. **吹牛　chuīniú**　brag, talk big
   他 就 爱 吹牛。
   Tā jiù ài chuīniú.
   He blows his own trumpet.

牛 is different from 午.　　　　　　　　　　**4 strokes**

ノ	⸍	二	牛								

肉

ròu   meat

The character depicts a slice of *meat* showing the grain of the flesh.

Radical: 冂 'border'

Index # 16

Character components: 冂 + 人 + 人

Character configuration:

Compounds, sentences and meanings

1. **肉** **ròu** meat
   许多 动物 的 肉 可以 吃。
   Xǔduō dòngwù de ròu kěyǐ chī.
   The flesh of many animals can be eaten.

2. **牛肉** **niúròu** beef
   我 喜欢 吃 牛肉 面。
   Wǒ xǐhuan chī niúròu miàn.
   I like beef noodles.

3. **肉片** **ròupiàn** sliced meat
   肉片、 肉丁、肉丝 一般 都 是 猪肉。
   Ròupiàn, ròudīng, ròusī yībān dōu shì zhūròu.
   Sliced meat, diced meat and shredded meat usually refer to pork.

4. **肉感** **ròugǎn** sexy
   她 穿起 那 条 短裙 非常 肉感。
   Tā chuānqǐ nà tiáo duǎnqún fēicháng ròugǎn.
   She looks very sexy in that short skirt.

5. **肉食** **ròushí** meat
   他 吃素，从 不 吃 肉食。
   Tā chī sù, cóng bù chī ròushí.
   He's a vegetarian and never touches meat.

End the second stroke of both 人 components firmly.   6 strokes

丨	冂	内	内	肉	肉						

A. Look at the 16-character grid and CIRCLE words or phrases. They can be written horizontally or vertically. (Look at the circled characters in the Key if you are unsure.) Copy the word or phrase next to the grid and write the pinyin and meaning.

橘	子	水	酒
杯	牛	羊	喝
菜	肉	鸡	蛋
单	面	炒	爱

	Word or phrase			Pinyin	Meaning
(i)	橘	子	水	júzishuǐ	orange juice
(ii)					
(iii)					
(iv)					

B. Using the characters in the 16-character grid, convert the pinyin sentences into characters and write the English meaning.

(i)	Zhè shì càidān, hē diǎn jiǔ ma?								
(ii)	Lái liǎng bēi júzishuǐ.								
(iii)	Nǐ ài chī chǎo jīdàn ma?								
(iv)	Bù, wǒ jiù yào ge niúròu miàn.								

C. Match the Chinese words with their English meaning.

(i)

shū 菜	cook
做菜	capacity for liquor
单身	cup, glass
酒量	drink a toast
pí 酒	vegetables
杯子	single (not married)
gān 杯	orange color
橘黄	beer

(ii)

炒菜	sack someone
炒 gǔ 票	butter
炒 yóuyú	meat
牛 pí 气	a stir-fried dish
牛 yóu	mutton
肉感	stubbornness
肉 shí	speculate on shares
羊肉	sexy

zì oneself

The character represents the pictograph of the nose 自 from which it came to mean *oneself* or *by oneself.*

Radical: 自 'oneself'

Character component: 自

Index # 147

Character configuration:

Compounds, sentences and meanings

1. **自 zì** naturally
   现在 多 用功， 将来 自 有 好处。
   Xiànzài duō yònggōng, jiānglái zì yǒu hǎochù.
   If you work hard now, you will reap the benefits later.

2. **自己 zìjǐ** self
   我 觉得自己住 比较 方便。
   Wǒ juéde zìjǐ zhù bǐjiào fāngbiàn.
   I think it's easier to live alone.

3. **自从 zìcóng** since
   我 自从 跳舞 以后，身体 好 多 了。
   Wǒ zìcóng tiàowǔ yǐhòu, shēntǐ hǎo duō le.
   Since I took up dancing, my health has improved a lot.

4. **自行车 zìxíngchē** bicycle
   我 不会 骑 自行车。
   Wǒ búhuì qí zìxíngchē.
   I can't ride a bicycle.

5. **自由 zìyóu** free, of one's choice
   我 父母 是 自由 恋爱 结合 的。
   Wǒ fùmǔ shì zìyóu liàn'ài jiéhé de.
   My parents arranged their own marriage.

There is equal spacing between the horizontal strokes.										6 strokes
′	亻	冂	白	自	自					

己　jǐ　self

The character resembles the beginning of a silk skein. It denotes the originator of *talk* or *doing*, that is, the speaker or *oneself*.

Radical: 己 'self'　　　　　　　　**Index # 62**

Character component: 己　　　　　**Character configuration:** ☐

Compounds, sentences and meanings

1. **己　jǐ　self**
   己 所 不 欲, 勿 施 于 人。
   Jǐ suǒ bú yù, wù shī yú rén.
   Don't treat others in a way you wouldn't like to be treated yourself.

2. **我自己　wǒ zìjǐ　myself**
   放心 吧, 我 会 照顾 我 自己 的。
   Fàngxīn ba, wǒ huì zhàogu wǒ zìjǐ de.
   Don't worry, I'll look after myself.

3. **你自己　nǐ zìjǐ　yourself**
   你 自己 想 办法 吧, 我 帮不了 你。
   Nǐ zìjǐ xiǎng bànfǎ ba, wǒ bāngbuliǎo nǐ.
   You work it out yourself, I can't help you.

4. **他自己　tā zìjǐ　himself**
   这 是 他 自己 的事, 我们 管不了。
   Zhè shì tā zìjǐ de shì, wǒmen guǎnbuliǎo.
   This is his affair, we shouldn't interfere.

5. **知己　zhījǐ　close friend**
   人生 难得 有 几 个 知己。
   Rénshēng nándé yǒu jǐ ge zhījǐ.
   In life, it's rare to have more than a few close friends.

The top left corner is completely open.										3 strokes
㇕	㇆	己								

niàn think

The character combines *now* 今 and *heart* 心, and represents the idea of what is 'now on the heart'. Thus it means an *idea, thought* or *intention*.

Radical: 心 'heart'

Index # 76

Character components: 今 + 心

Character configuration:

Compounds, sentences and meanings

1. **念 niàn** think of, miss (loved ones)
   我们 老 念着 你。
   Wǒmen lǎo niànzhe nǐ.
   We miss you very much.

2. **念课文 niàn kèwén** read aloud a text
   要 养成 大声 念 课文 的 习惯。
   Yào yǎngchéng dàshēng niàn kèwén de xíguàn.
   We should get into the habit of reading the text aloud.

3. **念书 niànshū** study
   我 弟弟 在 美国 念书。
   Wǒ dìdi zài Měiguó niànshū.
   My younger brother is studying in the United States.

4. **念头 niàntóu** thought, idea
   你 最好 放弃 这 个 念头。
   Nǐ zuìhǎo fàngqì zhè ge niàntóu.
   You'd better give up the idea.

5. **纪念 jìniàn** commemorate
   人们 集会纪念 这 位 伟大 的
   Rénmen jíhuì jìniàn zhè wèi wěidà de
   音乐家。
   yīnyuèjiā.
   They held a commemorative function for the great musician.

The last stroke of 今 does not touch the middle dot of 心.　　　　8 strokes

ノ	入	人	今	今	念	念	念				

shǐ beginning

The character combines *female* 女 and *platform* 台 to suggest the idea that in the female sex was traced the *beginning* of things. It came to mean *begin*.

Radical: 女 'female'　　　　　　　　　**Index # 65**

Character components: 女 + 厶 + 口　　　**Character configuration:**

Compounds, sentences and meanings

1. 始　shǐ　begin
   不 知 始 于 何时。
   Bù zhī shǐ yú héshí.
   It's not known exactly when this came into being.

2. 始末　shǐmò　beginning and end
   事情 的 始末 是 这样 的。
   Shìqing de shǐmò shì zhèyàng de.
   This is the story from A to Z.

3. 始终　shǐzhōng　from start to finish
   会议 始终 在 友好 的 气氛 中 进行。
   Huìyì shǐzhōng zài yǒuhǎo de qìfēn zhōng jìnxíng.
   The talks proceeded in a friendly atmosphere from start to finish.

4. 开始　kāishǐ　begin
   一 种 新的 工作, 开始 总 会
   Yī zhǒng xīnde gōngzuò, kāishǐ zǒng huì
   遇到 一些 困难。
   yùdào yīxiē kùnnan.
   You always run into some difficulties at the beginning of a new job.

5. 原始　yuánshǐ　primeval, primitive
   这 是 原始 森林。
   Zhè shì yuánshǐ sēnlín.
   This is a primeval forest.

The first stroke of 台 is a downward-left-bend.							8 strokes

| く | 女 | 女 | 如 | 始 | 始 | 始 | 始 | | | | |

fēi   not

The character is a phonetic used as a character. It can be thought of as *two rows of people standing side by side but facing different directions.*

Radical: 丨 'vertical stroke'   **Index # 3**

Character components: 丨 + 三 + 丨 + 三   **Character configuration:** ⊟

Compounds, sentences and meanings

1. 非 **fēi** not
   这 件 事 非 你 我 所 能 解决。
   Zhè jiàn shì fēi nǐ wǒ suǒ néng jiějué.
   This matter cannot be decided by you or me.

2. 非 ... 不 **fēi ... bù** must, have to
   要 学好 中文, 非 下 苦工 不行。
   Yào xuéhǎo Zhōngwén, fēi xià kǔgōng bùxíng.
   You have to work hard to learn Chinese properly.

3. 非常 **fēicháng** extraordinary, very
   街上 非常 热闹。
   Jiēshàng fēicháng rè'nao.
   The street is a hive of activity.

4. 非但 **fēidàn** not only
   非但 学生 答不出 连 老师 也
   Fēidàn xuésheng dábuchū, lián lǎoshī yě
   答不出。
   dábuchū.
   Not only the students, but the teacher too, didn't know the answer.

5. 非法 **fēifǎ** illegal
   盗版 软件被 宣布 为非法。
   Dàobǎn ruǎnjiàn bèi xuānbù wéi fēifǎ.
   Pirated software has been declared illegal.

Write the left component first, then the right component.   8 strokes

丨	㇏	ヨ	ヨ	非	非	非	非				

zhòng/chóng   heavy/repeat

The character combines *thousand* 千 and *mile* 里 to suggest the idea that something becomes *heavy* when carried for a long distance.

Radical: 丿 'downward-left stroke'   **Index # 4**

Character components: 千 + 日 + 二   **Character configuration:** ☐

Compounds, sentences and meanings

1. 重 **chóng** again
   把 生词 重 抄 一 遍。
   Bǎ shēngcí chóng chāo yí biàn.
   Copy the new words out again.

2. 重复 **chóngfù** repeat
   避免 不 必要 的 重复。
   Bìmiǎn bú bìyào de chóngfù.
   Avoid unnecessary repetition.

3. 重点 **zhòngdiǎn** focal point, key
   北京 大学 是 重点 大学。
   Běijīng Dàxué shì zhòngdiǎn dàxué.
   Peking University is an elite university.

4. 重视 **zhòngshì** emphasize
   大家 都 很 重视 这 件 事。
   Dàjiā dōu hěn zhòngshì zhè jiàn shì.
   Everyone takes the matter seriously.

5. 重要 **zhòngyào** important
   学 语言 最 重要 是 能 记住
   Xué yǔyán zuì zhòngyào shì néng jìzhù
   生词。
   shēngcí.
   The most important thing in learning a language is to be able to remember the new words.

The top horizontal stroke is the longest.   **9 strokes**

一	二	仨	盲	盲	盲	重	重	重				

 **jī** base

The character combines *earth* 土 and the phonetic 其 to suggest the idea of *base* or *foundation*.

Radical: 土 'sound' **Index # 40**
or 其 'such' **Index # 171**
Character components: 其 + 土 **Character configuration:**

Compounds, sentences and meanings

1. **基** **jī** foundation
   这 房子 的 地基 很 稳固。
   Zhè fángzi de dìjī hěn wěn'gù.
   The foundation of this house is very sturdy.

2. **基本** **jīběn** basically
   这 个 电影 基本 上 是 好 的。
   Zhè ge diànyǐng jīběn shàng shì hǎo de.
   On balance, it's a good movie.

3. **基本功** **jīběngōng** basic skill
   她的 语言 基本功 很 扎实。
   Tāde yǔyán jīběngōng hěn zhāshí.
   She has a solid mastery of basic language skills.

4. **基层** **jīcéng** grassroots level
   中国 现在 进行 基层 选举。
   Zhōngguó xiànzài jìnxíng jīcéng xuǎnjǔ.
   China is holding local elections.

5. **基督教** **Jīdūjiào** Christianity
   他 是 基督教徒。
   Tā shì Jīdūjiàotú.
   He is a Christian.

The middle horizontal stroke is the longest.										11 strokes
一	十	艹	艹	甘	其	其	其	其	基	基

功

gōng achievement

The character combines *work* 工 and *effort* 力 to suggest the idea that efforts bring *result*.

Radical: 工 'work' **Index # 39**
or 力 'strength' **Index # 31**
Character components: 工 + 力 **Character configuration:**

Compounds, sentences and meanings

1. **功** **gōng** achievement
   功 到 自然 成。
   Gōng dào zìrán chéng.
   Slow and steady wins the race.

2. **功课** **gōngkè** homework
   她 在 学校 里 门门 功课 都 很 好。
   Tā zài xuéxiào lǐ ménmén gōngkè dōu hěn hǎo.
   She does well in every subject at school.

3. **功能** **gōngnéng** function
   这 种 电脑 具有 多 种 功能。
   Zhè zhǒng diànnǎo jùyǒu duō zhǒng gōngnéng.
   This computer can perform many different functions.

4. **成功** **chénggōng** succeed, success
   你 要 坚持 才 会 成功。
   Nǐ yào jiānchí cái huì chénggōng.
   If you persevere, you will succeed.

5. **用功** **yònggōng** hardworking
   她 还 在 图书馆 里 用功 呢。
   Tā hái zài túshūguǎn lǐ yònggōng ne.
   She is still working hard in the library.

The last stroke of 工 lifts when written as a radical.				5 strokes
一	丁	工	功	功

xìn   letter, trust

The character is an ideogram which combines *people* 亻 and *word* 言 to suggest people communicate with words and ideas in a *letter*.

Radical: 亻 'upright person'

Index # 19

Character components: 亻 + 言

Character configuration:

Compounds, sentences and meanings

1. **信** **xìn** letter
   你 到 了 那儿 就 给 我 来 个 信。
   Nǐ dàole nàr jiù gěi wǒ lái ge xìn.
   Please send me a letter when you arrive.

2. **信不过** **xìnbuguò** distrust
   你 是 信不过 我, 所以 不肯 对 我
   Nǐ shì xìnbuguò wǒ, suǒyǐ bùkěn duì wǒ
   　讲　真话。
   jiǎng zhēnhuà.
   You are not telling me the truth because you don't trust me.

3. **信得过** **xìndeguò** trust
   你 要是 信得过 我, 就 交 给 我 办。
   Nǐ yàoshi xìndeguò wǒ, jiù jiāo gěi wǒ bàn.
   If you trust me, let me do it for you.

4. **信心** **xìnxīn** confidence, faith
   我 对 这 药 信心 不 大。
   Wǒ duì zhè yào xìnxīn bú dà.
   I haven't much faith in this medicine.

5. **信用** **xìnyòng** trustworthiness
   他 信用 好, 完全 可以 信任。
   Tā xìnyòng hǎo, wánquán kěyǐ xìnrèn.
   His credit is good. You can trust him.

The top horizontal stroke is longer than those below.									9 strokes
丿	亻	亻	信	信	信	信	信	信	

　　　　　　　　　　　　　　　Full form

门　mén　door

門

The full form of the character is a pictograph representing *a double door* and means a *gate*.

Radical: 门 'door'　　　　　　　　　**Index # 37**

Character component: 门　　　　　　**Character configuration:**

Compounds, sentences and meanings

1. **门** **mén** measure word
   她 在 学校 里 门门 功课 都 很 好。
   Tā zài xuéxiào lǐ ménmén gōngkè dōu hěn hǎo.
   She does well in every subject at school.

2. **门口** **ménkǒu** entrance
   我 在 门口 等候。
   Wǒ zài ménkǒu děnghòu.
   I'll wait at the gate.

3. **门路** **ménlù** social connections (Literally,
   doors and roads)
   办 这 种 事,他 有 门路。
   Bàn zhè zhǒng shì, tā yǒu ménlù.
   *He knows where to go to get this kind of job
   done.*

4. **门牌** **ménpái** street number; house number
   你 家 门牌 几 号?
   Nǐ jiā ménpái jǐ hào?
   What's the number of your house?

5. **门外汉** **ménwàihàn** layman
   对于 美术, 我 是 门外汉。
   Duìyú měishù, wǒ shì ménwàihàn.
   *Where the fine arts are concerned, I am only a
   layman.*

End the first dot firmly to the right.　　　　　　　　　　　　　　　**3 strokes**

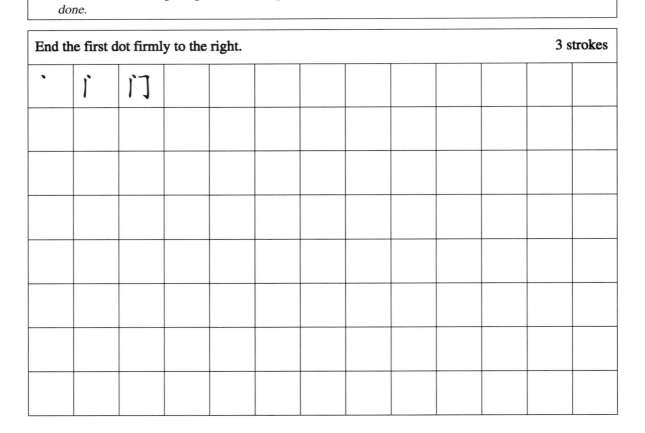

A. Look at the 16-character grid and CIRCLE words or phrases. They can be written horizontally or vertically. (Look at the circled characters in the Key if you are unsure.) Copy the word or phrase next to the grid and write the pinyin and meaning.

心	非	自	常
经	验	己	开
基	重	要	始
信	功	定	门

	Word or phrase			Pinyin	Meaning
(i)	自	己		zìjǐ	self
(ii)					
(iii)					
(iv)					

B. Using the characters in the 16-character grid, convert the pinyin sentences into characters and write the English meaning.

(i)	Wǒ shuō zìjǐ de xuéxí jīngyàn.									
(ii)	Wǒ juéde kāishǐ fēicháng zhòngyào.									
(iii)	Yídìng yào xiān xuéhǎo jīběngōng.									
(iv)	Yǒule xìnxīn, jiù yǒu xìngqù xué.									

C. Match the Chinese words with their English meaning.

(i)

自从	thought, idea
自 yóu	from start to finish
知己	illegal
jì 念	of one's choice
念头	since
始 zhōng	close friend
非常	commemorate
非法	extraordinary

(ii)

重 fù	hardworking
重 shì	homework
功 kè	confidence, faith
功 fu	repeat
用功	trustworthiness
信心	emphasize
信用	important
重要	time

坚　jiān　hard, solid

The full form of the character has three components: *official (minister)* 臣, *again* 又 and *earth* 土. By extension, it came to mean *strong*.

Radical: 土 'earth'

Index # 40

Character components: ⺆ + 又 + 土

Character configuration:

Compounds, sentences and meanings

1. 坚　**jiān**　solid
   坚 如 磐石。
   Jiān rú pánshí.
   Solid as a rock.

2. 坚持　**jiānchí**　persevere in
   她 每天 坚持 练习 写 汉字。
   Tā měitiān jiānchí liànxí xiě Hànzì.
   She perseveres with her daily practice of writing Chinese characters.

3. 坚定　**jiāndìng**　firm
   你 别 说 了,我的 立场 很 坚定。
   Nǐ bié shuō le, wǒde lìchǎng hěn jiāndìng.
   Don't try to talk me out of it, my stand in this matter is very firm.

4. 坚决　**jiānjué**　resolute
   我 坚决 反对 这样 做。
   Wǒ jiānjué fǎnduì zhèyàng zuò.
   I'm resolutely opposed to going about it in this way.

5. 坚强　**jiānqiáng**　strong
   他 是 一个 性格 坚强 的 人。
   Tā shì yí ge xìnggé jiānqiáng de rén.
   He is a person of strong character.

The first vertical stroke is shorter than the second one.								7 strokes
丨	刂	⺊	収	坚	坚	坚		

chí hold, grasp

The character combines *hand* 扌 and the phonetic 寺 to refer to the idea of *hold* or *grasp*.

Radical: 扌 'hand'　　　　　　　　　**Index # 48**

Character components: 扌 + 士 + 寸　　　**Character configuration:**

Compounds, sentences and meanings

1. **持 chí** persevere
   刻苦 学习, 持 之 以 恒。
   Kèkǔ xuéxí, chí zhī yǐ héng.
   Study hard, don't give up.

2. **持久 chíjiǔ** enduring
   他们 之间 的 感情 是 不会 持久 的。
   Tāmen zhījiān de gǎnqíng shì búhuì chíjiǔ de.
   Their love won't last.

3. **持有 chíyǒu** hold
   我 持有 美国 护照。
   Wǒ chíyǒu Měiguó hùzhào.
   I hold an American passport.

4. **支持 zhīchí** support
   我 完全 支持 这 个 建议。
   Wǒ wánquán zhīchí zhè ge jiànyì.
   I'm all for this proposal.

5. **维持 wéichí** maintain
   大家 都 想 维持 现状。
   Dàjiā dōu xiǎng wéichí xiànzhuàng.
   Everyone wants to maintain the status quo.

The middle horizontal stroke is the longest.　　　　**9 strokes**

| 一 | 十 | 扌 | 扩 | 扩 | 挂 | 挂 | 持 | 持 | | | |

cì position in a series

The character combines *ice* 冫 and *owe* 欠. It is not clear how this combination gives the idea of *order* or *place in a sequence*.

Radical: 冫 'ice'　　　　　　　　　　**Index # 7**

Character components: 冫 + 欠　　　　　**Character configuration:** ⊟

Compounds, sentences and meanings

1. 次 **cì** measure word
   今天 我 来 找过 你 两 次。
   Jīntiān wǒ lái zhǎoguo nǐ liǎng cì.
   I looked for you twice today.

2. 次数 **cìshù** number of times
   练习 的 次数 越 多, 熟练 的 程度
   Liànxí de cìshù yuè duō, shúliàn de chéngdù
   越 高。
   yuè gāo.
   The more you practice, the better you'll be.

3. 次序 **cìxù** order, sequence
   请 按次序 入场。
   Qǐng àn cìxù rùchǎng.
   Please stay in line as you come in.

4. 次要 **cìyào** less important
   把 这 个 问题 推到 次要 地位。
   Bǎ zhè ge wèntí tuīdào cìyào dìwèi.
   Give this problem lower priority.

5. 车次 **chēcì** train or bus service
   上下班 的 时候 车次 比较 多。
   Shàngxiàbān de shíhou chēcì bǐjiào duō.
   During peak hours, buses and trains are more frequent.

The last two strokes taper off.							6 strokes

丶	冫	冫	汃	汾	次				

bì certainly

The character combines *heart* 心 and *the sweeping stroke* 丿 to suggest the idea of that one has made a resolution and *must* carry it out.

Radical: 心 'heart'　　　　　　　　**Index # 76**

Character components: 心 + 丿　　　　**Character configuration:** ☐

Compounds, sentences and meanings

1. **必** **bì** must
   我 明天 下午 两点半 必 到。
   Wǒ míngtiān xiàwǔ liǎngdiǎnbàn bì dào.
   I'll definitely be there at 2:30 tomorrow.

2. **必得** **bìděi** have to
   你 必得 去 一 趟。
   Nǐ bìděi qù yī tàng.
   You simply must go.

3. **必定** **bìdìng** must
   她 必定 知道。
   Tā bìdìng zhīdao.
   She must have known it.

4. **必然** **bìrán** inevitable
   他 必然 失败。
   Tā bìrán shībài.
   He will certainly fail.

5. **必要** **bìyào** necessary
   我们 没有 必要 再 讨论 了。
   Wǒmen méiyǒu bìyào zài tǎolùn le.
   There's no need for us to discuss this any further.

必 and 心 are different.　　　　　　　　　　　5 strokes

丿	心	心	必	必							

Full form

须 **xū** must, have to

The full form of the character is made up of two parts: *feathery* 彡 and *page* 頁. It is not clear how this combination gives the meaning of *must*.

Radical: 彡 'feathery' **Index # 55**
or 页 'page' **Index # 140**
Character components: 彡 + 页 **Character configuration:**

Compounds, sentences and meanings

1. 须 **xū** must
   我们 须 作出 更大 的 努力。
   Wǒmen xū zuòchū gēngdà de nǔlì.
   We'll have to try even harder.

2. 须要 **xūyào** must, have to
   这 问题 需要 好好 研究 和 处理。
   Zhè wèntí xūyào hǎohǎo yánjiū hé chǔlǐ.
   This problem requires thorough investigation and careful handling.

3. 须知 **xūzhī** one should know that
   须知 得来 不易。
   Xūzhī délái búyì.
   Keep in mind that the victory is hard-won.

4. 无须 **wúxū** not necessary
   他 会 解释 清楚 的,你 无须 着急。
   Tā huì jiěshì qīngchǔ de, nǐ wúxū zháojí.
   He'll explain everything, there's no need to get excited.

End the last stroke firmly. **9 strokes**

| ノ | 彡 | 彡 | 纩 | 纩 | 纩 | 须 | 须 | 须 | | | |

àn according to

The character combines *hand* 扌 and the phonetic 安 to suggest the action of *pressing*.

Radical: 扌 'hand'　　　　　　　　　　**Index # 48**

Character components: 扌 + 安

Character configuration:

Compounds, sentences and meanings

1. **按 àn** press
   你 怎么 不 按 门铃 就 走进来 了?
   Nǐ zěnme bū àn ménlíng jiù zǒujìnlai le?
   How come you just walk in without ringing the doorbell?

2. **按理 ànlǐ** according to reason
   按理不 应当 这么 办。
   Ànlǐ bù yīngdāng zhème bàn.
   Logically, it should not be done this way.

3. **按次序 àn cìxù** in sequence
   词句按 拼音 字母 次序 排列。
   Cíjù àn pīnyīn zìmǔ cìxù páiliè.
   The words and phrases are listed in alphabetical order.

4. **按时 ànshí** on time
   我们 一定 按时 开会，不要 迟到。
   Wǒmen yídìng ànshí kāihuì, bùyào chídào.
   We will begin the meeting promptly. Don't be late.

5. **按照 ànzhào** according to
   按照 贡献 大小，分别 给 以 奖励。
   Ànzhào gòngxiàn dàxiǎo, fēnbié gěi yǐ jiǎnglì.
   Awards will be given in proportion to the contribution.

The sixth stroke is a horizontal-hook.										9 strokes
一	扌	扌	扌	扩	扩	护	按	按		

順 **shùn** follow

順

The full form is made up of two parts: *river* 川 and *page* 頁 which means *head* in this instance. With one *head* following the river, the character came to mean *follow*.

Radical: 页 'page'

Index # 140

Character components: 川 + 页

Character configuration:

Compounds, sentences and meanings

1. 順 **shùn** along
   顺着 这 条 路 走。
   Shùnzhe zhè tiáo lù zǒu.
   Follow this road.

2. 順便 **shùnbiàn** do something without extra effort
   你去 图书馆 的 时候， 顺便 把 我
   Nǐ qù túshūguǎn de shíhou, shùnbiàn bǎ wǒ
   这 本 书 还 了 吧。
   zhè běn shū huán le ba.
   When you go to the library, please return this book for me.

3. 順利 **shùnlì** successful
   工作 正在 顺利 进行。
   Gōngzuò zhèngzài shùnlì jìnxíng.
   The work is proceeding smoothly.

4. 順序 **shùnxù** sequence, order
   汉字 按 拼音 字母 顺序 排列。
   Hànzì àn pīnyīn zìmǔ shùnxù páiliè.
   The characters are arranged in alphabetical order.

5. 笔顺 **bǐshùn** stroke order
   写 汉字 要 注意 笔顺。
   Xiě Hànzì yào zhùyì bǐshùn.
   You have to pay attention to stroke order when writing characters.

End the last stroke firmly.

9 strokes

丿	川	川	川	川	川	顺	顺	顺				

498

yǎng   provide for

The full form of the character combines *sheep* 羊 and *food* 食 to represent delicious food. It means *healthy food* or *to feed*.

Radical: 羊 'sheep'

Index # 133

Character components: 羊 + 丶 + 丿丨

Character configuration:

Compounds, sentences and meanings

1. **养** **yǎng** provide for
   他 从小 没有 父母, 是 姑姑 把
   Tā cóngxiǎo méiyǒu fùmǔ, shì gūgu bǎ
   他 养 大的。
   tā yǎng dà de.
   He lost his parents when he was a child, and was brought up by his aunt.

2. **养神** **yǎngshén** rest to attain mental tranquility
   不要 打搅 他,他在 闭目 养神。
   Búyào dǎjiǎo tā, tā zài bìmù yǎngshén.
   Don't disturb him, he's resting.

3. **保养** **bǎoyǎng** take good care of one's health
   他 很 会 保养。
   Tā hěn huì bǎoyǎng.
   He knows how to take care of himself.

4. **修养** **xiūyǎng** accomplishment
   他 在 文学 上 很 有 修养。
   Tā zài wénxué shàng hěn yǒu xiūyǎng.
   He has a wide knowledge of literature.

5. **营养** **yíngyǎng** nutrition
   牛奶 的 营养 价值 很 高。
   Niúnǎi de yíngyǎng jiàzhí hěn gāo.
   Milk has a high nutritional value.

The bottom left stroke has a slight lift to the left.								9 strokes
丶	丷	兰	兰	兰	羊	养	养	养

惯　**guàn**　be used to

慣

The character combines *upright heart* 忄 and the phonetic 貫 to suggest the idea of getting used to something. It came to mean *be used to.*

Radical: 忄 'upright heart'

Index # 33

Character components: 忄 + 贯

Character configuration:

Compounds, sentences and meanings

1. 惯　**guàn**　get used to
   我 惯了 早 睡 早 起。
   Wǒ guànle zǎo shuì zǎo qǐ.
   I've got into the habit of going to bed early and getting up early.

2. 惯坏　**guànhuài**　spoil (a child)
   别 把 孩子 惯坏 了。
   Biè bǎ háizi guànhuài le.
   Don't spoil the child.

3. 惯例　**guànlì**　usual practice
   这样 做 会 打破 惯例。
   Zhèyàng zuò huì dǎpò guànlì.
   This is a break from the usual practice.

4. 习惯　**xíguàn**　be accustomed to
   这样　潮湿 的 天气 我 实在
   Zhèyàng cháoshī de tiānqì wǒ shízài
   不 习惯。
   bù xíguàn.
   I just can't get used to this damp weather.

End the last stroke firmly.

11 strokes

丶	丷	忄	忄ㄴ	忄口	忄𭅆	忄𭅏	忄甲	惯	惯	惯		

Full form

 jì record

The full form of the character combines *word* 言 and the phonetic 己, which also means *record* or *mark*, to suggest the idea of *putting down in writing* or *record*.

Radical: 讠 'word'

Index # 9

Character components: 讠 + 己

Character configuration:

Compounds, sentences and meanings

1. **记** jì jot down
   请 把 电话 号码 记下来。
   Qǐng bǎ diànhuà hàomǎ jìxiàlai.
   Please jot down the telephone number.

2. **记得** jìde remember
   我 完全 记不得了。
   Wǒ wánquán jìbude le.
   I simply don't remember it.

3. **记性** jìxìng memory
   她的记性 很 好。
   Tāde jìxìng hěn hǎo.
   She has a good memory.

4. **记住** jìzhù learn by heart
   我 记不住 这么 多 汉字。
   Wǒ jìbuzhù zhème duō Hànzì.
   I can't remember so many characters.

5. **忘记** wàngjì forgotten
   他 紧张地 工作，忘记了 去 吃
   Tā jǐnzhāngde gōngzuò, wàngjìle qù chī
   晚饭。
   wǎnfàn.
   He was working so hard that he forgot to go for dinner.

Note the difference between 己 and 已.   5 strokes

`	讠	记	记	记					

Quiz 50 (491–500)

A. Look at the 16-character grid and CIRCLE words or phrases. They can be written horizontally or vertically. (Look at the circled characters in the Key if you are unsure.) Copy the word or phrase next to the grid and write the pinyin and meaning.

要求	养	按
坚	持	次	成
习	笔	顺	每
惯	必	须	练

	Word or phrase		Pinyin	Meaning
(i)	要	求	yāoqiú	require
(ii)				
(iii)				
(iv)				

B. Using the characters in the 16-character grid, convert the pinyin sentences into characters and write the English meaning.

(i)	Yào jiānchí liànxí xiě Hànzì.							
(ii)	Měi cì bù yāoqiú xiě tài duō.							
(iii)	Dàn bìxū àn bǐshùn xiě.							
(iv)	Yǎngchéngle xíguàn, jiù néng jìzhù.							

C. Match the Chinese words with their English meaning.

(i)

坚决	enduring
持久	less important
zhī 持	must
次数	resolute
次要	inevitable
必得	support
必然	number of times
需要	necessary

(ii)

按理	smooth, successful
按时	usual practice
顺利	logically
xiū 养	remember
惯 lì	on time
记得	memory
记 xìng	forget
wàng 记	accomplishment

296

CHARACTER BUILDING 10 (451–500)

A. Memorize each of the following radicals and their English names. As a review exercise, write the pinyin and English meaning below:

1. [丶] 'dot'
    主 (＿＿＿＿) ＿＿＿＿＿＿＿ ; 为 (＿＿＿＿) ＿＿＿＿＿＿＿ .

2. [丨] 'vertical stroke'
    非 (＿＿＿＿) ＿＿＿＿＿＿＿ ; 旧 (＿＿＿＿) ＿＿＿＿＿＿＿ .

3. [丿] 'downward-left stroke'
    重 (＿＿＿＿) ＿＿＿＿＿＿＿ ; 向 (＿＿＿＿) ＿＿＿＿＿＿＿ .

4. [冫] 'ice'
    次 (＿＿＿＿) ＿＿＿＿＿＿＿ ; 冷 (＿＿＿＿) ＿＿＿＿＿＿＿ .

5. [讠] 'word'
    试 (＿＿＿＿) ＿＿＿＿＿＿＿ ; 记 (＿＿＿＿) ＿＿＿＿＿＿＿ .

6. [冂] 'border'
    肉 (＿＿＿＿) ＿＿＿＿＿＿＿ ; 周 (＿＿＿＿) ＿＿＿＿＿＿＿ .

7. [亻] 'upright person'
    休 (＿＿＿＿) ＿＿＿＿＿＿＿ ; 优 (＿＿＿＿) ＿＿＿＿＿＿＿ ;
    信 (＿＿＿＿) ＿＿＿＿＿＿＿ .

8. [又] 'again'
    鸡 (＿＿＿＿) ＿＿＿＿＿＿＿ ; 难 (＿＿＿＿) ＿＿＿＿＿＿＿ ;

9. [力] 'strength'
    功 (＿＿＿＿) ＿＿＿＿＿＿＿ ; 男 (＿＿＿＿) ＿＿＿＿＿＿＿ .

10. [氵] '3 drops of water'
    酒 (＿＿＿＿) ＿＿＿＿＿＿＿ ; 清 (＿＿＿＿) ＿＿＿＿＿＿＿ .

11. [忄] 'upright heart'
    惯 (＿＿＿＿) ＿＿＿＿＿＿＿ ; 快 (＿＿＿＿) ＿＿＿＿＿＿＿ .

12. [门] 'door'
    门 (＿＿＿＿) ＿＿＿＿＿＿＿ ; 问 (＿＿＿＿) ＿＿＿＿＿＿＿ .

13. [工] 'work'
    功 (＿＿＿＿) ＿＿＿＿＿＿＿ ; 工 (＿＿＿＿) ＿＿＿＿＿＿＿ .

14. [土] 'earth'
    境 (＿＿＿＿) ＿＿＿＿＿＿＿ ; 基 (＿＿＿＿) ＿＿＿＿＿＿＿ ;
    坚 (＿＿＿＿) ＿＿＿＿＿＿＿ ; 场 (＿＿＿＿) ＿＿＿＿＿＿＿ .

15. [艹] 'grass'
    茶 (＿＿＿＿) ＿＿＿＿＿＿＿ ; 菜 (＿＿＿＿) ＿＿＿＿＿＿＿ .

16. [扌] 'hand'
    持 (＿＿＿＿) ＿＿＿＿＿＿＿ ; 按 (＿＿＿＿) ＿＿＿＿＿＿＿ .

17. [小] 'small'
    尝 (＿＿＿＿) ＿＿＿＿＿＿＿ ; 常 (＿＿＿＿) ＿＿＿＿＿＿＿ .

18. [口] 'mouth'
    喝 (＿＿＿＿) ＿＿＿＿＿＿＿ ; 味 (＿＿＿＿) ＿＿＿＿＿＿＿ .

19. [饣] 'food'
饮 (_____) _____ ; 馆 (_____) _____ .

20. [己] 'self'
己 (_____) _____ ; 已 (_____) _____ .

21. [女] 'female'
奶 (_____) _____ ; 始 (_____) _____ .

22. [马] 'horse'
验 (_____) _____ ; 马 (_____) _____ .

23. [火] 'fire'
炒 (_____) _____ ; 烧 (_____) _____ .

24. [心] 'heart'
息 (_____) _____ ; 必 (_____) _____ .

25. [王] 'king'
主 (_____) _____ ; 环 (_____) _____ .

26. [木] 'tree'
杯 (_____) _____ ; 橘 (_____) _____ .

27. [牛] 'cattle'
牛 (_____) _____ ; 特 (_____) _____ .

28. [田] 'field'
累 (_____) _____ ; 男 (_____) _____ .

29. [米] 'rice'
料 (_____) _____ ; 糖 (_____) _____ .

30. [页] 'page'
须 (_____) _____ ; 顺 (_____) _____ .

31. [虫] 'insect'
蛋 (_____) _____ ; 虽 (_____) _____ .

32. [自] 'self'
自 (_____) _____ ; 息 (_____) _____ .

33. [舌] 'tongue'
甜 (_____) _____ ; 舒 (_____) _____ .

34. [其] 'such'
基 (_____) _____ ; 期 (_____) _____ .

B. Write the pinyin and meaning against the characters classified under the following radicals.

1. [歹] 'evil'   死   (_____) _____

2. [鸟] 'bird'   鸡   (_____) _____

3. [食] 'eat'   餐   (_____) _____

The following are words and phrases classified under parts of speech. Write their pinyin and meaning.

Nouns 饮料 (_____) _____ ; 饮用水 (_____) _____ ;

冷饮 (_____) _____ ; 奶茶 (_____) _____ ;

牛奶 (_____) _____ ; 茶叶 (_____) _____ ;

茶杯 (_____) _____ ; 杯子 (_____) _____ ;

世界杯 (_____) _____ ; 糖果 (_____) _____ ;

甜头 (_____) _____ ; 味道 (_____) _____ ;

气味 (_____) _____ ; 信息 (_____) _____ ;

利息 (_____) _____ ; 主见 (_____) _____ ;

主意 (_____) _____ ; 餐车 (_____) _____ ;

中餐 (_____) _____ ; 环节 (_____) _____ ;

环境 (_____) _____ ; 境地 (_____) _____ ;

优点 (_____) _____ ; 菜单 (_____) _____ ;

酒杯 (_____) _____ ; 酒量 (_____) _____ ;

橘子 (_____) _____ ; 公鸡 (_____) _____ ;

牛肉 (_____) _____ ; 鸡蛋 (_____) _____ ;

蛋白 (_____) _____ ; 蛋黄 (_____) _____ ;

自己 (_____) _____ ; 自行车 (_____) _____ ;

知己 (_____) _____ ; 经验 (_____) _____ ;

始末 (_____) _____ ; 基本功 (_____) _____ ;

功能 (_____) _____ ; 信用 (_____) _____ ;

门口 (_____) _____ ; 门路 (_____) _____ ;

门票 (_____) _____ ; 门外汉 (_____) _____ ;

笔顺 (_____) _____ ; 次数 (_____) _____ .

车次 (_____) _____ ;

Personal 我自己 (_____) _____ ; 你自己 (_____) _____ ;
Pronouns 他自己 (_____) _____ ; 她自己 (_____) _____ ;

Measure 杯 (_____) _____ ; 门 (_____) _____ .
Words

Verbs 料到 (_____) _____ ; 料理 (_____) _____ ;

料想 (_____) _____ ; 死记 (_____) _____ ;

死心 (_____) _____ ; 尝试 (_____) _____ ;

试味 (_____) _____ ; 试行 (_____) _____ ;

试用 (_____) _____ ;   休假 (_____) _____ ;

休息 (_____) _____ ;   休养 (_____) _____ ;

做菜 (_____) _____ ;   信不过 (_____) _____ ;

信得过 (_____) _____ ;   养神 (_____) _____ ;

记得 (_____) _____ ;   记住 (_____) _____ ;

开始 (_____) _____ ;   坚持 (_____) _____ ;

持有 (_____) _____ ;   习惯 (_____) _____ ;

Adjectives

好喝 (_____) _____ ;   美味 (_____) _____ ;

主要 (_____) _____ ;   环城 (_____) _____ ;

优美 (_____) _____ ;   单身 (_____) _____ ;

橘黄 (_____) _____ ;   非法 (_____) _____ ;

重点 (_____) _____ ;   用功 (_____) _____ ;

坚定 (_____) _____ ;   持久 (_____) _____ ;

次要 (_____) _____ ;   必要 (_____) _____ ;

Adverbs

…死了 (_____) _____ ;   单单 (_____) _____ ;

酒后 (_____) _____ ;   非常 (_____) _____ ;

顺便 (_____) _____ ;   需要 (_____) _____ ;

必得 (_____) _____ ;   必定 (_____) _____ ;

必然 (_____) _____ ;   按理 (_____) _____ .

Conjunction   非但 (_____) _____ .

Prepositions   自从 (_____) _____ ;   按照 (_____) _____ ;

按时 (_____) _____ .

WORD/SENTENCE PUZZLE 10

Find and circle words, phrases and sentences hidden in the puzzle. They can be found horizontally from left to right or vertically . The lines across and down are indicated by numbers. Write their meaning next to the pinyin. The first one is done for you.

ACROSS

1. Tā zhǐ shì jiǔròu péngyou, buhuì bāngzhù wǒ de.

   He's only a fair-weather friend. He won't help me.

3. Běijīng yǒu hěnduō měiwèi xiǎochī.

   _____

6. Xué yǔyán zuì zhòngyào shì néng
   jìzhù shēngcí. _____

7. diǎnlǐ _____

8. xìnxīn _____

9. shūxiě _____

10. nán'guò _____

11. (i) xiǎngfa _____

    (ii) Wǒ měitiān jiānchí xiě Hànzì. _____

12. chéngjiù _____

13. (i) yǒu dàoli _____

    (ii) huìhuà _____

14. zhǔyi _____

15. (i) gǎnqíng _____

    (ii) gōngnéng _____

18. Zhōumò de shíhou, chēcì bǐjiào duō. _____

DOWN

1. Běijīng Dàxué shì zhòngdiǎn dàxué. _____

3. Wǒ xiǎng zhīdao shìqing de shǐmò. _____

4. Tā zuì ài hējiǔ. _____

5. yìshí _____

6. Nǐ yàoshi xìndeguò wǒ jiù jiāo gěi wǒ bàn. _____

8. (i) kěnéng _____

   (ii) Wǒ jīntiān lái zhǎoguo nǐmen liǎng cì. _____

9. jìde _____

10. (i) jìbuzhù _____

    (ii) Nǐ yào jiānchí cái huì chénggōng. _____

11. nénglì _____

12. Wǒ yào mǎi Yīng-Hàn cídiǎn. _____

13. Xiě Hànzì yào zhùyì bǐshùn. _____

	1	2	3	4	5	6	7	8	9	10	11	12	13
1	他	只	是	酒	肉	朋	友	不	会	帮	助	我	的
2	双	正	改	界	种	难	绿	应	调	流	贯	要	验
3	北	京	有	很	多	美	味	小	吃	验	羊	买	容
4	京	厕	本	别	己	难	非	首	基	记	鸡	英	趣
5	大	帮	所	他	真	你	红	可	必	不	炒	汉	杯
6	学	语	言	最	重	要	是	能	记	住	生	词	跟
7	是	价	蓝	爱	像	是	紧	河	得	容	须	典	礼
8	重	首	成	喝	话	信	心	气	特	你	像	他	爸
9	点	银	敬	酒	张	得	做	我	别	要	按	书	写
10	大	知	我	体	难	过	会	今	台	坚	养	奶	汉
11	学	昨	想	法	请	我	每	天	坚	持	写	汉	字
12	向	把	知	回	成	就	城	来	灯	才	自	会	要
13	祝	有	道	理	糖	交	讲	找	楚	会	话	息	注
14	颜	决	事	请	饮	给	理	过	就	成	狗	主	意
15	语	感	情	新	累	我	休	你	死	功	能	题	笔
16	主	外	的	语	要	办	料	们	甜	间	力	因	顺
17	星	试	始	什	一	尝	讲	两	餐	优	境	环	馆
18	茶	周	末	的	时	候	车	次	比	较	多	白	味

Alphabetical Index

fǔyīn	辅音	294.4
fǔzhù	辅助	294.5
fù	附	351.1
fùdài	附带	351.2
fùjiāshuì	附加税	351.3
fùjìn	附近	351.4
fùshàng	附上	351.5

G

gāi	该	292.1
gāidāng	该当	292.2
gāisǐ	该死	292.3
gǎi	改	289.1
gǎibiàn	改变	289.2
gǎidiào	改掉	289.3
gǎigē	改革	289.4
gǎizhèng	改正	289.5
gānbēi	干杯	474.4
gānjú	柑橘	475.4
gǎn	感	271.1
gǎnjué	感觉	271.2
gǎnmào	感冒	271.3/438.5
gǎnqíng	感情	271.4
gǎnxiè	感谢	271.5
gāng	刚	386.1
gāngcái	刚才	269.5/386.2
gānggāng	刚刚	386.3
gānghǎo	刚好	386.4
gāngqiǎo	刚巧	386.5
gǎng	港	256.1
Gǎngbì	港币	256.5
gǎngkǒu	港口	256.2
gāo	高	308.1
gāo'ǎi	高矮	308.2
gāodà	高大	308.4
gāodī	高低	308.3
gāogēnxié	高跟鞋	280.5
gāojí	高级	405.5
gāoxìng	高兴	272.5/308.5
gào	告	281.1
gàobié	告别	281.2
gàojià	告假	281.3
gàosu	告诉	281.4

gē	歌	302.1
gēchàngjiā	歌唱家	305.5
gējùyuàn	歌剧院	302.3
gēmí	歌迷	302.4
gēshēng	歌声	302.5
gēxīng	歌星	302.2
gěi	给	313.1
gěile	给了	313.2
gēn	跟	280.1
gēn … yíyàng	跟 … 一样	280.2
gēnshàng	跟上	280.3
gēnzhe	跟着	280.4
gōng'ānjú	公安局	370.5
gōngjī	公鸡	477.4
gōng	功	488.1
gōngkè	功课	488.2
gōngnéng	功能	488.3
gōngjǐ	供给	313.4
gǔwán	古玩	344.5
gùkè	顾客	443.5
guā	刮	414.1
guāliǎn	刮脸	414.3
guāliǎndāo	刮脸刀	414.4
guā mù xiāng kàn	刮目相看	414.5
guāpò	刮破	414.2
guǎi	拐	358.1
guǎijiǎo	拐角	358.2
guǎiwān	拐弯	358.3
guǎiwān-mòjiǎo	拐弯抹角	358.4
guǎizhàng	拐杖	358.5
guǎn	馆	470.1
guàn	惯	499.1
guànhuài	惯坏	499.2
guànlì	惯例	499.3
guǎngchǎng	广场	361.2
guǒ	果	367.1
guǒrán	果然	367.3/418.5
guoduàn	果断	367.2

H

hǎigǎng	海港	256.3
hǎiwān	海湾	311.3
hángyè	行业	339.4

xiàngwǎng	向往	357.5
xiàng	相	330.1
xiàngmào	相貌	330.2
xiàngpiàn	相片	330.3
xiàngshēng	相声	330.4
xiàng	像	392.1
xiàngyàng	像样	392.2
xiǎoshēng	小声	266.3
xiǎoxīn	小心	320.5
xiàoróng	笑容	309.5
xié	鞋	383.1
xiédài	鞋带	383.2
xiéjiang	鞋匠	383.3
xiéyóu	鞋油	383.4
xiēxi	歇息	462.5
xīn	心	320.1
xīnlǐ	心理	320.2
xīnqíng	心情	320.3
xīnténg	心疼	320.4
xīn	新	385.1
xīnnián	新年	385.2
xīnqí	新奇	385.3
xīnwén	新闻	385.4
xīnwénjiè	新闻界	347.5
xīnxiān	新鲜	385.5
xìn	信	489.1
xìnbuguò	信不过	489.2
xìndeguò	信得过	489.3
xìnxīn	信心	489.4
xìnyòng	信用	489.5
xìnxī	信息	462.2
xīngfèn	兴奋	272.2
xìng	兴	272.1
xìngqù	兴趣	272.3/273.4
xìngtóu	兴头	272.4
xíng	行	339.1
xíngli	行李	339.2
xíngshǐ	行驶	339.3
xiū	休	461.1
xiūjià	休假	461.2
xiūxi	休息	461.3
xiūyǎng	休养	461.4
xiūyè	休业	461.5

xiūjiàn	修建	278.5
xiūyǎng	修养	498.4
xū	须	495.1
xūyào	须要	495.2
xūzhī	须知	495.3
xǔ	许	365.1
xǔduō	许多	365.2
xǔjiǔ	许久	365.3

Y

yán	言	261.1
yánlùn	言论	261.2
yántán	言谈	261.3
yánxíng	言行	261.4
yányǔ	言语	261.5
yán	颜	371.1
yánliào	颜料	371.2
yánmiàn	颜面	371.4
yánsè	颜色	371.3
yǎnjiè	眼界	347.3
yàn	厌	413.1
yànfán	厌烦	413.2
yànjuàn	厌倦	413.3
yànshízhèng	厌食症	413.4
yànwù	厌恶	413.5
yàn	验	275.1
yànxiě	验血	275.2
yǎng	养	498.1
yǎngshén	养神	498.2
yāoqiú	要求	296.5
yào	要	262.1
yàobù	要不	262.2
yàohǎo	要好	262.3
yàojǐn	要紧	262.4
yào	药	439.1
yàocái	药材	439.2
yàofāng	药方	439.3
yàodiàn	药店	439.4
yàoshuǐ	药水	439.5
yěxǔ	也许	365.5
yè	叶	426.1
yèzi	叶子	426.2
yè	夜	408.1

Radical Index

[女] #65		
如	rú	366
奶	nǎi	454
始	shǐ	484
要	yào	262

[纟] #68		
红	hóng	354
级	jí	405
给	gěi/jǐ	313
绿	lǜ	355

[马] #69		
验	yàn	275

4 strokes

[灬] #71		
然	rán	418
照	zhào	329

[方] #74		
放	fàng	321
旅	lǚ	338

[火] #75		
灯	dēng	356
炒	chǎo	476
烧	shāo	434

[心] #76		
心	xīn	320
必	bì	494
念	niàn	483
思	sī	445
息	xī	462
意	yì	444
感	gǎn	271
想	xiǎng	283

[户] #77		
所	suǒ	353

[礻] #78		
礼	lǐ	441
祝	zhù	448
神	shén	399

[王] #79		
主	zhǔ	463
环	huán	467
玩	wán	344
理	lǐ	300

[木] #81		
机	jī	333
极	jí	428
林	lín	430
杯	bēi	474
果	guǒ	367
相	xiàng	330
树	shù	429
橘	jú	475

[歹] #83		
死	sǐ	465

[车] #84		
辅	fǔ	294

[戈] #85		
划	huà	342
成	chéng	446

[止] #88		
正	zhèng	290

[日] #90		
易	yì	310
春	chūn	411
普	pǔ	253
景	jǐng	328
晴	qíng	403
量	liǎng/liàng	435
暖	nuǎn	420
香	xiāng	255

[日] #91		
曲	qū/qǔ	307
冒	mào	438
最	zuì	299

[牛] (牜) #95		
牛	niú	479
物	wù	442
特	tè	378

[手] #96		
拿	ná	395

[气] #98		
气	qì	400

[攵] #99		
改	gǎi	289
放	fàng	321
教	jiāo/jiào	312
敬	jìng	447

[斤] #101		
所	suǒ	353
新	xīn	385

[月] #103		
肥	féi	393
服	fú	389

[欠] #104		
歌	gē	302

[风] #105		
风	fēng	327

[水] #109		
水	shuǐ	345

5 strokes

[穴] #110		
穿	chuān	387
容	róng	309

KEY

Quiz 26 (251–260)

A.

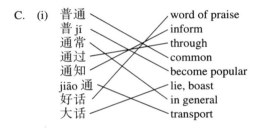

Word or phrase	Pinyin	English meaning
(i) 中国话	Zhōngguóhuà	Chinese language
(ii) 香港	Xiānggǎng	Hong Kong
(iii) 普通话	Pǔtōnghuà	Modern Standard Chinese
(iv) 听不懂	tīngbudǒng	can't understand

B.

Pinyin	Characters	Translation
(i) Hànyǔ jiù shì Zhōngguóhuà.	汉语就是中国话。	*Hanyu* has the same meaning as *Zhongguohua.*
(ii) Hànyǔ yòu jiào Pǔtōnghuà.	汉语又叫普通话。	*Hanyu* is also known as *Putonghua.*
(iii) Zài Xiānggǎng chūshēng de rén bù yídìng néng tīng dǒng Pǔtōnghuà.	在香港出生的人不一定能听懂普通话。	People who are born in Hong Kong don't necessarily understand *Putonghua* (Modern Standard Chinese).

C. (i)

普通 — common
普及 — become popular
通常 — in general
通过 — through
通知 — inform
jiāo 通 — transport
好话 — word of praise
大话 — lie, boast

(ii)

听见 — hear
听话 — obedient
出 cuò — make a mistake
出 fā — set out
定做 — made to order
一定 — definitely
懂 shì — understand
懂得 — mature

Quiz 27 (261–270)

A.

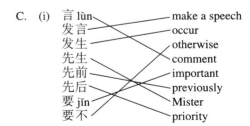

Word or phrase	Pinyin	English meaning
(i) 学拼音	xué pīnyīn	learn pinyin
(ii) 声调	shēngdiào	tone
(iii) 语言	yǔyán	language
(iv) 认读	rèndú	recognition reading

B.

Pinyin	Characters	Translation
(i) Pǔtōnghuà yǒu sì ge shēngdiào.	普通话有四个声调。	*Putonghua* has four tones.
(ii) Xué Hànyǔ yào xiān xué fāyīn, xué fāyīn yào xué Hànyǔ Pīnyīn, hái yào duō shuō cái huì yǒu jìnbù.	学汉语要先学发音，学发音要学汉语拼音，还要多说才会有进步。	When learning Chinese, you first need to learn pronunciation; when learning pronunciation, you need to learn pinyin, and you also need to speak it a lot to make any progress.

C. (i)

言 lùn — comment
发言 — make a speech
发生 — occur
先生 — Mister
先前 — previously
先后 — priority
要 jǐn — important
要不 — otherwise

(ii)

口音 — accent
声音 — sound
小声 — softly
调 chá — investigate
调 pí — mischievous
拼写 — spell
gāng 才 — just now
人才 — talent

Quiz 28 (271–280)

A.

对	感	跟	下
谈	兴	经	验
可	趣	本	建
交	流	书	议

	Word or phrase	Pinyin	English meaning
(i)	感兴趣	gǎn xìngqù	be interested in something
(ii)	经验	jīngyàn	experience
(iii)	交流	jiāoliú	exchange ideas
(iv)	建议	jiànyì	suggestion

B.

	Pinyin	Characters	Translation
(i)	Wǒ duì Hànzì hěn gǎn xìngqù.	我对汉字很感兴趣。	I'm very interested in Chinese characters.
(ii)	Kěyǐ tántan nǐde jīngyàn ma?	可以谈谈你的经验吗？	Can you talk about your experience?
(iii)	Wǒmen kěyǐ jiāoliú yíxiàr.	我们可以交流一下儿。	We can certainly exchange ideas on it.
(iv)	Wǒ jiànyì gēnzhe zhè běn shū xué.	我建议跟着这本书学。	I suggest that you follow this book.

C. (i)

感动 — be excited
感觉 — interest, delight
感谢 — feeling
高兴 — be touched by
兴 fèn — pleasure
趣 wèi — talk, conversation
lè 趣 — happy
谈话 — thanks

(ii)

验 xiě — exchange
shí 验 — popular
交流 — blood test
流 chuán — build
流 lì — establish
流 xíng — hand down
建 lì — experiment
xiū 建 — fluent

Quiz 29 (281–290)

A.

练	告	诉	习
讲	改	流	怕
想	正	利	就
多	得	开	口

	Word or phrase	Pinyin	English meaning
(i)	告诉	gàosu	tell
(ii)	改正	gǎizhèng	correct
(iii)	流利	liúlì	fluent
(iv)	开口	kāikǒu	speak (Literally, open your mouth)

B.

	Pinyin	Characters	Translation
(i)	Wǒ gàosu nǐ zěnyàng liànxí ba.	我告诉你怎样练习吧。	Let me tall you how to practice.
(ii)	Xiǎng jiǎngde liúlì jiù yào duō jiǎng.	想讲得流利就要多讲。	If you want to speak fluently, you have to speak a lot.
(iii)	Yào duō kāikǒu, búyào pà shuōcuò.	要多开口，不要怕说错。	You need to speak, and not be afraid of making mistakes.
(iv)	Cuòle jiù zhīdao zěnyàng gǎizhèng.	错了就知道怎样改正。	Only by making mistakes can you learn to correct them.

C. (i)

想 fa — talk, speak
想 niàn — fluent
讲话 — open to public use
讲 jià — way of thinking
讲 jiu — miss (someone)
流利 — bargain
开 fàng — begin
开 shǐ — be particular about

(ii)

怕 lěng — change, correct
错过 — normal
错 wù — dislike the cold
改 gē — miss
改 biàn — accurate
正 cháng — mistake
正 què — reform
正在 ——— right this moment

Quiz 30 (291–300)

A.

找	辅	应	该
语	导	理	音
要	发	正	确
求	想	法	最

	Word or phrase	Pinyin	English meaning
(i)	辅导	fǔdǎo	tutor, to give tuition
(ii)	应该	yīnggāi	ought to
(iii)	正确	zhèngquè	accurate
(iv)	想法	xiǎngfa	idea, what one has in mind

B.   **Pinyin**   **Characters**   **Translation**
      (i) Nǐ yīnggāi zhǎo ge Hànyǔ fǔdǎo.   你应该找个汉语辅导。   You should find a Chinese tutor.
      (ii) Yāoqiú tāde fāyīn zhèngquè.   要求她／他的发音正确。   You should be satisfied that she/he has
                                                                        accurate pronunciation.
      (iii) Hái yào néng jiǎng Hànyǔ yǔfǎ.   还要能讲汉语语法。   And that she/he can explain Chinese grammar.
      (iv) Zhǎo ge Zhōngguórén zuì lǐxiǎng. 找个中国人最理想。   It is ideal if you can find a Chinese person.

C.   (i)

应 dāng	plead
应 fū	seek advice
辅 zhù	confirm
导游	ought to
求 qíng	determine
求 jiào	assistance
确定	tourist guide
确认	deal with

(ii)

法 lǜ	best
法子	recently
最多	law
最好	way, method
最后	ideal
最近	reason
理想	at most
理 yóu	last

Character Building 6 (251–300)

A. 1. [一] 才 *cái*, just; 开 *kāi*, open; 正 *zhèng*,
            exact; 求 *qiú*, seek.
    2. [讠] 话 *huà*, language; 调 *diào/tiáo*, tone/adjust;
            议 *yì*, discuss; 诉 *sù*, tell; 谈 *tán*, talk;
            讲 *jiǎng*, talk, explain; 该 *gāi*, ought to.
    3. [八] 兴 *xìng*, joy, interest; 典 *diǎn*, classics.
    4. [儿] 儿 *ér*, son, child; 先 *xiān*, first; 元 *yuán*,
            dollar; 兄 *xiōng*, older brother.
    5. [又] 又 *yòu*, again; 发 *fā*, develop.
    6. [氵] 港 *gǎng*, harbor; 流 *liú*, flow; 法 *fǎ*, law.
    7. [忄] 怕 *pà*, afraid; 懂 *dǒng*, understand.
    8. [宀] 定 *dìng*, fix; 家 *jiā*, family.
    9. [广] 应 *yīng*, ought to; 床 *chuáng*, bed.
    10. [辶] 通 *tōng*, through; 道 *dào*, way, know.

    11. [士] 声 *shēng*, sound; 喜 *xǐ*, happy.
    12. [寸] 导 *dǎo*, guide; 对 *duì*, correct.
    13. [扌] 找 *zhǎo*, look for; 拼 *pīn*, put together.
    14. [口] 听 *tīng*, listen; 唱 *chàng*, sing.
    15. [女] 要 *yào*, want; 她 *tā*, she
    16. [心] 想 *xiǎng*, think; 感 *gǎn*, feel, sense
    17. [车] 车 *chē*, vehicle; 辅 *fǔ*, assist.
    18. [日] 普 *pǔ*, commonplace; 香 *xiāng*, fragrant.
    19. [曰] 最 *zuì*, most; 者 *zhě*, person.
    20. [钅] 错 *cuò*, wrong; 钟 *zhōng*, clock.
    21. [西] 要 *yào*, want; 西 *xī*, west.
    22. [竹] 第 *dì*, ordinal number; 算 *suàn*, calculate.
    23. [走] 趣 *qù*, interest; 起 *qǐ*, rise.
    24. [足] 跟 *gēn*, follow; 跑 *pǎo*, run.

B. 1. [刂] 利 *lì*, sharp
    2. [廴] 建 *jiàn*, build
    3. [凵] 出 *chū*, emerge
    4. [巳] 导 *dǎo*, guide, lead
    5. [王] 理 *lǐ*, reason

    6. [攵] 改 *gǎi*, change
    7. [石] 确 *què*, accurate
    8. [言] 言 *yán*, word
    9. [音] 音 *yīn*, sound

C. 1. [舌] 活 *huó*, live, alive;
            话 *huà*, language.
    2. [日] 音 *yīn*, sound;
            普 *pǔ*, commonplace.
    3. [斤] 听 *tīng*, listen;
            近 *jìn*, near.
    4. [禾] 香 *xiāng*, fragrant;
            利 *lì*, sharp.
    5. [白] 怕 *pà*, afraid;
            百 *bǎi*, hundred.

    6. [亥] 该 *gāi*, ought to;
            孩 *hái*, child.
    7. [取] 趣 *qù*, interest;
            最 *zuì*, most.
    8. [艮] 跟 *gēn*, follow;
            很 *hěn*, very.
    9. [业] 兴 *xīng*, joy, interest;
            应 *yīng/yìng*, ought to/respond.

Review 6 (251–300)

Nouns
普通话 *Pǔtōnghuà*, Modern Standard Chinese;   话 *huà*, language;
电话 *diànhuà*, telephone;   好话 *hǎohuà*, flattery;
语言 *yǔyán*, language;   外语 *wàiyǔ*, foreign language;
声调 *shēngdiào*, tone;   发音 *fāyīn*, pronunciation;
拼音 *pīnyīn*, pinyin;   兴趣 *xìngqù*, interest;
经验 *jīngyàn*, experience;   建议 *jiànyì*, suggestion;
辅导 *fǔdǎo*, coaching;   要求 *yāoqiú*, requirement, demand.

Ordinal number
第 *dì*, ordinal number.

Verbs

说话 *shuōhuà*, speak; 讲话 *jiǎnghuà*, speak, talk; 交谈 *jiāotán*, conversation; 建议 *jiànyì*, suggest; 听说 *tīngshuō*, hear, tell; 告诉 *gàosu*, tell; 看懂 *kàndǒng*, understand (by reading); 想 *xiǎng*, want, think; 讲 *jiǎng*, speak, explain; 错 *cuò*, make mistakes; 改正 *gǎizhèng*, correct mistakes;

通知 *tōngzhī*, inform; 交流 *jiāoliú*, exchange; 听 *tīng*, listen; 听见 *tīngjiàn*, hear; 懂 *dǒng*, understand; 懂得 *dǒngdē*, understand; 听懂 *tīngdǒng*, understand (by hearing); 谈 *tán*, talk; 怕 *pà*, be afraid of; 找 *zhǎo*, find; 辅导 *fǔdǎo*, coach.

Auxiliary Verbs

想 *xiǎng*, would like to; 要 *yào*, want to; 应该 *yīnggāi*, ought to.

Adjectives

普通 *pǔtōng*, common; 香 *xiāng*, fragrant; 理想 *lǐxiǎng*, ideal; 流利 *liúlì*, fluent;

Adverbs

一定 *yídìng*, definitely; 正 *zhèng*, just, precisely; 正在 *zhèngzài*, in the process of; 要不 *yàobù*, otherwise; 才 *cái*, just, only then; 最 *zuì*, most.

Preposition

跟 *gēn*, with.

Word/Sentence Puzzle 6

ACROSS

2. I still can't understand Mandarin.
4. exchange
5. There are four tones.
6. You have to learn pronunciation when learning a language.
9. requirement
10. interesting
11. I have a Chinese tutor.
12. grammar
14. pronounce something correctly.

DOWN

2. I'm interested in language exchange.
4. (i) Someone said …
   (ii) You have to speak more before you will improve.
6. (i) understand (by reading);
   (ii) To learn pronunciation, one has to study pinyin.
7. Grammar.
8. (i) A loud voice; (ii) confirm
9. talk
12. You should find yourself an English tutor.

	1	2	3	4	5	6	7	8	9	10	11	12	13
1						看			谈			你	
2	我	还	听	不	懂	普	通	话				应	
3		对		说								该	
4		交	流									找	
5		流		你			声	调	有	四		个	
6	学	语	言	要	先	学	发	音				英	
7		言		多		发		很				语	
8		感		说		音		大				辅	
9		兴		才		要	求					导	
10	有	趣		会		学							
11			我	有	个	汉	语	辅	导				
12			进		语	法							
13			步		拼								
14				发	音	正	确						
15					定								

Quiz 31 (301–310)

A.

高	民	歌	容
喜	首	曲	易
通	俗	唱	较
难	比	调	懂

Word or phrase	Pinyin	English meaning
(i) 民歌	*mín'gē*	folk song
(ii) 歌曲	*gēqǔ*	song
(iii) 容易	*róngyì*	easy
(iv) 通俗	*tōngsú*	popular

B.

Pinyin	Characters	Translation
(i) Nǐ xǐhuan tīng Zhōngguó mín'gē ma?	你喜欢听中国民歌吗？	Do you like to listen to Chinese folk songs?
(ii) Xǐhuan, dànshì mín'gē hěn nán chàng.	喜欢，但是民歌很难唱。	Yes, but folk songs are difficult to sing.
(iii) Wǒ bǐjiào xǐhuan tōngsú gēqǔ.	我比较喜欢通俗歌曲。	I prefer pop music.
(iv) Diàozi bú tài gāo, róngyì chàng.	调子不太高，容易唱。	The tunes are not too high, so they are easy to sing.

C. (i)
民 zhǔ
人民
唱歌
但是
不但
难得
难过
交易

sad
but
sing
people
democracy
transaction
rare
not only

(ii)
俗气
习俗
高大
高兴
歌曲
曲 jiě
xiào 容
容 rěn

happy
misinterpret
in poor taste
custom
put up with
song
tall and big
smile

Quiz 32 (311–320)

A.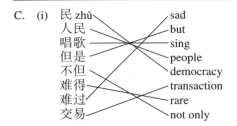

Word or phrase	Pinyin	English meaning
(i) 台湾	Táiwān	Taiwan
(ii) 月亮	yuèliang	the moon
(iii) 金曲	jīnqǔ	classic hit
(iv) 代表	dàibiǎo	represent

B.
Pinyin	Characters	Translation
(i) Wǒ xiǎng xué Táiwān tōngsú gēqǔ.	我想学台湾通俗歌曲。	I want to learn pop songs from Taiwan.
(ii) Nǐ néng jiāo gěi wǒ yì shǒu ma?	你能教给我一首吗?	Can you teach me one?
(iii) Méi wèntí. Zhè shì jīnqǔ lǎogē.	没问题,这是金曲老歌。	No problem. This is a golden oldie.
(iv) Jiào <Yuèliang Dàibiǎo Wǒde Xīn>.	叫《月亮代表我的心》	It is called "The moon represents my heart".

C. (i)
教师
教 táng
教 yù
首先
问题
话题
金 róng
现金

first of all
question
finance, banking
teacher
church
ready cash
education
topic of conversation

(ii)
明亮
月亮
代 jià
代 tì
表 dǎ
表 yǎn
心 lǐ
心 qíng

perform
express
bright, shining
mood
the moon
psychology
replace
price, cost

Quiz 33 (321–330)

A.

Word or phrase	Pinyin	English meaning
(i) 黄山	Huángshān	The Yellow Mountain
(ii) 照相	zhàoxiàng	take photographs
(iii) 打算	dǎsuàn	plan
(iv) 风景	fēngjǐng	scenery

B.
Pinyin	Characters	Translation
(i) Fàngjià shí, nǐ xiǎng qù nǎr wán?	放假时,你想去哪儿玩?	Where do you plan to go for your holidays?
(ii) Wǒ dǎsuàn qù Huángshān wán.	我打算去黄山玩。	I plan to go to the Yellow Mountain.
(iii) Huángshān fēngjǐng hěn měi.	黄山风景很美。	The scenery around the Yellow Mountain is really beautiful.
(iv) Nǐ kěyǐ zhào hěnduō xiàng.	你可以照很多相。	You can take heaps of photos.

C. (i)
假 zào
假 rú
假期
请假
打字
打听
打 sǎo
算 pán

sweep, clean
abacus
counterfeit
if
holiday
type
find out
take leave

(ii)
算 zhàng
山 dǐng
风趣
风 sú
景 sè
照 jiù
照 piàn
相 mào

as before
photograph
summit
scenery
work out accounts
appearance
humorous
custom

Quiz 34 (331–340)

A.

旅	快	贵	钱
行	飞	机	办
花	行	票	法
坐	怎	慢	太

Word or phrase	Pinyin	English meaning
(i) 旅行	lǚxíng	travel
(ii) 飞机	fēijī	aeroplane
(iii) 机票	jīpiào	plane ticket
(iv) 办法	bànfǎ	way, means

B.

Pinyin	Characters	Translation
(i) Nǐ zěnme qù Huángshān? Zuò huǒchē?	你怎么去黄山？坐火车？	How do you travel to the Yellow Mountain? By train?
(ii) Huǒchē tài màn, zuò fēijī kuài.	火车太慢，坐飞机快。	Trains are too slow, it is much faster by plane.
(iii) Fēijīpiào de jiàqián hěn guì ma?	飞机票的价钱很贵吗？	Is a plane ticket very expensive?
(iv) Méi bànfǎ, lǚxíng yào huāqián de.	没办法，旅行要花钱的。	There's nothing you can do about it, it costs money to travel.

C. (i)
机会 motorized
机动 speed
机 líng opportunity
快 cān value
快 lè price
快慢 clever
价 zhī happy
价钱 fast food

(ii)
讲价 work
办理 luggage
办 shì handle
花样 bargain
行 li travel
行 shǐ bank
行 yè variety
yín 行 profession

Quiz 35 (341–350)

A.

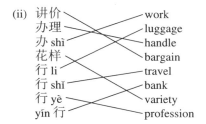

黄	河	江	行
玩	水	世	山
决	定	界	长
名	旅	计	划

Word or phrase	Pinyin	English meaning
(i) 黄河	Huánghé	the Yellow River
(ii) 世界	shìjiè	the world
(iii) 决定	juédìng	decide
(iv) 计划	jìhuà	plan

B.

Pinyin	Characters	Translation
(i) Shuōshuō nǐde lǚxíng jìhuà ba.	说说你的旅行计划吧。	Tell us about your travel plans.
(ii) Wǒ hái méi juédìng qù nǎr wán.	我还没决定去哪儿玩。	I haven't yet decided where to go.
(iii) Zhōngguó de shānshuǐ shìjiè yǒumíng.	中国的山水世界有名。	The scenery in China is world famous.
(iv) Chángjiāng de fēngjǐng hěn měi.	长江的风景很美。	The scenery along the Changjiang River is very pretty.

C. (i)
计较 epoch-making
计算 toy
划分 haggle over
划时代 divide
决心 planning
jiě 决 thing
玩 jù determination
玩 yìr resolve

(ii)
水 guǒ the world
水 píng Changjiang River
山水 huà level
世 jì landscape painting
世上 fruit
yǎn 界 century
界 xiàn limits
长江 field of vision

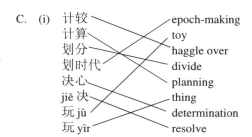
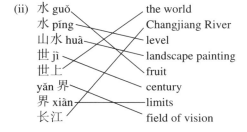

Character Building 7 (301–350)

A.
1. [一] 世 *shì*, the world; 表 *biǎo*, show, express.
2. [乛] 民 *mín*, people; 飞 *fēi*, fly.
3. [亠] 高 *gāo*, tall; 亮 *liàng*, bright.
4. [冫] 决 *jué*, definitely; 冷 *lěng*, cold.
5. [讠] 计 *jì*, calculate; 话 *huà*, language.
6. [刂] 划 *huà*, stroke (of a Chinese character); 利 *lì*, sharp.
7. [八] 首 *shǒu*, first; 兴 *xìng*, happy.
8. [亻] 但 *dàn*, but; 代 *dài*, replace; 假 *jiǎ/jià*, false/holiday; 价 *jià*, price; 俗 *sú*, custom.
9. [又] 难 *nán*, difficult; 又 *yòu*, again.
10. [力] 办 *bàn*, manage; 助 *zhù*, assistance
11. [氵] 湾 *wān*, bay; 江 *jiāng*, river.
12. [忄] 慢 *màn*, slowly; 快 *kuài*, fast.
13. [艹] 花 *huā*, flower; 黄 *huáng*, yellow.
14. [扌] 打 *dǎ*, strike; 找 *zhǎo*, look for.
15. [口] 唱 *chàng*, sing; 听 *tīng*, listen.
16. [彳] 行 *xíng*, capable, competent; 很 *hěn*, very.
17. [纟] 给 *gěi*, give; 练 *liàn*, practice.
18. [灬] 照 *zhào*, shine; 热 *rè*, hot.
19. [方] 旅 *lǚ*, travel; 放 *fàng*, put, place.
20. [心] 心 *xīn*, heart; 想 *xiǎng*, think
21. [王] 玩 *wǎn*, play; 理 *lǐ*, reason.
22. [木] 相 *xiàng*, appearance; 机 *jī*, machine.
23. [日] 景 *jǐng*, scenery; 易 *yì*, easy.
24. [曰] 曲 *qǔ*, song; 最 *zuì*, most.
25. [攵] 教 *jiāo*, teach; 放 *fàng*, release.
26. [欠] 歌 *gē*, song; 欢 *huān*, happy.
27. [戈] 划 *huà*, delimit; 我 *wǒ*, I.
28. [田] 界 *jiè*, delimit; 男 *nán*, male.
29. [西] 票 *piào*, ticket; 要 *yào*, want.
30. [竹] 算 *suàn*, calculate; 第 *dì*, ordinal number.

B.
1. [风] 风 *fēng*, wind
2. [山] 山 *shān*, mountain
3. [水] 水 *shuǐ*, water
4. [穴] 容 *róng*, easy
5. [示] 票 *piào*, ticket
6. [页] 题 *tí*, topic
7. [金] 金 *jīn*, gold
8. [舟] 船 *chuán*, boat

C.
1. [口] 哥 *gē*, older brother; 歌 *gē*, song.
2. [谷] 俗 *sú*, custom; 容 *róng*, hold, contain.
3. [方] 放 *fàng*, put, place; 旅 *lǚ*, travel.
4. [廾] 开 *kāi*, open; 算 *suàn*, calculate.
5. [元] 玩 *wán*, play; 远 *yuǎn*, far.
6. [介] 价 *jià*, price; 界 *jiè*, boundary.
7. [夬] 快 *kuài*, fast; 决 *jué*, definitely.
8. [戈] 划 *huà*, stroke (of a Chinese character); 找 *zhǎo*, look for.
9. [首] 首 *shǒu*, first and foremost; 道 *dào*, way, road.

Review 7 (301–350)

Nouns
人民 *rénmín*, people;
歌星 *gēxīng*, a singing star;
歌唱家 *gēchàngjiā*, vocalist;
习俗 *xísú*, custom;
曲子 *qǔzi*, song;
台湾 *Táiwān*, Taiwan;
首都 *shǒudū*, capital;
问题 *wèntí*, question, problem;
月亮 *yuèliang*, the moon;
心理 *xīnlǐ*, psychology;
计算机 *jìsuànjī*, computer;
黄山 *Huángshān*, the Yellow Mountain;
风俗 *fēngsú*, custom;

民歌 *mín'gē*, folk song;
歌声 *gēshēng*, sound of singing;
俗话 *súhuà*, saying;
作曲家 *zuòqǔjiā*, composer;
海湾 *hǎiwān*, bay;
教师 *jiàoshī*, teacher;
现金 *xiànjīn*, cash;
话题 *huàtí*, topic of conversation;
表面 *biǎomiàn*, surface;
假期 *jiàqī*, holiday;
黄金 *huángjīn*, gold;
山城 *shānchéng*, mountain city;
风趣 *fēngqù*, humor;

风景 *fēngjǐng*, scenery;
机会 *jīhuì*, opportunity;
价钱 *jiàqián*, price;
办理 *bànlǐ*, handle;
计算 *jìsuàn*, calculate;
世界 *shìjiè*, the world;
长江 *Chángjiāng*, Changjiang River (the Yangtze);

飞机 *fēijī*, aeroplane;
快慢 *kuàimàn*, speed;
办法 *bànfǎ*, way, method;
旅行 *lǚxíng*, travel;
山水 *shānshuǐ*, scenery;
江山 *jiāngshān*, landscape;
黄河 *Huánghé*, the Yellow River.

Verbs

唱歌 *chànggē*, sing; 作曲 *zuòqǔ*, compose a song;
代办 *dàibàn*, act as agent for; 代表 *dàibiǎo*, represent;
放心 *fàngxīn*, be at ease; 请假 *qǐngjià*, ask for leave;
打电话 *dǎ diànhuà*, dial a number; 打算 *dǎsuàn*, plan;
讲价 *jiǎngjià*, bargain; 花钱 *huāqián*, spend money;
划分 *huàfēn*, divide; 决心 *juéxīn*, be determined;

交易 *jiāoyì*, transact; 教书 *jiāoshū*, teach;
放大 *fàngdà*, enlarge; 放假 *fàngjià*, have a holiday;
打听 *dǎtīng*, find out; 打字 *dǎzì*, type;
照相 *zhàoxiàng*, take photograph;
花样 *huāyàng*, style; 计划 *jìhuà*, plan;
决定 *juédìng*, decide.

Adjectives

难过 *nán'guò*, sad; 难得 *nándé*, rare;
高兴 *gāoxìng*, happy; 容易 *róngyì*, easy;
明亮 *míngliàng*, bright; 小心 *xiǎoxīn*, careful;
计时 *jìshí*, reckon by time.

通俗 *tōngsú*, popular; 高大 *gāodà*, tall and big;
首要 *shǒuyào*, of first importance;
机动 *jīdòng*, motorized; 快活 *kuàihuó*, happy;

Adverbs

首先 *shǒuxiān*, first and foremost;
照常 *zhàocháng*, as usual; 慢慢 *mànmàn*, slowly;
飞快 *fēikuài*, fast; 决不 *juébù*, definitely not.

Conjunctions

但是 *dànshì*, but; 不但 *búdàn*, not only.

Word/Sentence Puzzle 7

ACROSS

1. He intends to go to the Yellow Mountain for a holiday.
3. customs
4. ocean view
5. The moon represents my heart.
8. It's a good opportunity, don't let it slip.
10. Taipei
11. bay
12. (i) plane ticket;   (ii) touring, travel
14. I've decided to invite her to come along.
15. Think of a good topic.

DOWN

2. It's light already.
5. I want to give this movie ticket to her.
7. He's not in a good mood today.
9. It would be great if I could go to Taiwan for a holiday.
11. The scenery around the Yellow Mountain is beautiful.
12. Don't worry, there won't be any problems.

	1	2	3	4	5	6	7	8	9	10	11	12	13
1							他	打	算	去	黄	山	玩
2							今				山		
3							天				风	俗	
4		天					的			海	景		
5	月	亮	代	表	我	的	心				很		
6		了			想		情		有		美		
7					把		不		机				
8					这	是	好	机	会	不	要	放	过
9					张				去			心	
10					电				台	北		吧	
11					影			海	湾			不	
12			飞	机	票				旅	游		会	
13					给				游			出	
14	我	决	定	请	她	去			就			问	
15							想	个	好	的	话	题	
16									了			的	

Quiz 36 (351–360)

A.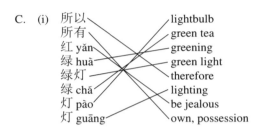

Word or phrase	Pinyin	English meaning
(i) 红绿灯	hónglǜdēng	traffic lights
(ii) 厕所	cèsuǒ	toilets
(iii) 拐弯	guǎiwān	turn a corner
(iv) 附近	fùjìn	nearby

B.

Pinyin	Characters	Translation
(i) Qǐngwèn, fùjìn yǒu méiyǒu cèsuǒ?	请问,附近有没有厕所?	Excuse me, is there a toilet nearby?
(ii) Zài qiánmiàn hónglǜdēng, xiàng yòu guǎi.	在前面红绿灯,向右拐。	Turn right when you get to the lights.
(iii) Dào dì'èr ge lùkǒu, zuǒ guǎiwān.	到第二个路口,左拐弯。	Turn left at the second intersection.
(iv) Zài zǒu 50 mǐ, yǒu gōnggòng cèsuǒ.	再走 50 米,有公共厕所。	Walk another 50 meters, there is a public toilet.

C. (i)
所以 — therefore
所有 — own, possession
红 yǎn — be jealous
绿灯 — green light
绿 chá — green tea
灯 pào — lightbulb
灯 guāng — lighting

(with "greening" option)

(ii)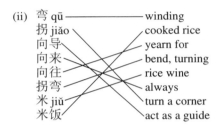
弯 qū — winding
拐 jiǎo — turn a corner
向导 — act as a guide
向来 — always
向往 — yearn for
拐弯 — bend, turning
米 jiǔ — rice wine
米饭 — cooked rice

Quiz 37 (361–370)

A.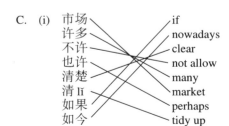

Word or phrase	Pinyin	English meaning
(i) 商场	shāngchǎng	arcade
(ii) 银行	yínháng	bank
(iii) 清楚	qīngchu	clear
(iv) 往回走	wǎng huí zǒu	go back (from previous direction)

B.

Pinyin	Characters	Translation
(i) Shāngchǎng lǐ yǒu méiyǒu yínháng?	商场里有没有银行?	Is there a bank in the shopping mall?
(ii) Wǒ bú tài qīngchu, yěxǔ méiyǒu.	我不太清楚,也许没有。	I'm not sure, maybe not.
(iii) Rúguǒ méiyǒu, nǐ wǎng huí zǒu.	如果没有,你往回走。	If there isn't one, go back.
(iv) Yóujú duìmiàn yǒu yì jiā yínháng.	邮局对面有一家银行。	Opposite the post office there's a bank.

C. (i)
市场 — market
许多 — many
不许 — not allow
也许 — perhaps
清楚 — clear
清 lǐ — tidy up
如果 — if
如今 — nowadays

(ii)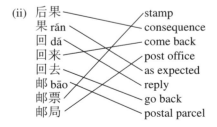
后果 — consequence
果 rán — as expected
回 dá — reply
回来 — come back
回去 — go back
邮 bāo — postal parcel
邮票 — stamp
邮局 — post office

Quiz 38 (371–380)

A.

Word or phrase	Pinyin	English meaning
(i) 白色	báisè	white
(ii) 颜色	yánsè	color
(iii) 特别	tèbié	special
(iv) 容易	róngyì	easy

B.

Pinyin	Characters	Translation
(i) Nǐ xǐhuan shénme yánsè?	你喜欢什么颜色？	What colors do you like?
(ii) Wǒ xǐhuan hēisè.	我喜欢黑色。	I like black.
(iii) Hēisè róngyì chèn biéde yánsè.	黑色容易衬别的颜色。	Black goes with most colors.
(iv) Wǒ juéde lánsè bú chèn huángsè.	我觉得蓝色不衬黄色。	I don't think blue goes with yellow.

C. (i)
颜 miàn — face, prestige
色 zé — set off
黑 ān — darkness
衬 shān — shirt
衬 tuō — color and luster
白 fēi — waste
白天 — daytime
别人 — other people

(ii)
别 zhī — in order to
特色 — special features
特长 — special skill
yuán 因 — reason
因 cǐ — thus
为了 — because
为什么 — why
因为 — unique

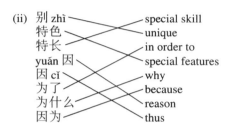

Quiz 39 (381–390)

A.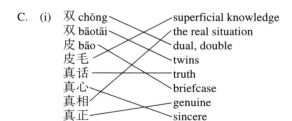

Word or phrase	Pinyin	English meaning
(i) 运动鞋	yùndòngxié	sports shoes
(ii) 皮鞋	píxié	leather shoes
(iii) 舒服	shūfu	comfortable
(iv) 穿起来	chuānqǐlái	put on

B.

Pinyin	Characters	Translation
(i) Zhè shuāng píxié zhēn hǎokàn.	这双皮鞋真好看。	These shoes are really pretty.
(ii) Shì xīn de, shàng xīngqī gāng mǎi de.	是新的，上星期买的。	They are new. I bought them last week.
(iii) Búguò chuānqilái hái bù shūfu.	不过穿起来还不舒服。	But they still don't feel comfortable.
(iv) Nǐ mànmàn jiù juéde shūfu le.	你慢慢就觉得舒服了。	You'll wear them in eventually.

C. (i)
双 chóng — dual, double
双 bāotāi — twins
皮 bāo — briefcase
皮毛 — superficial knowledge
真话 — truth
真心 — sincere
真相 — the real situation
真正 — genuine

(ii)
刚才 — just now
刚好 — exactly
新 xiān — fresh
穿过 — go across
舒 chàng — free from worry
服从 — obey
服 wù — service
pò 旧 — old and shabby

Quiz 40 (391–400)

A.

Word or phrase	Pinyin	English meaning
(i) 紧身	jǐnshēn	tight fit
(ii) 合适	héshì	suitable
(iii) 衣服	yīfu	clothes
(iv) 神气	shénqì	cocky, impressive

B.

Pinyin	Characters	Translation
(i) Wǒ xǐhuan chuān jǐnshēn yīfu.	我喜欢穿紧身衣服。	I like wearing tight clothes.
(ii) Zhè jiàn hǎoxiàng féi le diǎnr.	这件好像肥了点儿。	This one seems to be a bit loose.
(iii) Qǐng bǎ nà jiàn ná gěi wǒ kànkan.	请把那件拿给我看看。	Please show me that one.
(iv) Zhèng héshì, nǐ chuānzhe zhēn shénqì!	正合适,你穿着真神气!	It's really fits, you look cool.

C. (i)
紧 zhāng — nervous
紧 jǐ — urgent
像样 — presentable
好像 — seem, be like
肥大 — loose, large
肥 pàng — fat, obese
把 wò — certainty
拿手 — be good at

(ii)
合口 — be to one's taste
合理 — reasonable
适合 — suit, fit
着 liáng — catch a cold
着 xiǎng — consider
神经 — nerve
气候 — climate
气 wèi — smell

Character Building 8 (351–400)

A. 1. [丶] 为 wèi, for; 半 bàn, half

2. [丨] 旧 jiù, old; 中 zhōng, middle

3. [丿] 向 xiàng, toward; 千 qiān, thousand

4. [讠] 许 xǔ, allow; 计 jì, calculate

5. [十] 真 zhēn, real; 直 zhí, straight

6. [刂] 刚 gāng, just now; 别 bié, other

7. [人] 合 hé, join, suit; 舒 shū, stretch

8. [亻] 像 xiàng, resemble; 但 dàn, but

10. [又] 双 shuāng, double, pair; 难 nán, difficult

11. [氵] 清 qīng, clear; 湾 wān, bay

12. [辶] 适 shì, appropriate; 过 guò, pass

13. [艹] 蓝 lán, blue; 黄 huáng, yellow

14. [扌] 把 bǎ, object marker; 拐 guǎi, turn

15. [口] 因 yīn, reason; 回 huí, return

16. [女] 如 rú, resemble; 好 hǎo, good

17. [纟] 红 hóng, red; 绿 lǜ, green

18. [木] 果 guǒ, fruit; 相 xiàng, photograph

19. [斤] 所 suǒ, place; 新 xīn, new

20. [月] 肥 féi, fat; 服 fú, submit

21. [穴] 穿 chuān, wear; 容 róng, complexion

22. [白] 白 bái, white; 百 bǎi, hundred

23. [页] 颜 yán, face; 题 tí, topic

B. 1. [厂] 厕 cè, toilet

2. [阝] 附 fū, attach

3. [刀] 色 sè, color

4. [尸] 局 jú, bureau

5. [弓] 弯 wān, curve

6. [火] 灯 dēng, lights

7. [礻] 神 shén, god

8. [牛] 特 tè, special

9. [衤] 衬 chèn, set off

10. [疋] 楚 chǔ, clear (as in qīngchu)

11. [羊] 着 zhe, verbal suffix

12. [系] 紧 jǐn, tight

13. [革] 鞋 xié, shoes

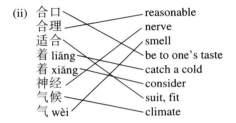

C. 1. ［艮］银 *yín*, silver;
        跟 *gēn*, follow

    2. ［巴］肥 *féi*, fat;
        把 *bǎ*, object marker.

    3. ［舌］适 *shì*, appropriate;
        话 *huà*, language

    4. ［斤］新 *xīn*, new;
        听 *tīng*, listen

    5. ［另］拐 *guǎi*, turn;
        别 *bié*, other

Review 8 (351–400)

Nouns
附近 *fùjìn*, nearby;
厕所 *cèsuǒ*, toilet;
绿灯 *lǜdēng*, green light;
弯路 *wānlù*, winding road;
米饭 *mǐfàn*, cooked rice;
银行 *yínháng*, bank (financial);
邮票 *yóupiào*, stamp;
颜面 *yánmiàn*, face;
黑人 *hēirén*, black people;
蓝色 *lánsè*, blue;
别人 *biérén*, other people;
特点 *tèdiǎn*, characteristics;
双人床 *shuāngrénchuáng*, double bed;
皮鞋 *píxié*, leather shoes;
真相 *zhēnxiàng*, real situation;
穿着 *chuānzhuó*, dress, apparel;
神经 *shénjīng*, nerve;
气色 *qìsè*, complexion.

女厕 *nǚcè*, female toilet;
红绿灯 *hónglǜdēng*, traffic lights;
向导 *xiàngdǎo*, guide;
弯子 *wānzi*, curve;
商场 *shāngchǎng*, shopping mall;
银色 *yínsè*, silver color;
邮局 *yóujú*, post office;
颜色 *yánsè*, color;
衬衣 *chènyī*, shirt;
别的 *biéde*, other;
特长 *tècháng*, special skill;
特色 *tèsè*, special character;
皮毛 *pímáo*, superficial knowledge;
真话 *zhēnhuà*, truth;
新年 *xīnnián*, new year;
服务 *fúwù*, service;
气候 *qìhòu*, climate;

Interrogative Pronouns
为什么 *wèishénme*, why.

Measure Word
双 *shuāng*, a pair of.

Verbs
附上 *fùshàng*, attach; 向往 *xiàngwǎng*, yearn for;
回来 *huílái*, come back; 回去 *huíqù*, go back;
为期 *wéiqī*, be completed by a definite date;
合不来 *hébulái*, can't get along with; 适合 *shìhé*, suit, fit;
着想 *zhuóxiǎng*, consider the interests of somebody or something.

拐弯 *guǎiwān*, turn; 清理 *qīnglǐ*, clean, tidy up;
为难 *wéinán*, make things difficult for;
穿过 *chuānguò*, go through; 服从 *fúcóng*, obey;

Adjectives
所有 *suǒyǒu*, all; 弯弯 *wānwān*, curving;
许多 *xǔduō*, many; 黄色 *huángsè*, yellow;
特有 *tèyǒu*, peculiar; 真心 *zhēnxīn*, sincere;
舒适 *shūshì*, cozy; 肥大 *féidà*, loose-fitting;
合口 *hékǒu*, be to one's taste;
适宜 *shìyí*, appropriate;

弯曲 *wānqū*, winding; 清楚 *qīngchu*, clear;
黑白 *hēibái*, black and white; 特别 *tèbié*, special;
真正 *zhēnzhèng*, genuine; 舒服 *shūfu*, comfortable;
拿手 *náshǒu*, good at;
合理 *hélǐ*, reasonable; 合适 *héshì*, suitable;
适中 *shìzhōng*, well-situated.

Adverbs
向来 *xiànglái*, always; 许久 *xǔjiǔ*, for a long time;
如今 *rújīn*, nowadays; 白天 *báitiān*, daytime;
刚好 *gānghǎo*, just right.

不许 *bùxǔ*, not allow; 也许 *yěxǔ*, maybe;
刚才 *gāngcái*, just then; 刚刚 *gānggāng*, just now;

Conjunctions
因为 *yīnwèi*, because; 所以 *suǒyǐ*, therefore;
如果 *rúguǒ*, if.

Prepositions
为了 *wèile*, in order to; 把 *bǎ*, object marker

Word/Sentence Puzzle 8

ACROSS

1. This pair of shoes is very comfortable.
4. Please don't make things difficult for me.
6. (i) Arrived in Beijing not long ago.
   (ii) voice/sound
8. When he speaks, his facial expression is just like his father.
13. Why didn't you say it clearly?
16. It takes a lot of time to learn a foreign language.

DOWN

1. The size of this pair of shoes is just right.
3. He's studying English because he wants to leave the country.
5. This behavior is unacceptable.
7. reasonable
9. Her accent is quite peculiar.
11. I seem to have met him somewhere before.
13. He doesn't get along with his father.

	1	2	3	4	5	6	7	8	9	10	11	12	13
1	这				这	双	鞋	穿	起	来	很	舒	服
2	双				种								
3	鞋				行				她		这		
4	大		请	别	为	难	我		的		个		
5	小				真				口		人		他
6	刚	来	北	京	不	久		声	音		我		跟
7	合				像				很		好		他
8	适		他	说	话	的	神	气	特	别	像	他	爸
9			学						别		在		爸
10			英								哪		合
11			语		请	问	邮	局	在	哪	儿		不
12			是								见		来
13			你	为	什	么	不	讲	清	楚	过		
14			了			理							
15			出										
16	学	外	国	语	要	花	很	多	时	间			

Quiz 41 (401–410)

A.

风	预	力	阴
南	报	夜	间
最	高	快	级
向	晴	气	温

Word or phrase	Pinyin	English meaning
(i) 预报	yùbào	forecast
(ii) 夜间	yèjiān	night time
(iii) 最高	zuìgāo	highest
(iv) 气温	qìwēn	temperature

B.

Pinyin	Characters	Translation
(i) Tiānqì yùbào shuō jīntiān qíngtiān.	天气预报说今天晴天。	The weather forecast says today will be sunny.
(ii) Fēngxiàng nán fēng, fēnglì èrjí.	风向南风,风力二级。	There will be a southerly, force 2 wind.
(iii) Zuìgāo qìwēn 18 dù.	最高气温18度。	The maximum temperature will be 18 degrees.
(iv) Yèjiān zuìdī qìwēn 9 dù.	夜间最低气温9度。	The overnight minimum temperature will be 9 degrees.

C. (i)

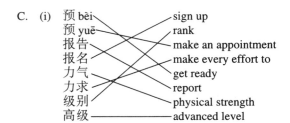

预 bèi — sign up
预 yuē — rank
报告 — make an appointment
报名 — make every effort to
力气 — get ready
力求 — report
级别 — physical strength
高级 — advanced level

(ii)

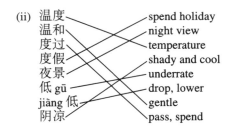

温度 — spend holiday
温和 — night view
度过 — temperature
度假 — shady and cool
夜景 — underrate
低 gū — drop, lower
jiàng 低 — gentle
阴凉 — pass, spend

Quiz 42 (411–420)

A.
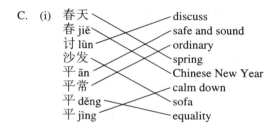

Word or phrase	Pinyin	English meaning
(i) 刮风沙	guā fēngshā	duststorm
(ii) 虽然	suīrán	although
(iii) 讨厌	tǎoyàn	what a nuisance
(iv) 平常	píngcháng	generally

B.
Pinyin	Characters	Translation
(i) Běijīng chūntiān hái bǐjiào lěng.	北京春天还比较冷。	Spring in Beijing is still quite cold.
(ii) Zuì tǎoyàn shì guā fēngshā.	最讨厌是刮风沙。	The most annoying aspect is that it is dusty.
(iii) Qìwēn píngcháng 10 dù zuǒyòu.	气温平常10度左右。	The temperature is generally around 10 degrees.
(iv) Suīrán lěng, dàn wūlǐ yǒu nuǎnqì.	虽然冷,但屋里有暖气。	Although it is cold, there is central heating.

C. (i)
春天 — spring
春 jié — Chinese New Year
讨 lùn — discuss
沙发 — sofa
平 ān — calm down
平常 — ordinary
平 děng — equality
平 jīng — safe and sound

(ii)
然后 — then, afterwards
然 ér — but, however
hū 然 — suddenly
果然 — sure enough
屋子 — room
房屋 — housing
暖气 — central heating
温暖 — warm

Quiz 43 (421–430)

A.

Word or phrase	Pinyin	English meaning
(i) 凉快	liángkuāi	cool
(ii) 漂亮	piāoliang	pretty
(iii) 季节	jìjié	season
(iv) 郊外	jiāowài	countryside

B.
Pinyin	Characters	Translation
(i) Běijīng de qiūtiān hěn liángkuāi.	北京的秋天很凉快。	Autumn in Beijing is nice and cool.
(ii) Shì lǚyóu de hǎo jìjié.	是旅游的好季节。	It is a good season for touring.
(iii) Rénmen dào jiāowài qù kàn qiūyè.	人们到郊外去看秋叶。	People go to the countryside to see autumn leaves.
(iv) Huángde, hóngde piàoliangjíle!	黄的,红的,漂亮极了。	The leaves are yellow and red, it's really pretty.

C. (i)
凉 shuǎng — nice and cool
凉鞋 — sandals
秋季 — autumn
节 shí — rhythm
节 zòu — program (TV etc.)
节 mù — on a diet
郊 qū — suburb
郊游 — outing

(ii)
漂亮话 — high-sounding words
极大 — enormous
极 duān — extreme
极力 — do one's utmost
树叶 — leaves
树 lì — establish
树阴 — shade of a tree
sēn 林 — forest

Quiz 44 (431–440)

A.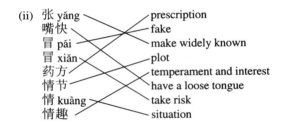

	Word or phrase	Pinyin	English meaning
(i)	感冒	gǎnmào	have the flu
(ii)	体温	tǐwēn	body temperature
(iii)	发烧	fāshāo	run a temperature
(iv)	张开	zhāngkāi	open wide

B.

	Pinyin	Characters	Translation
(i)	Wǒ bìngle. Tóutòng, fāshāo.	我病了，头痛，发烧。	I'm sick, I have a headache and I am running a temperature.
(ii)	Liángliang tǐwēn ba, qǐng zhāngkāi zuǐ.	量量体温吧，请张开嘴。	Let me check your temperature. Open your mouth.
(iii)	38 dù, bú yàojǐn, gǎnmào le.	38度，不要紧，感冒了。	It's 38 degrees. It's not serious. You have the flu.
(iv)	Chī diǎn yào, guò jǐ tiān jiù hǎo le.	吃点药，过几天就好了。	Take some medicine and you'll get better in a few days.

C. (i)

病人 — patient
头发 — hair
头脑 — brains, mind
痛苦 kǔ — suffering
痛快 — delighted
痛心 xīn — distressed
气量 — tolerance
力量 — strength

(ii)

张 yáng — make widely known
嘴快 — have a loose tongue
冒 pái — fake
冒 xiǎn — take risk
药方 — prescription
情节 — plot
情 kuàng — situation
情趣 — temperament and interest

Quiz 45 (441–450)

A.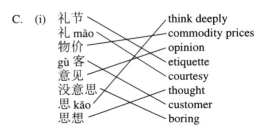

	Word or phrase	Pinyin	English meaning
(i)	礼物	lǐwù	gift
(ii)	客气	kèqi	polite, courteous
(iii)	快乐	kuàilè	happy
(iv)	意思	yìsi	meaning

B.

	Pinyin	Characters	Translation
(i)	Zhè shì gěi nǐ de shēngrì lǐwù.	这是给你的生日礼物。	This is a gift for your birthday.
(ii)	Nín tài kèqi le!	您太客气了！	You are too kind.
(iii)	Yīdiǎn xiǎo yìsi, bù chéng jìngyì.	一点小意思，不成敬意。	It is only a little something, it's nothing really.
(iv)	Zhù shēngrì kuàilè, wànshì-rúyì!	祝生日快乐，万事如意。	I hope you have a happy birthday, many happy returns!

C. (i)

礼节 — etiquette
礼 mào — courtesy
物价 — commodity prices
gù 客 — customer
意见 — opinion
没意思 — boring
思 kǎo — think deeply
思想 — thought

(ii)

成就 — achievement
wán 成 — finish
zūn 敬 — respect
qǐng 祝 — celebrate
乐 guān — optimistic
音乐 — music
事情 — matter
事 gù — accident

Character Building 9 (401–450)

A. 1. [丶] 头 *tóu*, head; 为 *wèi*, on behalf of.

2. [一] 平 *píng*, level; 事 *shì*, matter.

3. [丿] 乐 *lè*, happy; 向 *xiàng*, toward.

4. [亠] 夜 *yè*, night; 交 *jiāo*, hand over.

5. [冫] 凉 *liáng*, cool; 冷 *lěng*, cold.

6. [讠] 讨 *tǎo*, discuss; 许 *xǔ*, permit.

7. [厂] 厌 *yàn*, dislike; 厕 *cè*, toilet.

8. [刂] 刮 *guā*, scrape; 刚 *gāng*, just now.

9. [亻] 低 *dī*, low; 但 *dàn*, but.

10. [阝] 阴 *yīn*, dark; 附 *fù*, attach.

11. [阝] 郊 *jiāo*, outskirts; 邮 *yóu*, mail.

12. [力] 力 *lì*, strength; 办 *bàn*, do.

13. [氵] 沙 *shā*, sand; 温 *wēn*, mild in temperature; 漂 *piāo/piǎo/piào*, adrift/bleach/pretty; 清 *qīng*, clear.

14. [忄] 情 *qíng*, emotion; 忙 *máng*, busy.

15. [宀] 客 *kè*, guest; 定 *dìng*, fixed.

16. [广] 度 *dù*, degree; 应 *yīng/yìng*, ought to/answer.

17. [艹] 节 *jié*, festival; 药 *yào*, medicine.

18. [扌] 报 *bào*, report; 把 *bǎ*, object marker.

19. [口] 叶 *yè*, leaf; 虽 *suī*, although; 嘴 *zuǐ*, mouth.

20. [尸] 屋 *wū*, room; 局 *jú*, bureau.

21. [纟] 级 *jí*, grade; 红 *hóng*, red.

22. [灬] 然 *rán*, correct; 热 *rè*, hot.

23. [火] 烧 *shāo*, burn; 灯 *dēng*, light.

24. [心] 意 *yì*, idea; 思 *sī*, think.

25. [礻] 礼 *lǐ*, politeness; 祝 *zhù*, congratulation.

26. [木] 林 *lín*, forest; 极 *jí*, extremely; 树 *shù*, tree; 果 *guǒ*, fruit

27. [戈] 成 *chéng*, become; 我 *wǒ*, I.

28. [日] 春 *chūn*, spring; 晴 *qíng*, sunny; 量 *liáng/liàng*, measure/quantity; 暖 *nuǎn*, warm.

29. [曰] 冒 *mào*, give off; 最 *zuì*, most.

30. [牛] 物 *wù*, thing; 特 *tè*, special.

31. [攵] 敬 *jìng*, respect; 改 *gǎi*, change.

32. [疒] 病 *bìng*, sickness; 痛 *tòng*, pain.

33. [禾] 秋 *qiū*, autumn; 季 *jì*, season.

34. [页] 预 *yù*, prepare; 题 *tí*, topic.

B. 1. [艮] 服 *fú*, submit; 报 *bào*, report.

2. [月] 阴 *yīn*, dark; 肥 *féi*, loose-fitting.

3. [舌] 刮 *guā*, scrape; 适 *shì*, suitable.

4. [至] 屋 *wū*, room; 到 *dào*, arrive.

5. [寸] 讨 *tǎo*, discuss; 对 *duì*, accurate.

6. [京] 凉 *liáng*, cool; 就 *jiù*, then.

Review 9 (401–450)

Nouns
预报 *yùbào*, forecast;
力气 *lìqì*, physical strength;
温度 *wēndù*, temperature;
夜间 *yèjiān*, night time;
夜景 *yèjǐng*, night scene;
春节 *Chūnjié*, Chinese New Year;
沙发 *shāfā*, sofa; 沙子 *shāzi*, sand;
暖气 *nuǎnqì*, central heating; 秋季 *qiūjì*, autumn;
凉鞋 *liángxié*, sandals; 季节 *jìjié*, season;
节假日 *jiéjiàrì*, holidays and festivals;
城郊 *chéngjiāo*, outskirts; 叶子 *yèzi*, leaves;
树阴 *shùyīn*, shade of trees; 山林 *shānlín*, mountain forest;
南极 *Nánjí*, the South Pole; 病假 *bìngjià*, sick leave;
头发 *tóufa*, hair; 头脑 *tóunǎo*, brains;
气量 *qìliàng*, forbearance; 感冒 *gǎnmào*, flu;
药水 *yàoshuǐ*, mixture (medicine); 情节 *qíngjié*, plot;
情人 *qíngrén*, lover; 事情 *shìqing*, matter;
礼节 *lǐjié*, etiquette; 动物园 *dòngwùyuán*, zoo;
主意 *zhǔyi*, idea; 思路 *sīlù*, train of thought;
成就 *chéngjiù*, achievement; 音乐 *yīnyuè*, music.

力量 *lìliang*, power;
级别 *jíbié*, rank;
风度 *fēngdù*, demeanor;
夜生活 *yèshēnghuó*, night life;
春天 *chūntiān*, spring;
春风 *chūnfēng*, spring breeze;
屋子 *wūzi*, room; 房屋 *fángwū*, housing;
秋色 *qiūsè*, autumn colors; 秋天 *qiūtiān*, autumn;
季候风 *jìhòufēng*, monsoon; 冬季 *dōngjì*, winter;
郊外 *jiāowài*, countryside;
树叶 *shùyè*, leaves; 树林 *shùlín*, forest;
漂亮话 *piàolianghuà*, fine words;
病情 *bìngqíng*, state of illness; 病人 *bìngrén*, patient;
量词 *liàngcí*, measure word;
药方 *yàofāng*, prescription;
情趣 *qíngqù*, temperament and interest;
物价 *wùjià*, prices; 礼物 *lǐwù*, gift;
意见 *yìjiàn*, opinion; 意思 *yìsi*, meaning;
思想 *sīxiǎng*, thought; 敬意 *jìngyì*, respect;

Measure Word
节 *jié* (for lessons)

Verbs
报告 *bàogào*, report; 报名 *bàomíng*, sign up;
度假 *dùjià*, go vacationing;
头痛 *tóutòng*, have a headache;
量力 *liànglì*, estimate one's ability;
张嘴 *zhāngzuǐ*, open one's mouth.

力求 *lìqiú*, strive to; 度过 *dùguò*, spend time in;
漂游 *piāoyóu*, lead a wandering life;
发烧 *fāshāo*, run a temperature;
张开 *zhāngkāi*, open wide;

Adjectives
中级 *zhōngjí*, middle grade; 高级 *gāojí*, high grade;
阴凉 *yīnliáng*, cool and shady;
不讨好 *bùtǎohǎo*, not have one's labor rewarded;
凉快 *liàngkuài*, cool (the weather);
痛快 *tòngkuài*, delighted; 痛心 *tòngxīn*, distressed;
嘴快 *zuǐkuài*, have a loose tongue; 客气 *kèqi*, courteous;

温暖 *wēnnuǎn*, warm; 阴黑 *yīnhēi*, dark (the weather);
讨厌 *tǎoyàn*, detestable/annoying;
暖和 *nuǎnhuo*, nice and warm;
漂亮 *piàoliang*, pretty; 极大 *jídà*, enormous;
紧张 *jǐnzhāng*, nervous;
没意思 *méi yìsi*, boring; 快乐 *kuàilè*, happy.

Adverbs
平常 *píngcháng*, normally; 然后 *ránhòu*, then;
事先 *shìxiān*, beforehand; 事后 *shìhòu*, after the event.

果然 *guǒrán*, true enough; 极力 *jílì*, do one's utmost;

Conjunctions
虽然 *suīrán*, although; 虽说 *suīshuō*, although.

Word/Sentence Puzzle 9

ACROSS
2. It's been windy every day. It's annoying.
4. I saw a movie and then went home.
7. Chinese and Western etiquette are different.
9. I don't understand what you mean.
12. (i) make a decision.
    (ii) clean up
14. It's cold outside, you'll catch a cold.

DOWN
1. I like the Mid-autumn Festival.
3. It's clearing up.
4. A small gift as a token of my regard.
6. (i) telephone
    (ii) I can't sleep during the day.
7. the countryside
8. Cars are expensive outside China.
9. consequence
10. clear-thinking
11. What time are you going home?
13. Autumn has arrived; the leaves on the trees have turned red.

	1	2	3	4	5	6	7	8	9	10	11	12	13
1											你		秋
2		每	天	刮	风	真	讨	厌			几		天
3			晴							点			到
4	我	看	了	一	场	电	影	然	后	就	回	家	了
5	喜			点		话		果		家			树
6	欢			小			郊						上
7	中	国	的	礼	节	跟	外	国	不	一	样		的
8	秋			物			外						叶
9	节		我	不	明	白	你	的	意	思			子
10			成		天		汽		路				都
11			敬		我		车		很				红
12		拿	主	意		睡		很		清	理		了
13			不			贵		楚					
14	外	面	冷	容	易	着	凉						

Quiz 46 (451–460)

A.

错	甜	点	心
奶	尝	饮	糖
茶	得	料	喝
里	味	道	吧

Word or phrase	Pinyin	English meaning
(i) 甜点心	tián diǎnxīn	pastry
(ii) 奶茶	nǎichá	tea with milk
(iii) 饮料	yǐnliào	drinks
(iv) 味道	wèidao	taste, flavor

B.

Pinyin	Characters	Translation
(i) Nǐ hē shénme yǐnliào?	你喝什么饮料?	What would you like to drink?
(ii) Nǎichá ba, búyào táng.	奶茶吧,不要糖。	I'll have tea with milk but no sugar.
(iii) Zhèlǐ de tián diǎnxīn búcuò.	这里的甜点心不错。	The pastries here are good.
(iv) Shì ma? Nà wǒ děi chángchang wèidao.	是吗?那我得尝尝味道。	Really? In that case we must try some.

C. (i)

(ii)

Quiz 47 (461–470)

A.

<table>
<tr><td></td><td></td><td></td><td></td><td>Word or phrase</td><td>Pinyin</td><td>English meaning</td></tr>
<tr><td>饿</td><td>休</td><td>般</td><td>馆</td><td>(i) 休息</td><td>xiūxi</td><td>rest</td></tr>
<tr><td>优</td><td>息</td><td>主</td><td>意</td><td>(ii) 主意</td><td>zhǔyi</td><td>idea, suggestion</td></tr>
<tr><td>美</td><td>餐</td><td>店</td><td>又</td><td>(iii) 优美</td><td>yōuměi</td><td>excellent</td></tr>
<tr><td>快</td><td>环</td><td>境</td><td>累</td><td>(iv) 环境</td><td>huánjìng</td><td>surrounding, environment</td></tr>
</table>

B.

Pinyin	Characters	Translation
(i) Nǐ xiǎng xiūxi yíxià ma?	你想休息一下吗?	Would you like a little rest?
(ii) Hǎo zhǔyi! Lèisǐ wǒ le!	好主意!累死我了!	Good idea! I'm dead tired.
(iii) Zhè ge kuàicāndiàn huánjìng yōuměi.	这个快餐店环境优美。	This fast food joint is in a beautiful setting.
(iv) Jiù zài zhèlǐ xiūxi yíxià ba.	就在这里休息一下吧。	Let's take a break here.

C. (i)

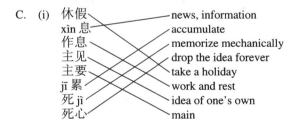

(ii)

Quiz 48 (471–480)

A.

<table>
<tr><td></td><td></td><td></td><td></td><td>Word or phrase</td><td>Pinyin</td><td>English meaning</td></tr>
<tr><td>橘</td><td>子</td><td>水</td><td>酒</td><td>(i) 橘子水</td><td>júzishuǐ</td><td>orange juice</td></tr>
<tr><td>杯</td><td>牛</td><td>羊</td><td>喝</td><td>(ii) 牛肉</td><td>niúròu</td><td>beef</td></tr>
<tr><td>菜</td><td>肉</td><td>鸡</td><td>蛋</td><td>(iii) 菜单</td><td>càidān</td><td>menu</td></tr>
<tr><td>单</td><td>面</td><td>炒</td><td>爱</td><td>(iv) 鸡蛋</td><td>jīdàn</td><td>egg</td></tr>
</table>

B.

Pinyin	Characters	Translation
(i) Zhè shì càidān, hē diǎn jiǔ ma?	这是菜单，喝点酒吗？	Here's the menu. Would you like some alcoholic drinks?
(ii) Lái liǎng bēi júzishuǐ.	来两杯橘子水。	We'll have two glasses of orange juice.
(iii) Nǐ ài chī chǎo jīdàn ma?	你爱吃炒鸡蛋吗？	Do you like scrambled eggs?
(iv) Bù, wǒ jiù yào ge niúròu miàn.	不，我就要个牛肉面。	No thanks. I'll have beef noodles.

C.

(i)
shū 菜 — cook
做菜 — capacity for liquor
单身 — cup, glass
酒量 — drink a toast
pí 酒 — vegetables
杯子 — single (not married)
gān 杯 — orange color
橘黄 — beer

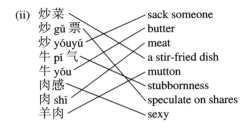

(ii)
炒菜 — sack someone
炒 gǔ 票 — butter
炒 yóuyú — meat
牛 pí 气 — a stir-fried dish
牛 yóu — mutton
肉感 — stubbornness
肉 shǐ — speculate on shares
羊肉 — sexy

Quiz 49 (481–490)

A.

心	非	自	常
经	验	己	开
基	重	要	始
信	功	定	门

Word or phrase	Pinyin	English meaning
(i) 自己	zìjǐ	self
(ii) 经验	jīngyàn	experience
(iii) 开始	kāishǐ	begin
(iv) 重要	zhòngyào	important

B.

Pinyin	Characters	Translation
(i) Wǒ shuō zìjǐ de xuéxí jīngyàn.	我说自己的学习经验。	Let me tell you about my learning experience.
(ii) Wǒ juéde kāishǐ fēicháng zhòngyào.	我觉得开始非常重要。	I think it's very important to have a good start.
(iii) Yídìng yào xiān xuéhǎo jīběngōng.	一定要先学好基本功。	First of all, you should learn the basic skills properly.
(iv) Yǒule xìnxīn, jiù yǒu xìngqù xué.	有了信心，就有兴趣学。	Once you've acquired confidence, you'll want to keep learning.

C.

(i)
自从 — thought, idea
自 yóu — from start to finish
知己 — illegal
jì 念 — freedom
念头 — since
始 zhōng — close friend
非常 — commemorate
非法 — extraordinary

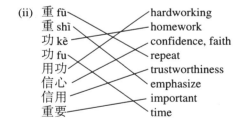

(ii)
重 fù — hardworking
重 shì — homework
功 kè — confidence, faith
功 fu — repeat
用功 — trustworthiness
信心 — emphasize
信用 — important
重要 — time

Quiz 50 (491–500)

A.

要	求	养	按
坚	持	次	成
习	笔	顺	每
惯	必	须	练

Word or phrase	Pinyin	English meaning
(i) 要求	yāoqiú	requirement
(ii) 坚持	jiānchí	persevere
(iii) 习惯	xíguàn	be used to
(iv) 笔顺	bǐshùn	stroke order

B.   **Pinyin**   **Characters**   **Translation**

(i) Yào jiānchí liànxí xiě Hànzì.   要坚持练习写汉字。   You have to persevere when you practice
                                                                          writing characters.

(ii) Měi cì bù yāoqiú xiě tài duō.   每次不要求写太多。   It's not necessary to write a lot of
                                                                          characters on each occasion.

(iii) Dàn bìxū àn bǐshùn xiě.   但必须按笔顺写。   But it is imperative to follow the stroke
                                                                          order.

(iv) Yǎngchéngle xíguàn, jiù néng jìzhù.   养成了习惯，就能记住。   Once you've developed the habit, you'll
                                                                          remember the character.

C.   (i) 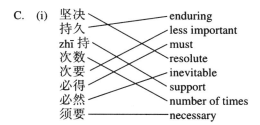   (ii)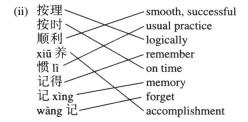

Character Building 10 (451–500)

A. 1.   [丶] 主 zhǔ, main; 为 wèi, on behalf of.

2.   [丨] 非 fēi, not; 旧 jiù, old.

3.   [丿] 重 zhòng/chóng, heavy/repeat; 向 xiàng,
toward.

4.   [冫] 次 cì, position in a series; 冷 lěng, cold.

5.   [讠] 试 shì, try; 记 jì, remember.

6.   [冂] 肉 ròu, meat; 周 zhōu, week.

7.   [亻] 休 xiū, rest; 优 yōu, excellent; 信 xìn,
letter.

8.   [又] 鸡 jī, chicken; 难 nán, difficult.

9.   [力] 功 gōng, achievement; 男 nán, male.

10. [氵] 酒 jiǔ, alcohol; 清 qīng, clear.

11. [忄] 惯 guàn, be used to/indulge in; 快 kuài,
fast.

12. [门] 门 mén, door; 问 wèn, ask.

13. [工] 功 gōng, achievement; 工 gōng, work.

14. [土] 境 jìng, territory; 基 jī, foundation.
坚 jiān, hard; 场 chǎng, field.

15. [艹] 茶 chá, tea; 菜 cài, vegetables.

16. [扌] 持 chí, hold; 按 àn, according to.

17. [小] 尝 cháng, taste; 常 cháng, often.

18. [口] 喝 hē, drink; 味 wèi, flavor.

19. [饣] 饮 yǐn, drink; 馆 guǎn, dwelling.

20. [己] 己 jǐ, self; 已 yǐ, already

21. [女] 奶 nǎi, milk; 始 shǐ, origin.

22. [马] 验 yàn, check; 马 mǎ, horse.

23. [火] 炒 chǎo, stir-fried; 烧 shāo, burn.

24. [心] 息 xī, rest; 必 bì, must.

25. [王] 主 zhǔ, main; 环 huán, surround.

26. [木] 杯 bēi, cup/glass; 橘 jú, orange

27. [牛] 牛 niú, cattle; 特 tè, special.

28. [田] 累 lèi, tired; 男 nán, male.

29. [米] 料 liào, material; 糖 táng, sugar.

30. [页] 须 xū, must; 顺 shùn, follow.

31. [虫] 蛋 dàn, egg; 虽 suī, although.

32. [自] 自 zì, self; 息 xī, rest.

33. [舌] 甜 tián, sweet; 舒 shū, stretch.

34. [其] 基 jī, foundation; 期 qī, period.

B. 1.   [歹] 死 sǐ, die
2.   [鸟] 鸡 jī, chicken

3.   [食] 餐 cān, meal

Review 10 (451–500)

Nouns

饮料 *yǐnliào*, drinks; 饮用水 *yǐnyòngshuǐ*, drinking water;

冷饮 *lěngyǐn*, cold drink; 奶茶 *nǎichá*, Western tea with milk; 牛奶 *niúnǎi*, milk; 茶叶 *cháyè*, tea leaves;

茶杯 *chábēi*, teacup; 杯子 *bēizi*, cup/glass; 世界杯 *Shìjièbēi*, World Cup;

糖果 *tángguǒ*, confectionary; 甜头 *tiántóu*, incentive (as an inducement);

味道 *wèidao*, flavor; 气味 *qìwèi*, smell, odor; 信息 *xìnxī*, news, information;

利息 *lìxī*, interest (investment); 主见 *zhǔjiàn*, thoughts of one's own;

主意 *zhǔyi*, suggestion; 餐车 *cānchē*, dining car (on a train); 中餐 *Zhōngcān*, Chinese meal; 环节 *huánjié*, link;

环境 *huánjìng*, surroundings; 境地 *jìngdì*, circumstances; 优点 *yōudiǎn*, strong point; 菜单 *càidān*, menu;

酒杯 *jiǔbēi*, wine glass; 酒量 *jiǔliàng*, capacity for liquor; 橘子 *júzi*, orange (fruit); 公鸡 *gōngjī*, rooster;

牛肉 *niúròu*, beef; 鸡蛋 *jīdàn*, chicken egg; 蛋白 *dànbái*, egg white; 蛋黄 *dànhuáng*, yolk;

自己 *zìjǐ*, self; 自行车 *zìxíngchē*, bicycle; 知己 *zhījǐ*, close friend; 经验 *jīngyàn*, experience;

始末 *shǐmò*, beginning and end; 基本功 *jīběngōng*, basic skills; 功能 *gōngnéng*, function;

信用 *xìnyòng*, trustworthiness; 门口 *ménkǒu*, entrance; 门路 *ménlù*, social connections;

门票 *ménpiào*, admission; 门外汉 *ménwàihàn*, layman; 笔顺 *bǐshùn*, stroke order;

次数 *cìshù*, number of times; 车次 *chēcì*, bus/train service.

Personal Pronouns

我自己 *wǒzìjǐ*, myself; 你自己 *nǐzìjǐ*, yourself;

他自己 *tāzìjǐ*, himself.

她自己 *tāzìjǐ*, herself.

Measure Words

杯 *bēi* (for cup/glass); 门 *mén* (for academic subjects).

Verbs

料到 *liàodào*, expect; 料理 *liàolǐ*, take care of; 料想 *liàoxiǎng*, expect; 死记 *sǐjì*, learn mechanically;

死心 *sǐxīn*, drop the idea forever; 尝试 *chángshì*, try; 试味 *shìwèi*, try for taste; 试行 *shìxíng*, try out;

试用 *shìyòng*, try out (a product); 休假 *xiūjià*, take a holiday; 休息 *xiūxi*, rest; 休养 *xiūyǎng*, recuperate;

做菜 *zuòcài*, cook; 信不过 *xìnbùguò*, distrust; 信得过 *xìndeguò*, trust;

养神 *yǎngshén*, rest to retain mental tranquility; 记得 *jìde*, remember; 记住 *jìzhù*, remember;

开始 *kāishǐ*, begin; 坚持 *jiānchí*, persevere; 持有 *chíyǒu*, hold; 习惯 *xíguàn*, be used to.

Adjectives

好喝 *hǎohē*, tasty (drink); 美味 *měiwèi*, delicious; 主要 *zhǔyào*, main;

环城 *huánchéng*, surrounding the city; 优美 *yōuměi*, excellent;

单身 *dānshēn*, single (not married); 橘黄 *júhuáng*, orange color; 非法 *fēifǎ*, illegal;

重点 *zhòngdiǎn*, focal point; 用功 *yònggōng*, hardworking; 坚定 *jiāndìng*, resolute; 持久 *chíjiǔ*, enduring;

次要 *cìyào*, less important; 必要 *bìyào*, necessary.

Adverbs

···死了 *...sǐle*, extremely; 单单 *dāndān*, only; 酒后 *jiǔhòu*, under the influence of liquor;

非常 *fēicháng*, extraordinary; 顺便 *shùnbiàn*, (do sth.) in addition to what one is already doing;

需要 *xūyào*, must; 必得 *bìdé*, must; 必定 *bìdìng*, certainty; 必然 *bìrán*, inevitable;

按理 *ànlǐ*, logically.

Conjunction

非但 *fēidàn*, not only.

Prepositions

自从 *zìcóng*, since; 按照 *ànzhào*, according to;

按时 *ànshí*, on time.

Word/Sentence Puzzle 10

ACROSS

1. He's only a fair-weather friend. He won't help me.
3. Beijing is famous for its many delicious snacks.
6. When learning a language, it is most important to remember new words.
7. ceremony
8. confidence
9. hand-written
10. sad
11. (i) way of thinking
    (ii) Every day I make a point of writing characters.
12. achievement
13. (i) reasonable
    (ii) conversation
14. idea, suggestion
15. (i) feeling, emotion
    (ii) function
18. On weekends, there are more bus/train services.

DOWN

1. Peking University is an elite university.
3. I want to know the whole story of the matter.
4. He loves drinking alcohol.
5. momentarily
6. If you trust me, let me do it for you.
8. (i) probable, maybe
    (ii) I came over to look for you twice today.
9. remember
10. (i) can't remember
    (ii) You must persevere to succeed.
11. ability
12. I want to buy an English–Chinese dictionary.
13. You have to pay attention to stroke order when you write Chinese characters.

	1	2	3	4	5	6	7	8	9	10	11	12	13
1	他	只	是	酒	肉	朋	友	不	会	帮	助	我	的
2												要	
3	北	京	有	很	多	美	味	小	吃			买	
4	京									记		英	
5	大			他		你		可		不		汉	
6	学	语	言	最	重	要	是	能	记	住	生	词	
7	是			爱		是			得			典	礼
8	重			喝		信	心			你			
9	点			酒		得		我		要		书	写
10	大	我			难	过		今		坚			汉
11	学		想	法		我	每	天	坚	持	写	汉	字
12			知		成	就		来		才			要
13		有	道	理		交		找		会	话		注
14			事			给		过		成		主	意
15	感	情				我		你		功	能		笔
16		的				办		们			力		顺
17		始		一				两					
18		周	末	的	时	候	车	次	比	较	多		